T0419149

Academic Bildung in Net-based Higher Education

The explosive emergence of net-based learning in higher education brings with it new possibilities and constraints in teaching and learning environments. This edited collection considers how the concept of Academic Bildung – a term suggesting a personal educational process beyond actual learning – can be applied to net-based higher education, drawing on Scandinavian research to address the topic from both a theoretical and practical standpoint. Chapters explore the facilitation of online courses and argue how and why universities should involve dimensions of Academic Bildung on both a strategic and technological pedagogical content level.

The book is structured in three parts: Part I frames the current state of net-based learning and introduces Bildung as a concept; Part II contains a set of four case studies in Norway, Sweden and Denmark, also including a fifth study that looks at Scandinavian approaches to teaching and learning in comparison with data from the USA, the UK, Australia and Canada; Part III provides a synthesis of theories and cases to examine whether a Scandinavian orientation can be discerned. Contributions suggest that in order to address one of the fundamental functions of higher education, the ability to produce new knowledge, the Academic Bildung of the students has to be in focus.

Grounded in theoretical and empirical discussion, this book will appeal to researchers and academics in the field of higher education as well as personnel who work with teaching and learning with technology, and academics interested in the question of Academic Bildung.

Trine Fossland is Associate Professor at the Centre for Teaching, Learning and Technology, UiT The Arctic University of Norway, Norway.

Helle Mathiasen is Professor at the Faculty of Science, Department of Science Education, University of Copenhagen, Denmark.

Mariann Solberg is Postdoctoral Research Fellow at the Centre for Teaching, Learning and Technology, UiT The Arctic University of Norway, Norway.

Routledge Research in Higher Education

Academic Bildung in Net-based Higher Education

Moving beyond learning

**Edited by Trine Fossland,
Helle Mathiasen and Mariann Solberg**

Routledge
Taylor & Francis Group

LONDON AND NEW YORK

First published 2015
by Routledge
2 Park Square, Milton Park, Abingdon, Oxon OX14 4RN

and by Routledge
711 Third Avenue, New York, NY 10017

Routledge is an imprint of the Taylor & Francis Group, an informa business

© 2015 T. Fossland, H. Mathiasen and M. Solberg

British Library Cataloguing in Publication Data
A catalogue record for this book is available from the British Library.

Library of Congress Cataloging in Publication Data
Academic bildung in net-based higher education: moving beyond
learning/edited by Trine Fossland, Helle Mathiasen, Mariann
Solberg.
pages cm. — (Routledge research in higher education)
Includes bibliographical references and index.
1. Internet in higher education—Scandinavia. 2. Professional
education—Web-based instruction—Scandinavia. I. Fossland, Trine,
editor of compilation.
LB2395.7.A24 2015
371.33′44678—dc23
2014030151

ISBN: 978-1-138-80933-8 (hbk)
ISBN: 978-1-315-75005-7 (ebk)

Typeset in Baskerville
by Swales and Willis Ltd, Exeter, Devon, UK

Contents

Illustrations

Figures

Tables

Contributors

Søren S. E. Bengtsen is Assistant Professor at the Centre for Teaching Development and Digital Media, Aarhus University, Denmark. His main areas of research include doctoral supervision and education, online supervision and educational philosophy. He has published articles and book chapters within these fields of research. One of his present interests is how net-based digital tools influence the conditions for supervisory dialogues in doctoral supervision settings.

Christian Dalsgaard is Associate Professor at the Centre for Teaching Development and Digital Media, Aarhus University, Denmark. His main area of research is online learning with a specific focus on the unique learning potentials of the web. He has published articles within the fields of learning theory, online learning, personal learning environments, digital learning resources and mobile learning.

Claire Englund is Assistant Lecturer and Educational Developer at the Centre for Teaching and Learning, Umeå University, Sweden. She has worked at the university since 2005 as an educational technologist and educational developer. Previously, she worked at the National Swedish Centre for Flexible Learning as a course designer in the field of technology-enhanced distance learning. Englund is also a part-time PhD student at the Department of Education researching teachers' approaches to teaching and learning with technology and its implications for professional development in higher education.

Trine Fossland is Associate Professor at the Centre for Teaching, Learning and Technology, Result, UiT The Arctic University of Norway. She has worked with net-based education since 2004, and is teaching at the Teacher Training Course in Higher Education at UiT. Fossland is working specifically with pedagogy and ICT and is the deputy chairman on the board of the Norwegian network for university pedagogics. She is also a member of the Norwegian University expert group "Quality in ICT Supported Higher Education" and has written articles and edited books on ICT in higher education.

Gunnar Grepperud is Professor at the Centre for Teaching, Learning and Technology, Result, UiT The Arctic University of Norway. He has several years of experience in teacher education, and has taken part in a number of research and development projects on the facilitation of teaching and learning for adults. The main focus in Grepperud's research is the conditions for adult education, ICT and learning, and flexible education.

Finn Thorbjørn Hansen is Professor in Philosophical and Dialogical Practice at Centre for Dialogue and Organization, University of Aalborg, Denmark. For the past 15 years he has conducted research on and led continuing education in philosophical and dialogical praxis. Areas of specialisation are philosophical counseling, philosophy of education, existential pedagogy in higher education, citizenship education, and the phenomenology of wonder.

Frank Holen is a postdoctoral scholar at the Centre for Teaching, Learning and Technology, Result, UiT The Arctic University of Norway. Holen has worked with flexible and net-based education since 2000. He has several years of experience from management education, and has taken part in a number of research and development projects concerning knowledge development in work life. The main focus of his research is on institutional frameworks for development of ICT and net-based education, ICT and learning, and flexible education.

Heather Kanuka is Professor in Educational Policy Studies, Faculty of Education, University of Alberta, Canada. In 2004 she was awarded a Canada Research Chair in net-based teaching and learning in higher education. Kanuka's past and present research revolves around the relationships of teaching, learning and technology, within the context of effective strategies for teaching development. Most recently her research has focused on exploring the opinion, conceptions and attitudes – or the philosophical orientations – of academics who are educational technologists, and the influences these philosophical orientations have on net-based teaching and learning.

Helle Mathiasen is Professor at the Faculty of Science, University of Copenhagen, Department of Science Education, Denmark. Since the mid-'90s her research has revolved around use of digital media and net-based teaching and learning environments in high school and higher education. Mathiasen has been a member of national and international boards concerning pedagogy, teaching, learning and use of IT in the educational system, and has served as a guest professor. She has written several articles and edited books on the field.

Mariann Solberg, Dr. art. in philosophy, is a postdoctoral Research Fellow at the Centre for Teaching, Learning and Technology, Result, UiT The

Arctic University of Norway. Since 2008, she has worked as an advisor of project-oriented educational development of studies using ICT and digital media, in addition to conducting research in the area. Since 2011 Solberg has been teaching at the Teacher Training Courses in Higher Education at UiT. She has published on pedagogical philosophy, philosophy in the working life, epistemology, philosophy of science and net-based teaching, and learning in higher education.

Maria Wester is Senior Lecturer and Educational Developer at the Centre for Teaching and Learning, Umeå University, Sweden. She has been a teacher since the mid-'80s, and has taught at secondary school, teacher education, and is currently working with teaching and pedagogical development in higher education. Wester's research field is different aspects of teaching, mainly relational aspects such as gender, motivation and learning.

Acknowledgments

We thank the Center for Teaching, Learning and Technology (Result) at UiT The Arctic University of Norway, the Center for Teaching and Learning at Umea University and the Centre for Teaching and Digital Media, Aarhus University for hosting and helping us financially. A special thanks to colleagues in the field who have read and commented upon early versions of the chapters, this has been vital for the creative process.

Our contact person and editors at Routledge, who have all been very encouraging and a pleasure to work with. Routledge has ensured that deadlines were held, and given us very professional help and feedback.

A special thanks goes to Helen Hed, who is an academic Librarian at Umea University Library who has followed us during the whole process and to our external reader, Associate Professor Norm Friesen, who gave us important feedback, only one month before the final deadline. Many thanks to you all!

Introduction

Trine Fossland, Helle Mathiasen and
Mariann Solberg

Mass commodification, market orientation, standardisation and digitalisation are some of the reform elements in higher education that may potentially affect the development of the individual student in a negative way. For us this has caused a concern for student development and learning in net-based education. This book is the result of two years of work in a Scandinavian research group with a common interest in net-based higher education. We started out with a sense of there being something different in the Scandinavian way of conducting net-based higher education, and at the same time were concerned with the developmental processes of the net-based students towards being citizens of academia. If we look at the possible trajectory of a student who conducts all her higher education studies on the net, from the introductory course up to the PhD, using the present versions of our net-based educational courses and programmes, what do we believe would be the outcome? Will the student have developed her own voice as an academic? We fear that something would be lacking. Of course there could be a number of different dimensions lacking in any student development, regardless of learning environment. But when it comes to our present net-based courses and programmes, our hypothetical assumption is that the Academic Bildung of the students would suffer.

The idea of learning and, in particular, strategies for effective student learning, has for some time been the focus in university pedagogy, replacing teaching as the centre of attention. In many ways, this has been a fortunate shift. However, in order to address one of the fundamental functions of higher education, the ability to produce new knowledge, the focus has to be not only on learning but also on development of the students' Academic Bildung. Academic Bildung is connected to becoming an academically oriented person. It is a question of being socialised into an academic culture, as well as a matter of self-Bildung, of becoming an academic with the necessary integrity and expected creativity. Academic Bildung in this sense addresses the normative side of the student's development, her higher education citizenship, which is not covered in the concept of learning.

This book is thus first of all a contribution to the discussions on net-based education, where we have chosen to make the concept of Academic Bildung the lens through which we view net-based education. Our premise is that higher education, and in particular net-based higher education, will look different when achievement of Academic Bildung is seen as a goal. We conduct our investigations on micro-, meso- and macro-levels, examining the terms of net-based teaching and learning environments, institutional conditions and societal influence, respectively. At the same time, we look at the field with a multi-disciplinary lens, where philosophy, pedagogics, didactics, sociology and professional knowledge domains are involved. We provide examples of how the development of Academic Bildung can take place in different net-based educational settings, and we also provide examples showing how difficult this can be in the everyday life of net-based academia. In this way we analyse the conditions for both possibilities and challenges related to the development of Academic Bildung in net-based higher education. The point of departure is not that net-based environments are better or worse than face-to-face teaching and learning environments. Every environment has potentials, constraints and pitfalls. In net-based studies, however, the focus on facilitation of Academic Bildung seems even more important. A particular reason for this is that teachers have new opportunities and challenges for relating to the students. This is also the case concerning the students' opportunities to meet each other and the teachers involved. All are challenged by the new opportunities and constraints. Confronted with an explosive use of net-based education, the main question is: "How can universities educate students through net-based education and at the same time facilitate Academic Bildung?"

The structure of the book

The book is sectioned in three parts. If the theoretical framework of Part I is not of interest, the reader can choose to go directly to Part II. Part III consists of a discussion founded on the two earlier parts.

Part I: Framing the book

Part I consists of four chapters. Chapter 1, "Moving beyond learning in net-based higher education?", is written by Trine Fossland. In this chapter she frames the book in terms of a societal perspective on net-based higher education. This chapter presents the conceptual frames and introduces the core issues discussed in the book.

Chapter 2, "Net-based environments: Creating conditions for communication", is written by Helle Mathiasen. The focus of this chapter is on net-based teaching environments and the prerequisites for communication in such settings. Communication is here considered as the key to understanding the core values of net-based teaching. The concept of communication presented is meant to serve as an eye-opener, where the focus is on the prerequisites and maintenance of communication in net-based environments.

Chapter 3, "On Academic Bildung in higher education: A Scandinavian approach", is written by Mariann Solberg and Finn Thorbjørn Hansen. The chapter develops and presents a concept of Academic Bildung based on Humboldtian philsophy as well as more existentially oriented approaches to Bildung, relying in particular on Kant's and Gadamer's thinking. The authors turn to enlightenment traditions within Scandinavian public education and adult education in their search for the fundamental ideas of net-based education in Scandinavia.

Chapter 4, "Strategies for net-based education in Scandinavian universities" by Frank Holen, focuses on the explicit strategies at three Scandinavian universities. He poses the question: "What ideals are manifested in these strategies and practices, and what are the educational consequences?"

Part II: Case studies

The second part of the book consists of four case studies from net-based higher education courses in Norway, Sweden and Denmark, starting with a fifth study that looks at Scandinavian approaches to net-based higher education in comparison to practices from the USA, the UK, Australia and Canada. The case studies describe courses, teaching environments and student activities, and contribute to a discussion about rethinking course design and the use of ICT (information and communications technology) in light of Academic Bildung. The case studies discuss the role of communication and its conditions, the learning environment and course design on specific educational levels. An essential focus is the discussion concerning the possibilities, limitations, barriers and pitfalls inherent in organising teaching as fully or partially net-mediated courses. The case studies vary in theoretical lenses and themes, but they all look for Academic Bildung.

Chapter 5, "Philosophical orientations of teaching and technology: A Scandinavian case study", by Heather Kanuka from University of Alberta, Canada, opens Part II. She explores the question: "How do conceptions and attitudes – or the philosophies – of teaching and technology held by educational technologists within the higher education sector affect their teaching methods and the way they use technologies?" She examines how Scandinavian academics articulate their philosophical orientations on teaching and technology.

In Chapter 6, "Educating pharmacists: The perfect prescription?" Claire Englund and Maria Wester use a net-based bachelor programme in pharmacy as an example. The study focuses on the question of whether and how educational technologies can facilitate the acquisition of Academic Bildung in the professional identity necessary for the students' education and future profession.

In Chapter 7, "Net-based guerrilla didactics", Søren S. E. Bengtsen, Helle Mathiasen and Christian Dalsgaard present a study of net-based communication between students, and between students and teachers, in the master's education programme course: "IT educational design". The research questions posed in this chapter are: "How can technologies facilitate communication and learning in different teaching/learning environments, and what do the findings indicate when the focus is on pedagogic and didactic perspectives and initiatives in net-based communication in higher education?"

In Chapter 8, "Learning, meaning and Bildung? Reflections with reference to a net-based MBA programme", Gunnar Grepperud and Frank Holen ask to what extent do the MBA students display learning at a higher taxonomic level, and what explains their learning behaviour? The chapter reflects on how students approach learning in an experience-based master's programme, and relate that to the ideas and ideals of Bildung. The authors link and discuss the divide between the ideals of Bildung and the actual learning approaches of the master's program.

In Chapter 9, "Interprofessional net-based health education: A possibility to move beyond learning?", Trine Fossland studies a first semester net-based course involving 650 healthcare students from ten different disciplines. In this chapter she focuses on the particular course design to identify dimensions of Academic Bildung found in different empirical sources.

Part III: Rethinking university education

The case studies in Part II are the foundation for Part III, "Rethinking university education", where the central findings presented in the case studies are discussed within the philosophical Academic Bildung framework introduced in Part I. In addition to this theme, Part III presents a discussion concerning didactical perspectives. The book concludes with a summary, including new research questions.

In Chapter 10, "Pedagogical considerations: A new discourse based on Academic Bildung", Mariann Solberg, Gunnar Grepperud and Finn Thorbjørn Hansen look at the different dimensions and conceptions of Bildung found in the case studies and discuss these in relation to the concept of Academic Bildung developed in Part I. On the basis of the case studies, they ask whether and where digital media and IT can "add value" to the Bildung dimension.

Chapter 11, "Rethinking net-based higher education? The facilitation of a four-voiced pedagogy", is written by Trine Fossland. In this chapter she returns to the overall question of the book: "How can universities educate students through net-based education and at the same time facilitate Academic Bildung?" She asks whether it is necessary to rethink the pedagogical dimensions of net-based higher education.

In "Concluding remarks", Helle Mathiasen and Mariann Solberg make a short recapitulation and point out new perspectives and research questions.

Part I

Framing the book

1 Moving beyond learning in net-based higher education?

Trine Fossland

Net-based teaching and learning environments have changed the way higher education is approached. During the last decade net-based courses are no longer a core business only for universities with specialised distance education as a mission; they have been systematically integrated as an expanding pathway to higher education by predominately campus-based universities also. Universities worldwide have embraced technology as an essential solution to increase their global outreach and advance their competitiveness. At the same time, issues related to the later changes within higher education, such as new public management thinking, increased participation rates, and a greater diversity within the student population have been the subject of vigorous debate. Of particular concern is how these changes may challenge the quality of net-based education. Is there a reason for academic staff to be afraid of losing their responsibility for the students' development, or can these new net-based frames open up unexplored landscapes? As an increasing number of today's college and university students are enrolled in net-based courses, the facilitators' role and the quality of their facilitation of knowledge, skills and competences within these courses have become of current interest. Learning is not enough. The academic orientation of the students must be addressed and advanced. We want to take a closer look at this facilitation, as we argue that it is more important than ever to ask how we educate, to take responsibility and facilitate the students as academics and to face the challenges found within net-based higher education.

In this chapter, we discuss whether net-based higher education needs to be rethought in order for the students to move beyond learning. We present some of the underlying premises to consider when focusing on the development of Academic Bildung in net-based education. Additionally, the core concepts "net-based education" and "Academic Bildung" are highlighted, to provide a framework for the book[1].

Is there a need to rethink net-based higher education?

The increased complexity and mobility within society has affected higher education. The need and desire for reaching new student groups, the mass commodification of higher education, and the requirement for more flexible and effective communication and collaboration methods have led to a widespread and increasing popularity of net-based higher education. Many terms have been used to describe net-based education and the use of digital learning resources and information and communication technology (ICT, or simply IT) within higher education. Net-based education may range from 100 per cent internet-based lessons, through a combination of net- and campus-based instruction, to almost 100 per cent campus-based delivery for some courses. As different net-based courses have emerged, there have been critical views of this type of education, as national surveys have demonstrated that digital learning resources and IT are mainly used to administrate and distribute learning content within higher education (Ørnes et al. 2011). The idea of net-based education as more democratic with new opportunities for widening participation has, according to many critics, developed at the expense of educational quality. Net-based education has been characterised by critical voices as an easier way to higher education, less regulated, with consequences that will undermine the core ideas connected to research, teaching and learning. Student diversity, and the perception of students not being as involved as before, have strengthened this negative impression, since these challenges did not exist one generation ago (Biggs and Tang 2011). At the same time there are now more extensive demands related to higher education in general, often expressed in terms of increased workloads and administration requirements, and the new public management mentality pervading higher education at the expense of research and teaching. Furthermore, students are expected to develop into responsible citizens equipped with work-related and generic skills, such as information literacy, ability to collaborate, communicate, be creative and innovative, and develop problem-solving skills. As large and diversified student groups pursue their studies in net-based environments, this prompts a need for facilitation that addresses these new challenges.

The idea that higher education is losing its credibility and position within society is not new. Researchers like Pelikan (1992) and Barnett (1992) warned against a development towards making higher education not sufficiently challenging. Jaraslav Pelikan (1992) claimed in his book, *The idea of the university: A re-examination*, that "[a] modern society is unthinkable without the university" and that "the university is in a state of crisis and is in danger of losing credibility" (p. 13). Pelikan discussed the university's role in society, assessing its guiding principles, aims and practical functions. He demonstrated the inseparability of research and teaching on both intellectual and practical grounds, and argued that the core issues of the university – free inquiry, scholarly honesty, toleration of diverse beliefs, trust in rationality and public verifiability – must be practiced and taught by the university (op. cit.). These characteristic dimensions must also be seen as key values when it comes to developing and facilitating net-based course designs.

In his book, *The beautiful risk of education*, Biesta (2013) addressed the last two decades' push towards standardising education in advanced capitalist societies, linking this to neoliberal accountability mechanisms and technologies, as he presented the term "learnification of education". It is important to understand Biesta's distinction between learning and education, and what he called "the new language of learning", which he referred to as a discursive shift away from education to learning. Biesta earlier in 2006 discussed the problematic linkage between education and the economy, whereby "questions about the content and purpose of education became subject to the forces of the market instead of being the concern of professional judgment and democratic deliberation" (p. 31). The language, he argued, facilitates an *economic* understanding of the process of education (p. 24). This fosters ideas of a net-based education where all learning activities have to be closely aligned with the intended learning outcomes in each particular course. According to Ellis et al. (2009), the quality of student approaches to learning has been found to be closely associated with the quality of their learning outcomes. But, is it enough to fulfil the requirements of learning outcomes? Stephenson and Mantzs' (2012) closer analysis of the focus on learning outcomes in higher education, indicated that much of what is considered under learning outcomes, key skills, and employability is about documentation and appearing to make a difference in limited and defined learning outcomes. They argued that there has been resistance to some of these new ideas, but few attempts to articulate an alternative conception (op. cit.).

Many indicators and pressure factors tell us that there is a need to rethink net-based education. New challenges, increased complexity and mobility within society highlight the importance of the facilitators' approach to students' development as academics. Becoming an academic can be expressed through Barnett's (1997) notion of "critical being" which includes thinking, self-reflection and action, as "[c]ritical persons are more than just critical thinkers. They are able critically to engage with the world and with themselves as well as with knowledge" (ibid., p. 1). This can be seen as an approach to the world, to thinking and criticality that a university-educated person should aspire to. At the university, the students' struggle to become critical beings has to be facilitated, stimulated and approached – it does not just happen in net-based studies. Becoming an academic necessitates facilitation within higher education that engages and addresses threshold concepts and ideas, and deals with "troublesome knowledge" (Meyer and Land 2003). The development of intellectual and ethical dimensions can be seen as one of the key goals of education that enables transformative learning. According to Bryson (2014) transformation is difficult, because it

requires movement out of comfort zones, taking risks and embracing uncertainly. Strong engagement is a prerequisite to that. The more advanced or sophisticated ways of knowing imply an open-mindedness, academic self-confidence, reflectivity and an ability to relate to others which infer that the individual both wishes to engage and is already engaged.

(p. 11)

Within net-based courses, the students need to be brought out of their comfort zones in order to be challenged and engaged. University education within a changing world needs to address real challenges and opportunities within society, both in relation to specific disciplines and to foster wider perspectives. To succeed with this mission, net-based education needs to move beyond the restricted achievement expressed in limited perspectives on "learning outcomes" and "constructive alignment" (Biggs 2011), which in the Bologna Process and the European Qualification Framework are proposed as the required knowledge, skills and competences that are to provide future societal needs, often referred to as twenty-first century skills. Kreber (2014, p. 7) argued that there is a growing tension between higher education's intellectual, critical, theoretical and moral purposes, and those of a more practical and economic nature, oriented towards providing service to society. The question is whether there is a need for a special didactical approach to combine these interests, to confront the new challenges within net-based education. But first let us take a closer look into what these interests and qualifications can look like.

Twenty-first century skills in a world of super-complexity

In their article "Defining twenty-first century skills", Binkley et al. (2012) argued that the shifts in advanced economies, the specialisation and expansion of knowledge, and the transformation of work and social relationships through information and communication technology have defined new skills that are important for coping with the demands and challenges of today's society. Decentralised decision making, information sharing, teamwork, and demands for so-called innovative and creative thinking are seen as of increasing importance. Bingley argued that there is a need to replace past expectations of basic skills and knowledge with updated university standards for what students should be able to do. To encounter these challenges, he argued that universities must be transformed in ways that will enable students to acquire the "sophisticated thinking, flexible problem solving, collaboration and communication skills they will need to be successful in work and life" (p. 18). As a reaction to the pressures on today's universities, the need to develop courses and/or programmes that encourage and educate students from different disciplines to be thoughtful, ethical, and confident global citizens and citizens of academia (Solberg 2011) seems inevitable in order to maintain the universities' positions and the students' reflexive relation to a complex and global society. In line with Binkley, universities need to create opportunities for students to grow and thrive in all aspects of their education, and this involves rethinking teaching and learning environments and available learning resources. Several generic qualifications are expected of the students to adjust to working life.

Binkley and colleagues (2012) provided a list of twenty-first century skills based on their analysis of twelve relevant frameworks drawn from a number of countries. The list serves as an example of how to *approach* assessment of twenty-first century skills. They expect that educators, as they consider their model, may need to make adaptations that fit their own context as they design assessments appropriate for their students.

Ways of thinking

1   Creativity and innovation
2   Critical thinking, problem-solving, decision making
3   Learning to learn, metacognition

Ways of working

1   Communication
2   Collaboration (teamwork)

Tools for working

1   Information literacy
2   ICT literacy

Living in the world

1   Citizenship – local and global
2   Life and career
3   Personal and social responsibility

The list demonstrates that a university-educated person needs to open up to the world, as well as become critical and reflective about it. According to Søby (2003, p. 6) *digital literacy* describes the ability to develop the potential and innovative use of technology in learning and work activities. Søby (op. cit.) argue that there is an affinity between the concepts *information literacy* and *digital literacy* that gives meaning to what he calls "digital *Bildung*" and digital competence. *Information literacy* refers to:

- Fundamental IT skills that include searching, locating, evaluating, manipulating and controlling information from diverse digital sources and formats.
- The development of communicative competence, in the sense of a critical, interpretative and analytical relationship to sources, digital genres and media forms.

Digital competence is one of the eight key competences for lifelong learning, as acknowledged by the European Commission[2]. In the 2013 European Commission report "DIGCOMP: A framework for developing and understanding digital competence in Europe", Ferrari defined digital competence as "the confident, critical and creative use of IT to achieve goals related to work, employability, learning, leisure, inclusion and/or participation in society." He argued that digital competence enables us to acquire other key competences (e.g. language, mathematics, learning to learn, cultural awareness), as this is an transversal key competence. But is this enough? If we follow Barnett's and Pelikan's warnings into the halls of academia, what does this mean to the facilitation of net-based higher education? Is it possible to face the new issues by facilitating more active forms of collaboration, more authentic, problem- and inquiry-based challenges? Can we facilitate new possibilities for the students to expand their horizons and challenge the complexity of the world they live in? Do we need to address critical skills that form the foundation for the twenty-first century labour market suggested by Binkley et al. into every programme at tomorrow's universities? How can this be facilitated in order to develop the students' need for more authenticity within approaches to higher education?

Becoming an academic and striving for authenticity and autonomy

Student engagement, marked by both the teachers' and students striving for authenticity and autonomy, seems significant when the goal is to become an academically oriented person at the university. Becoming an academic can be understood as an identity project, where the students' social, cultural, economic, and symbolic capital comes into play (Bourdieu 1998). This also involves the transition whereby students come into more academic ways of approaching their studies. Students' opportunities to develop as academics are related to their social capital within a student group, whether this capital can be mobilised both socially and academically, whether students are socialised into the academic culture and so on (Solberg and Fossland, 2013). Whether they can afford to study instead of taking an extra job is another example of important factors that can affect their approach to higher education. Bryson (2014, p. 9) referred to three "ways of being a student", in which the student's experience and identity are constructed from the combination of:

- The nature of the personal project: What is the purpose or outcome of their degree for them, i.e. why are they at the university?
- The degree of integration into university life.
- The level of the intellectual engagement with the subject.

The engagement with the subject of study includes professional development and the development of disciplinary knowledge. The student's reasons for being at university is also something Barnett (2007, p. 70) argued as essential in his book *A will to learn*, where he linked the onto- logical with the epistemological dimensions of higher education. The student's approach to higher education is fundamental:

> Without self, without a will to learn, without a being that has come into itself, her effort to know and to act within a program of study cannot even begin to form with any assuredness.

Bryson (2014) argued that the students' sense of engagement with their experience as a student is enhanced by feeling part of something: a sense of belonging, affiliation and a feeling of being integrated. He understands stu- dents' engagement as much more than just doing. Being and becoming are addressed as ontological and epistemological considerations and important aspects of the students' approach, as well as the facilitators' mediation of students' engagement (SE):

> Student engagement is about what a student brings to Higher Educa- tion in terms of goals, aspirations, values and beliefs and how these are shaped and mediated by their experience whilst a student. SE is constructed and reconstructed through the lens of the perceptions and identities held by students and the meaning and sense a student makes of their experiences held by students and the meaning and sense of the perceptions and identities of their experiences and interactions.
>
> (Bryson, p. 19)

To facilitate students' engagement presupposes that the teacher is also engaged. This involves authenticity, a fundamental element in teaching. According to Kreber (2014), several authors have argued that there is a need for more authenticity in university teaching to address the students' personal engagement and their development into academics. In the 2014 book *Authenticity in and through teaching in higher education* Kreber argued that with a "particular engagement with their teaching teachers become more authentic", and that "being a scholar of teaching is an ongoing transformative learning process that is intimately bound up with becom- ing authentic" (p. 5). Teachers striving for authenticity in their teaching can develop the students' own authenticity, and "authenticity through teaching" refers therefore to teachers moving towards greater authenticity with the ultimate goal of promoting students' learning, development and authenticity (op. cit.). Kreber argued that "authenticity through teaching highlights that there is a relation between how teachers engage with their teaching and their students' development towards greater authenticity" (p. 9). She further argued that authenticity in teaching requires "that we orient ourselves to the shared ideas, purposes and values that underpin our practice as academic teachers" (p. 60). Kreber wrote that the teacher's (facilitator's) role must not be limited to doing what needs to be done to satisfy external demands (learning outcomes), or doing what is of value to us personally. Instead she insisted that "it must also include doing what is in the important interests of students and that they grow into their own authenticity" (op. cit.). Universities, at their best, are traditionally known as institutions that foster a student's hopes, imagination, wonderment, visions, integrity and critical thinking, making students invest in their own future as well as in their education. According to Kreber,

> authenticity involves not just being able to make rational choices; it also implies owning them, being personally invested in them, or feeling a deep inner commitment to them. Investing oneself in this way requires courage, but also empathy and compassion.
>
> (p. 10)

If we are going to address current challenges within net-based higher education, we need to address student engagement, autonomy and authenticity in our approach to the use of technology.

Can the use of technology be a driver for change?

In a world of "super-complexity" (Barnett 2004, p. 242) strategic development of educational technologies has become an important matter for nearly all universities over the last decade. According to Dutton and Loader (2004) IT is shaping the future of education, research and the sciences through access: information access, access to people, access to services, and access to technology. In their book *Rethinking pedagogy for a digital age,* Beetham and Sharpe (2013) address the question of student engagement as related to design, sharing and the facilitation of learning activities. Salomon (1996) defines a net-based learning environment as a specific group of conditions, including learning facilities and technologies, recognised behaviours and shared expectations in addition to teaching and learning tasks and activities, all gathered around and related to specific educational aims and content, like student learning and learning outcomes. The important question addressed here is whether the multiplicity of learning technologies used within these courses provides new opportunities for teachers to facilitate the students' development as critical beings. Can net-based courses address the qualifications, socialisation and subjectification – as Biesta (2010, 2013) understands the three domains, or functions – of education? Can these courses open up new possibilities for more authentic approaches to becoming an academically oriented person who is ready to enter the differentiated, individualised, complex and changing society? Can technology also become a stimulating frame for the students' process of approaching and handling this complexity, as well as an aid to their journey to become academics? The diversity of learning technologies, also beyond what is facilitated within particular university courses, has the potential to open up new landscapes for educational activities, like user-generated inputs, access to digital resources, and contact with others across the world that can challenge the students' development of Academic Bildung.

In this book we go into several empirical case studies from different theoretical angles. Can we find uses of technology that promote authentic examples, variation, new possibilities for exam revisions, student engagement, preparation, involvement and motivation which promote the students' development of Academic Bildung? Does use of technology contribute positively to the way students are integrated in the academic community, through providing new forms of collaboration that stimulate sharing of resources, more supervision, peer feedback and national or international collaboration with networks, and academic key personnel, with the potential to enhance the students' development of Academic Bildung, and develop and train their own academic voices? Can we find student activity where the use of technology promotes more active and authentic forms of learning that are inquiry- and problem-based, using, for example, social media or filmed cases as a starting point for critical discussions? Are there other approaches to Academic Bildung that allow students to, for instance, create their own authentic content in relation to their qualification requirements, potentially encourage their own creation process and authenticity, and develop their own "academic voice"? This makes the content represent more personal and creative commitments and investments, and this approach has the potential to transform knowledge in a way that influences the students' development of Academic Bildung. For instance, the use of technology can be used to make classrooms or learning spaces virtually in contact with workplaces (inviting interesting people to teaching/discussions via digital tools), or connect students with digital resources relevant for different occupations. Can we find both teachers and students who will make use of authentic digital material in ways that stimulate the students' development of Academic Bildung? Can we find uses of technology that enhance the students' thinking, flexible problem solving, collaboration and communication skills needed to be successful in work and life (referred to as twenty-first century skills)? Can we find innovative and updated ways to approach the students' academic journeys that can develop their Academic Bildung?

In the preface of their 2003 book *Effective teaching with technology in higher education,* Bates and Poole asked this important question: "If technology is the answer, what is the question?" Do we need to move away from the question of how technology can improve teaching, and instead turn the focus to how to serve the learners and their development as academics? One of the reasons why, over ten years later, this is still an important question is that we know from national surveys that digital learning resources and IT are mainly used to administrate and distribute learning content within higher education (Ørnes et al. 2011). Using technology for knowledge distribution and sharing content is not enough if the purpose is to develop the students and facilitate their approach to become academics at the university. So what do we need to do then, in order move the students beyond learning? In this book we want to investigate this when we ask: "How can universities educate students through net-based education and at the same time facilitate Academic Bildung?"

Moving beyond learning – A double-tracked concept of Academic Bildung

In Chapter 3 of this book, we present a concept of Academic Bildung that is based on a Humboldtian model as well as more existentially oriented approaches to Bildung that rely on Kant's and Gadamer's thinking on autonomy and authenticity. Humbolt's ideals, related to academic freedom and research-based education, are often referred to when Academic Bildung is discussed; the concept can be defined as mutual engagement of self and world, and as the formation of a student who operates both inside and outside the educational institution (Bostad and Ottersen 2011).

The "double-tracked" Bildung concept and Bildung pedagogy, outlined in Chapter 3, describes the concept as a developmental process of persons heading toward "something better – a tacit or explicit normative ideal, value or vision of ethical, existential, aesthetical or spiritual quality – in an educational setting" (p. 31). When defining the concept as double-tracked, authors Solberg and Hansen say that this is connected to both:

- "critical thinking, society-oriented reflection and autonomy", and
- "ethical dimensions of human formation and self-formation, existential- and being-oriented reflection and authenticity" (op. cit. p. 28).

When seen in relation to students in higher education in general, this involves both the critical emancipatory society-oriented dimension (the striving for autonomy) and the identity formation process (the striving for authenticity) associated with the search for meaning that is specific to teaching, learning, and research in higher education (op. cit). Can these values and dimensions be found within the different net-based courses presented in this book?

This volume connects Academic Bildung to the cultural and geographical scene of Scandinavia, meaning: 1) its perspectives are connected to Scandinavia, and 2) it examines empirical cases from different universities in Scandinavian countries. Our interest is linked to the facilitation of Academic Bildung in different models of teaching and learning environments of net-based higher education. This facilitation can be more or less successful, and conditions must be taken into consideration in every case. This book will discuss in more detail what this means in practice with regard to significant parts of the facilitation process in net-based courses, with perspectives from different disciplinary viewpoints. In this book we have defined Academic Bildung as becoming an academically oriented person, which concerns socialisation into an academic culture, critical and society-oriented thoughts, ethical-existential dimensions and being-oriented reflections. Academic Bildung is therefore also connected to a student's own expectations and knowledge, as well as the skills and general competences that are required in today's complex society.

Notes

1 These concepts are presented in more detail in Chapters 2 and 3 in this book.
2 With the 2006 "European recommendation on key competences," *Official Journal* L 394, 30 Dec. 2006.

References

Barnett, R. (1992), *Improving higher education: Total quality care.* Society of Research into Higher Education & Open University Press: Buckingham, UK.

Barnett, R. (1997), *Higher education: A critical business.* SHRE: London.

Barnett, R. (2004), "Learning for an unknown future". *Higher Education Research and Development*, vol. 23, no. 3, pp. 247–60.

Barnett, R. (2007), *A will to learn: Being a student in an age of uncertainty.* Open University Press: New York.

Bates, A. W., and Poole, G. (2003), *Effective teaching with technology in higher education: Foundations for success.* Jossey-Bass: San Francisco.

Beetham, H. and Sharpe, R. (2013), *Rethinking pedagogy for a digital age: Designing and delivering e-learning.* Routledge: New York.

Biesta, G. (2010), *Good education in an age of measurement: Ethics, politics, democracy.* Paradigm Publishers: Boulder, CO.

Biesta, G. (2013), *The beautiful risk of education.* Paradigm: London.

Biggs, J. and Tang, C. (2011), *Teaching for quality learning at university,* 4th edn. Open University Press/McGraw-Hill: Buckingham, UK.

Binkley et al. (2012), "Defining twenty-first century skills". In: Griffin, P., ed., *Assessment and teaching of 21st century skills.* Springer: New York.

Bonnett, M. and Cuypers, S. (2003), "Autonomy and authenticity in education". In: Blake, N., Smeyers, P., Smith, R. and Standish, P., eds., *The Blackwell guide to the philosophy of education*, pp. 326–40. Blackwell Publishing: Oxford.

Bostad, I. and Ottersen, O. P. (2011), "Dannelse i kryssild". In: Hagtvet, B. and Ognjenovic, G., eds., *Dannelse. Tenkning – modning – refleksjon*, pp. 56–69. Dreyer Forlag A/S: Oslo.

Bourdieu, P. (1998), *Distinction.* Routledge: London.

Bryson, C. (2014), *Understanding and developing student engagement.* Routledge: New York.

Dutton, W. H. and Loader, B. D. (2004), *Digital academe: New media in higher education and learning.* Routledge: London.

Ellis, R., Ginns, P. and Piggott, L. (2009), "E-learning in higher education: Some key aspects and their relationship to approaches to study". *Higher Education Research and Development*, vol. 28, no. 3, pp. 303–18.

Ferrari, A. (2013), "DIGCOMP: A Framework for Developing and Understanding Digital Competence in Europe". Available online at Competence in Europe, http://ftp.jrc.es/EURdoc/JRC83167.pdf (accessed 17 June 2014).

Fossland, T. (2013), "Digitalisering er ikke nok". In: Nordkvelle, Y. T., Fossland, T., and Netteland, G., eds. *Digital vurdering, nye kvalitetskrav og institusjonelt ansvar*, pp. 175–94. Akademika Forlag: Oslo.

Fossland, T. (2014), *Digitale læringsformer i høyere utdanning*. Universitetsforlaget: Oslo.

Gibbs, B. (1979), "Autonomy and authority in education". *Journal of Philosophy of Education*, vol. 13, pp. 119–32.

Kember, D., Ho, A. and Hong, C. (2010), "Characterising a teaching and learning environment capable of motivating student learning". *Learning Environment Research*, vol. 13, no. 1, pp. 43–57.

Kreber, C. (2014), *Authenticity in and through teaching: The transformative potential of the scholarship of teaching*. Routledge: London.

Ørnes, H. et al. (2011), "Digital tilstand i høyere utdanning", *Rapporten fra Norgesuniversitetets Nasjonale Undersøkelse*, Jan. 2011. Norgesuniversitetet: Oslo.

Pelikan, J. (1992), *The idea of the university: A re-examination*. Yale University Press: New Haven, CT.

Salomon, G. (1996), "Studying novel learning environments as patterns of change". In: Vosniadou, S., De Corte, E., Glaser, R. and Mandl, H., eds., *International perspectives on the design of technology-supported learning environments*. Lawrence Erbaum Associates: Mahwah, NJ/Routledge: New York.

Søby, M. (2003), "Digital competences: from ICT skills to digital 'bildung'", p. 6. Available online at http://www.ituarkiv.no/filearchive/Dig_comp_eng.pdf

Solberg, M. (2011), "Educating the citizen of academia online?" *International Review of Research in Open and Distance Learning*, vol. 12, no. 4, pp. 77–87.

Solberg, M. and Fossland, T. (2013), "Akademisk danning – Et mulig prosjekt for voksne studenter i fleksible studier?" In: Arbo, P., ed., *Utdanningssamfunnet og livslang læring: Festskrift til Gunnar Grepperud*, pp. 46–62. Gyldendal Akademisk: Oslo.

Stephenson, J. and Mantzs, Y. (2012), *Capability and quality in higher education*. Routledge: London.

2 Net-based environments

Creating conditions for communication

Helle Mathiasen

Introduction

The focus of this chapter is on net-based teaching environments and the prerequisites for communication in such settings. Communication is the key to understanding the core values of net-based teaching. The concept of communication is presented here as an eye-opener, where the focus is on the prerequisites for communication and its maintenance in net-based environments.

The concept of communication is pivotal, given that this concept is intricately entwined with the teaching process. Communication is central to both synchronous and asynchronous net-based environments and to both wholly and partly net-based course designs. The concept of learning, and thus knowledge construction, will be introduced in relation to the concept of teaching.

This chapter will draw on the concept of Academic Bildung, when considering the prerequisites, possibilities and constraints for the development of knowledge, skills, competences and Academic Bildung in net-based teaching environments in higher education. We suggest that Academic Bildung should be seen as a phenomenon that spans the borders between the dimensions of knowledge, skills and competences and be considered as a phenomenon beyond these concepts. The book offers different approaches to Academic Bildung, where we discuss the question posed in the introduction: "How can universities educate students through net-based education and at the same time facilitate Academic Bildung?" Hence an essential underlying condition for dealing with the question is whether the approach to Academic Bildung is seen through an ontological or a constructivist conceptual lens.

The discussion will provide an essential background for the readers' own reflections, particularly on the empirical studies that form the cases that comprise Part II of this volume. These studies have the dual purpose of drawing attention to the concept of net-based teaching environments and also the prerequisites for the development of Academic Bildung. The theoretical approaches in the case studies take different points of departure. By means of the concept of communication presented here, namely the prerequisites for communication, its maintenance and the proposed lens for an analytic approach to the concept of teaching and learning environments, the reader is offered a lens for critical reflection when considering the development of Academic Bildung, as discussed in Part III.

Communication

There are many perspectives on the concept of communication in the literature. For the purpose of this introduction, where the focus is net-based education, the preferred definition will be one that emphasises the requirement of a minimum of two persons and that these persons must focus their attention on the activity before a communication unit is actualised. Consequently, communication is not seen as the transfer of knowledge, and information is not seen as substance being transferred from one person to another (Shannon and Weaver [1949] 1971). This prerequisite means that all parties (teachers and students) play an active role in communication activities. Thus the concept of communication and the prerequisites for communication form a perspective where the teaching environment, seen as a potential environment for learning, is both designed and discussed.

Students can for instance pay attention to a lecture by listening, taking notes and posing questions on the appropriate net-based forum, the teachers can pay attention to the communication in the net-based forum by posting answers and contributing with further questions, literature suggestions, etc. In net-based group work, for example, both students and teachers play an active role by reading contributions posted in the group forums and participating in the forum by making contributions to an ongoing discussion.

Inspired by the German sociologist Niklas Luhmann we will introduce a concept of communication which draws on his systems theoretical approach to communication, teaching and learning. From a systems theory perspective our definition of communication would be considered as a synthesis of three selections: first, the selection of information; second, the selection of utterance (selected by the utterer, e.g. the teacher); and third, the selection of understanding (selected by the addressee, e.g. the student). Thus from this viewpoint you need a minimum of two persons to make a communication unit, which is considered to be a social system. We can observe the utterance, regardless whether the utterance is in oral or written form, but we cannot observe the third selection. The selection of understanding is, so to speak, invisible; that is, its operations are internal to the specific person.

If one conceptualizes communication as the synthesis of three selections, as the unity of information, utterance, and understanding, then communication is realized if and to the extent that understanding comes about. Everything else happens "outside" the unity of an elemental communication and presupposes it. This is especially true for a fourth type of selection: for the acceptance or the rejection of the specific meaning that was communicated. One must distinguish the addressee's understanding of the selection of meaning that has taken place from acceptance or rejection as a premise of the addressee's own behavior. This distinction is of considerable theoretical importance.

(Luhmann 1995, p. 147)

In addition to communication, defined as a synthesis of the three selections mentioned, we also want to focus attention on the conditions for acceptance or rejection of the uttered information. This fourth type of selection is an equally important element in a communication process; although not actually part of a communication unit it is something that is essential for the continuation of the communication. Both the communication unit and the fourth type of selection actualise the concept of Academic Bildung by making communication essential to its development. In other words you can choose to accept or reject "the specific meaning that was communicated" and at the same time you "must distinguish the addressee's understanding of the selection of meaning that has taken place from acceptance or rejection as a premise of the addressee's own behaviour"(ibid.). It is the communication environment that provides the opportunity to develop abilities for critical thinking, autonomy and authenticity, which also include a dimension of critical and society-oriented reflection and a dimension of ethical-existential and being-oriented reflection. Academic Bildung also encompasses socialisation into the academic culture and the question of self-Bildung, as an academic with the necessary integrity and expected creativity.

What is communicated in a net-based course and in what way seems essential for the process of developing Academic Bildung, and for students to become participants in an academic community.

Using the above conception of communication we have the possibility to focus on the conditions for the development of the "double-tracked" Bildung-concept, briefly presented in Chapter 1, and to further consider the main question posed in this book: "How can universities educate students through net-based education and at the same time facilitate the development of Academic Bildung?"

When endeavouring to make fruitful environments for the growth of all aspects of Academic Bildung the theoretical approach outlined above challenges both teachers and students to rethink the teaching environment and their roles in this setting, both on campus and when participating online.

Teaching

In this book the focus is on students' development of Academic Bildung in wholly or partly net-based teaching environments. Further, our definition of the concept of "teaching" is inspired by systems theory and builds on a definition of teaching as a highly sophisticated form of communication with the intention to change systems (Luhmann 2002).

In line with the definition above, students are seen as psychic systems, which operate in and maintain themselves via conscious activities like thoughts, emotions and intuitions. A person is a construction, in the sense that a person cannot be observed "an sich" (the thing in itself), but will be observed and constructed, depending on the observer (Luhmann 1995). The term *person* is related to communication and hence to social systems (cf. the definition of a communication unit). A human being encompasses several systems, in addition to the psychic systems of, for instance, the nervous system and digestive system, which are all self-referential.

> The theory of self-referential systems maintains that systems can differentiate only by self-reference, which is to say, only insofar as systems refer to themselves (be this to elements of the same system, to operations of same systems, or to the unity of the system) in constituting their elements and their elemental operations. To make this possible, systems must create and employ a description of themselves; they must at least be able to use the difference between system and environment within themselves, for orientation and as a principle for creating information. Therefore self-referential closure is possible only in an environment, only under ecological conditions. The environment is a necessary correlate of self-referential operations because these out of all operations cannot operate under the premise of solipsism. [. . .] The (subsequently classical) distinction between "closed" and "open" systems is replaced by the question of how self-referential closure can create openness.
>
> (Luhmann 1995, p. 9)

Teaching environments, meanwhile, are defined as social systems that operate in and maintain themselves through communication. Social systems are seen as environments for psychic systems and vice versa. In general these systems are characterised as being operationally closed and autonomous, but not closed in the same manner as autarchic systems, which are self-sufficient (Luhmann 1995, p. 411). Conversely, both social and psychic systems are dependent on their environments and thus their operations are self-governed and internal to the specific systems. To maintain themselves systems need nourishment from the environment and systems need to be "disturbed" by their environment to maintain themselves.

> One of communication's most important achievements is sensitizing the system to chance, disturbances, and "noise" of all kinds. In communication, one can make understandable what is unexpected, unwell known, and disappointing.
>
> (Luhmann 1995, p. 172)

Each psychic system has the opportunity to put itself at the disposal of other systems, by paying attention or contributing to a discussion, for example, as is the case when students contribute to a net-based discussion forum. Both students' and teachers' approaches to and participation in the actualized teaching environment is crucial when the focus is on maintaining communication and the conditions for the continuous development of Academic Bildung.

In other words, systems gain nourishment from their environment by observing their environment, thus the point of departure is that a system and its environment are mutually dependent – there is no system without an environment and vice versa.

The coupling of systems definitions and systems characteristics with the concept of communication leads to a manner of thinking where it is impossible to work with the idea that thoughts can leave a person. This also has some decisive consequences for, among other things, a discussion of teaching environments and the opportunities for the development of Academic Bildung. The distinction between system and environment, e.g. students and their teaching environment, give us the opportunity to discuss the facilitation and development of Academic Bildung from a point of departure where communication is pivotal.

Systems theory draws on a series of inspiring theoretical approaches and its condensation of exciting and creative thoughts generated mutually from science, the humanities, and social sciences is evocative in relation to the overall question asked in this book. In this context one of the essential theorists is Husserl (1936) and his phenomenologically inspired concept of intentional actions in connection with the concept of communication. Thus intentional action is linked with persons (observed as a psychic system) participating in a communication.

Even though social systems and psychic systems are operationally closed (self-reproductive), they can be coupled structurally through communication. If the students observe the communication in class or in a discussion forum and then make a contribution, we have a social system. Teaching, the specific form of intentional communication that aims to bring about change, is seen as a possible facilitator for learning processes and the development of knowledge, skills, competences and Academic Bildung. The concept of learning, inspired by the systems theoretical lens, is accordingly defined as individual mental constructions.

This has of course implications for the specific teaching environment. In this chapter we use the term "teaching environment" when we focus on communication and the term "learning environment" when the focus is on the students' learning processes. Thereby, learning is, so to speak, linked to psychic systems and teaching to social systems, and as mentioned above these two systems are structurally coupled and support each other, which highlights the need for communication. Since the point of departure is that thoughts never leave a person, for example a student, as thoughts but as a communicative reconstruction, according to the theoretical approach presented, we need to rethink the premises for teaching and education. The creation of the necessary conditions for communication and for its maintenance is a pivotal base for rethinking the possibilities for Academic Bildung.

Communication is what takes place when constructing understanding and knowledge based on the social system in play. Thus the focus is on the use of a variety of teaching environments, or communication forums, available to teachers and students.

The intention of this chapter has been to suggest and describe concepts that offer a possibility to be more precise about what we want to discuss. Furthermore, we see the clarification of the concepts used as a way to qualify the discussion about pedagogical and didactical premises for teaching and learning, including the facilitation and development of Academic Bildung. Therefore we do not subscribe to the concept of "blended learning" that often appears in the literature on this subject because it is hard to identify what, exactly, is "blended" in learning. Inspired by the theoretical frame presented we suggest the term "blended learning environments", and thereby focus on the environment where the variety or mix of teaching and learning environments are actualised. Our view is that this framework allows us to discuss the blending of different learning environments such as communication forums (net-based/on campus), learning resources and tools. It also encompasses how combining these environments may facilitate the students in their learning activities and achievement of academic goals, and at the same time offers new options for assessment. Like "blended learning", the terms "e-learning" or "elearning" are not used in this volume. The use of these terms tends to be imprecise and overemphasises the electronic aspect, which does not reflect the foundation and framework of educational settings. Instead, this book uses the term "net-based", as this provides a more exact description of the teaching and learning contexts under discussion.

Environments and conditions – The development of Academic Bildung?

Technology can never in itself transform how we approach teaching and learning within higher education without involving the pedagogical, attitudinal and content aspects involved in the educational planning of specific course designs. When approaching this complexity, Academic Bildung is seen as an important point of orientation to bear in mind. Both wholly and partly net-based teaching environments have consequences for the development of Academic Bildung through teaching and learning activities. As a consequence of a system's characteristics, some systems may be labelled non-trivial when we cannot predict the outcome of a well-known input (von Foerster and Pörksen 2006; Luhmann 2002). Such non-trivial systems may be described as operationally closed, self-referential, autono-mous, analytically indeterminable, unpredictable, and dependent on the previous operations and the concrete context.

When looked at from the perspective of teaching and learning envi-ronments, this means we cannot predict the outcome of a defined input, regardless of whether we choose face-to-face class teaching and learning environments or a net-based teaching environment. We do not know what happens in the system, that is, how the specific system operates in its self-referential mode. Whether a student has listened to a lecture on campus or a podcasted lecture one cannot foretell the outcome. While teachers' intentions concerning students' knowledge construction is one thing, the students' own construction of knowledge is another. However, if teachers and students have the opportunity to communicate about the content dur-ing or after the lecture, the teachers have the possibility to gain insight into what the students have understood of the uttered information in the lecture and the students have the possibility to test their understanding of the imparted knowledge.

If these possibilities are not present, we can talk about "one way knowl-edge conveyance" rather than communication. This approach reinforces the idea that the reproduction of teacher-communicated information is the purpose. There is no guarantee, and there has never been such a guaran-tee, that the students' development of Academic Bildung will take place in such a system.

The premises for communication are different in different environ-ments. For instance, communication in a face-to-face context will involve the use of multiple senses to control the selected understanding of the com-munication, and intonation, pauses and bodily movement also come into play. On the other hand, when it comes to written net-based communication forums, several of the communicative modes are not available, leaving only written text, graphics, smileys and other textual means to facilitate the social system's continuous self-reproduction (autopoiesis), bearing in mind that systems are closed, self-referential and autonomous, and that they operate in, constitute, reproduce and maintain themselves through communication (Mathiasen 2007). Research has on the other hand demonstrated that even small possibilities to communicate provide some students with the opportu-nity to participate in a manner that suits their way of being a student. For instance, some students stated that writing in a net-forum gives them the possibility to reflect on the content and form of the message, to write with-out breaks, to reintroduce previous messages when needed, to reflect on the finished message, and to consider if it should even be sent (Mathiasen 2005). The premises vary of course depending on the "bandwidth" of the communication, in the sense that face-to-face settings have many commu-nicative coupling possibilities compared to net-based written discussion forums (Mathiasen 2002). Net-based learning environments that use for example video conferencing offer possibilities from the third selection in the communication unit: an understanding that lies outside the conventional face-to-face or asynchronous-based teaching environment. Because we limit our focus to net-based environments in this book, the development of Academic Bildung is seen in relation to communication in different net-based learning and teaching environments, which the case studies will illustrate and analyse.

Each environment has its disadvantages and advantages for maintaining communication and the choice of teaching environment will ideally depend on, among other things, the possibilities for the development of Academic Bildung. The possibility for both students and teachers to respond or give feedback has different prerequisites within different settings, depending on the teaching and learning environment: such as face-to-face or written, synchronous or asynchronous.

Net-based teaching and learning technologies

When we use the concept "net-based" in relation to Academic Bildung and communication, it can include a variety of IT-tools, learning resource and types of communication forums. The figure below serves as an approach to different, partly overlapping perspectives and categories of educational technologies. We have to take complexity into account for psychic systems such as students and teachers, and also for social systems such as classes, universities and the educational system. All these systems can be considered unpredictable, non-trivial and dependent on the concrete context.

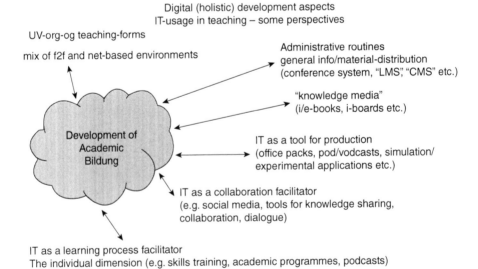

Figure 2.1 Net-based teaching and learning technologies to underpin communication processes.

That is the presupposition when we discuss teaching environments and thus the presupposition for communication and learning. The question in relation to the prerequisites for communication is how universities can provide teaching environments that enable the students to have the best possibilities to learn what is required, and to develop themselves in the ways required.

In this book we use the concept of net-based teaching and learning in higher education, where the teaching environments apply institutional platforms, net-mediated communication forums, tools for different types of production, digital learning resources and teaching materials that are in line with the intended learning goals of the course in question. This means that the organisational frames for teaching and learning may range from wholly net-based, through different combinations of net- and campus-based, to almost wholly campus-based. What it takes to succeed and achieve the learning goals and strengthen the students' development of Academic Bildung is an empirical question.

The case studies' empirical focus is manifold, with regard to the specific education, teaching activities and empirical and theoretical approaches. The studies all focus on the conditions necessary for communication and learning in teaching environments and on the opportunities for the development of Academic Bildung.

The next chapter will offer an exhaustive description of the concept of Academic Bildung.

References

Husserl, E. (1982), *Ideas pertaining to a pure phenomenology and to a phenomenology philosophy*, vol. 2., tr. Kersten, F. Martinus Nijhoff: The Hague.

Luhmann, N. (1995), *Social systems,* tr. Bednartz, J. Jr. and Baecker, D. Stanford University Press: Stanford, CA.

Luhmann, N. (2002), *Daserziehungssystem der gesellschaft.* Suhrkamp: Frankfurt.

Mathiasen, H. (2002), *Personlige bærbare computere i undervisningen.* DPU Forlag: Copenhagen.

Mathiasen, H. (2005), "Project and web-based teaching: An invitation to develop student and teacher roles". In: Buhl, M., Sørensen, B. and Meyer, B., eds., *Media and ICT: Learning potentials.* DPU Press: Copenhagen.

Mathiasen, H. (2007), "Teaching and learning in a variety of communication forums: An invitation to rethink learning environments and related student and teacher roles" [conference book], pp. 67–74. Coventry University Technocenter: UK.

Mathiasen, H. and Schrum, L. (2010), "New technologies, learning systems and communication: Reducing complexity in the educational system". In: Khine, M. and Saleh, I., eds., *New science of learning: Cognition, computers and collaboration in education.* Springer Publishing: New York.

Shannon, E. C. and Weaver, W. ([1949] 1971), *The mathematical theory of communication.* University of Illinois Press: Urbana, IL.

von Foerster, H. and Pörksen, B. (2006), *Wahrheit ist die erfindung eines lügners. Gespräche für skeptiker.* Carl-Auer Verlag: Heidelberg.

3 On Academic Bildung in higher education

A Scandinavian approach

Mariann Solberg and Finn Thorbjørn Hansen

And he has never lived
who wise became
on things he didn't love.
N. F. S. Grundtvig
(1783–1872)[1]

Introduction

Are there specific qualities or traits of a Scandinavian concept of Academic Bildung to be found in higher education in the Scandinavian countries today? If there are, can and should we expect to find such traits in students going through net-based education?

In this chapter we discuss what Academic Bildung is and should be in general, and what it is, or has a potential to be, in higher education institutions. Bildung is a pedagogical concept which dates back to Greek antiquity, and it points to personal development processes that the individual engages in when meeting the physical and cultural reality. We explain how we see Bildung relating to specific Scandinavian conceptions of education, which is to say welfare state conceptions of education, as well as adult education, "people's enlightenment", and "enlightenment for life". Through this, we hope to identify some specific capacities of a Scandinavian concept of Academic Bildung, a concept that will be relevant to higher education in general, and thus also to net-based higher education.

We present and argue for a "double-tracked" Bildung concept and Bildung pedagogy which has a dimension of critical, emancipatory and society-oriented reflection, as well as a dimension of ethical-existential and being-oriented reflection. We will elaborate on the notion of Academic Bildung as a concept which captures the human striving and longing for both autonomy[2] and authenticity[3], a will to master and rationally take control of one's life, as well as a recognition of the meaningfulness and existential values in life which cannot be constructed and mastered in a discursive and rational way but are rather experiences of meaningfulness to be immersed in. Our aim is to provide the theoretical background necessary for understanding the overall question of this book: "How can we educate students through net-based education and at the same time facilitate Academic Bildung?"

We assume that there are challenges and opportunities concerning Academic Bildung that are specific to net-based education. This might imply that there are specific forms of didactics that can be applied for achieving Academic Bildung in net-based courses. This is connected to the particular conditions for communication available, even if all forms of teaching can be seen as intentional communication that aims to bring about change, as argued in Chapter 2 of this book. What do we – from the viewpoint of Academic Bildung here laid out – tentatively assume can be done in order to teach in a way that facilitates development of Academic Bildung in net-based courses?

In this chapter we are not going to elaborate on *how* this Scandinavian concept of Academic Bildung may be fleshed out in concrete practices and perspectives in net-based learning in higher education. However, the case studies in Part II present aspects of the everyday reality in Scandinavian net-based higher education, and they all look for Bildung dimensions in the courses and programs under scrutiny. While the present chapter lays out the theoretical and normative foundations for a general Scandinavian concept of Academic Bildung, the case studies give descriptions of the empirical net-based reality with this concept as the authors' point of orientation. The researchers and educational developers who are the authors of the case studies reflect on cases in which they have been, or still are, involved. This means that the answer to what Scandinavian Academic Bildung *is* can probably be found somewhere in the dialogue between the theoretical and the empirical reality. Furthermore, Chapter 10 analyses how, and to what extent, net-based higher education, judging from the case studies, seems to enable or block development of Academic Bildung in students. Some reflections on the consequences of the empirical investigations, for a relevant and updated Scandinavian concept of Academic Bildung, and thus for a theory of Bildung in general, are also provided in Chapter 10. Chapter 11 points out how we as teachers and facilitators can use the opportunities in net-based learning environments and overcome the difficulties in the effort to support the net-based students' development of Academic Bildung. Hopefully, this will give a basis for further thinking about and working with Academic Bildung for both researchers and practitioners.

A Digital world with a human face?

The Swiss novelist Max Frisch wrote in his novel *Homo Faber* ([1957] 1994): "Technology is the knack of arranging the world so we need not experience it." A basic question in line with this view is often raised when talking about Bildung in connection with net-based learning and ICT today. Is there a risk that the use of ICT and net-based learning in higher education to some degree can eliminate what seems to be one of the unique human conditions? Do we only think of the existence and freedom of "the living word" and the "living dialogue" as it emerges, and maybe can only emerge, in the physical (and not technologically mediated) presence of the other, that is, when the students and teacher are present in a real time situation at the same place in a face-to-face-relation? What is lost if this is true, and what part, if any, of Academic Bildung will then disappear in net-based courses in higher education? And does it matter? If so, how can we as educational researchers and practitioners then find ways to supplement the "lack" of this mysterious and very difficult to comprehend "human presence" and I-thou relationship (Buber [1923] 2004)? Can we learn from the tradition of Bildung in order to better work with this dialogical and relational "being-dimension", and what could we do in practice? How do we describe, understand and give voice to this tacit experience and saturated being-dimension that might slip away or be reduced in a too technological- and net-based learning situation? Moreover, are there practices and structures in face-to-face education at the physical campuses that are impossible to recreate and remediate in net-based education? Or are there structures within the use of ICT and digital media in net-based higher education that give new opportunities for widening and further developing the human condition and experience of presence and authenticity in the learning situation? Can this be done in ways that can expand the possibilities for development of Academic Bildung for our students?

Neil Postman writes in his famous book *Technopolis: The surrender of culture to technology* (1993):

> New technologies alter the structure of our interests: the things we think *about*. They alter the character of our symbols: the things we think *with*. And they alter the nature of community: the arena in which thoughts develops.
>
> (p. 20)

We are not sure whether the Danish philosopher, poet and founder of the Nordic tradition of people's enlightenment *(folkeopplysning)*, N. F. S. Grundtvig, or Max Frisch, would look upon the new communication technology and its entry into higher education as a threat and as cultural decay. On the contrary, they might – open and imaginative as they were – indeed have welcomed the new technology and the unknown possibilities of learning, dialogues and insights that it might bring with it. The tragic story of "The Sorcerer's Apprentice" who became a servant of the technology and not the other way around might not be the case here. At least not if we are cautious about what these information and communication technologies might change on an imperceptible level in what we are forced or encouraged to think about, think with, and think from in the settings of higher education of today, and what we no longer think about, with and from.[4]

In the following we also unfold some new and prospering ideas in higher education research developed by the British professor Ronald Barnett (2004, 2007 and 2011) who offers us a framework and language to consider the overlooked being-dimension in higher education theory and research. We see the aims of facilitation of Academic Bildung as close to Barnett's thoughts on student development and learning. We will however point to some limitations we find in his view, and this will prepare the way for why and how we see the relevance and importance of rethinking the concept of Academic Bildung in higher education, and why the Scandinavian approach to Academic Bildung might have something fruitful to offer with its double-tracked understanding. The discussion of Barnett's thinking will hopefully also help in introducing the non-Scandinavian and non-German reader to the Scandinavian-German understanding of Academic Bildung, as a counterpart to the British understanding of the phenomenon of Bildung, and for the same reason we will briefly touch on the Anglo-American tradition of liberal education.

What is Bildung and why the concept of Academic Bildung?

However, before we go into Barnett's thinking, let us give a short introduction to the concept of Bildung and the reasons why we see a need for keeping it as a core concept of higher education. Bildung, or in Danish and Norwegian *dannelse*, in Swedish *bildning*, (in English often translated as "formation", "education" or "cultivation")[5] is a concept that has been stretched in quite a few different directions over time. In general, the idea of Bildung describes a personal development processes that a person is going through when he or she meets the world. In our understanding it not only describes a process of socialisation, as socialisation can be passive. Bildung is more correctly seen as a reciprocal process of formation between the individual as a self and the world, where the individual meets the world actively. In pedagogy and formal education Bildung is a basic concept, and thus on the same level as the concepts of learning and education.[6] In higher education there is a specific form of Bildung that we expect to occur in the student related to formal and informal learning. This is what we call Academic Bildung. The world the student meets here is that of the thoughts and practices, and the particular take on a part of reality, existent in a discipline or profession. Unlike the concepts of socialisation and learning, the concept of Bildung is normative. The notion is not neutral because some specific values and attitudes are always connected to it when used in concrete situations. Furthermore, it is a concept describing a developmental process toward something better – a tacit or explicit normative ideal, value or vision of ethical, existential, aesthetic or spiritual qualities – in an educational setting. It is connected to critical thinking, society-oriented reflection and autonomy on the one hand, and to ethical dimensions of human formation and self-formation, existential- and being-oriented reflection and authenticity on the other hand. The concept thus has one foot in enlightenment thinking and one foot in the romantic tradition in the history of ideas. The concept of Bildung has always been about culture and education and the combination of these, where the individual's development as a human not only concerns knowledge but also cultural sensibility. It has been about development of the individual's wider potential through education. While there may be a loose relation between education and one's personality, there is an intrinsic relation between Bildung and personality.

Within Scandinavian higher education the concept has been revived repeatedly, and different hyphenated concepts of Bildung have been put to use in the everyday language of academia. Instead of talking about the concept of Bildung, one could rather nowadays speak of a multitude of concepts of Bildung, to some extent overlapping each other in content.[7] Many of the new ways of using the concept, for instance the use of "digital *dannelse*" can seem to be far from the concept as it was conceived by Wilhelm von Humboldt. The Norwegian educator Lars Løvlie has introduced the somewhat wider notion of *teknokulturell danning* (In English "techno-cultural Bildung") in order to describe what Bildung can be in a postmodern technological society, where he sees Bildung as analogous to the notion of interface. The meeting between subject and world is in focus in both concepts. In net-based education this is an unquestionable condition. In a report released in 2011 by the Norwegian Association of Higher Education Institutions, "Dannelsesaspekter i utdanning. Rapport fra en arbeidsgruppe nedsatt av UHRs utdanningsutvalg", we find seven different concepts of Bildung. The question then is: why not abandon the concept? Why not just talk about academic skills, thinking skills, or graduate attributes? Or, as Jørgen Fossland poses the question:

> Why insist on using a concept that in addition to the bourgeois intellectual snobbery and dusty philology is also reminiscent of the darkest chapter in European history? Is it not better to reformulate the valuable aspects of the German tradition of formation without simultaneously waving the flag for ideals with the stressful inscription of Bildung?
>
> (2012, p. 168, our translation)

The reasons why we do not want to leave the concept behind are many. One of the reasons is that in student-centred pedagogy, Bildung is more relevant, not less. Bildung is about becoming a subject in the meeting with a physical and cultural reality. In order to speak and think from within the student's perspective, and not only from the needs of, for example, the labour market, concepts other than graduate attributes and specific skills are called for. And it is in particular the existential value of acquisition and production of new knowledge, the satisfaction of inquiring into culture, nature and society that are put out of sight when Bildung is left behind. Another reason is that we want to be in dialogue with our history and traditions. We want to be able to describe and discuss the existential, ethical, societal, cultural, and material foundations for Academic Bildung, and in order to do so we need to be able to see and refer to the way in which changes in the basic conditions of the educational systems and society at large and the varying ways and places and social strata for mediation of the phenomenon influence the concept. The concept has been a lens through which to look at education for a very long time, even if both the concept itself and the basic conditions for education have changed on the way to the present situation.[8]

There is an attitudinal side to Bildung that is lacking when we only focus on knowledge, skills, and competence, and moreover there is a content-oriented side to Bildung that will turn invisible if neglected. The attitudinal side deals with the formation of identity, thus both the ethical and the existential aspects of education. This means that there is a normative side to the concept of Bildung that we do not necessarily catch if we confine ourselves to talking about academic skills or graduate attributes. The content-side of Bildung deals with the kinds of cultural content, in a wide sense, that students meet in their education. Throughout history there have been different kinds of content that have been recommended as particularly relevant or essential for the successful process of Bildung to take place. This has generally either taken the form of a canon, i.e. classical readings etc., that has been regarded as eminent and time transcendent, or it has taken form as encyclopedic content, encompassing as wide an encounter with cultural expressions as possible. When considering this content intrinsically to the concept, we have what we would call a substantial concept of Bildung, as opposed to a formal concept of Bildung, where no specific content is considered to be intrinsic to the concept itself. If we confined ourselves to academic skills, we would not see the need for a connectedness to a specific content, albeit not a predefined or prescribed content. So, we stick with a concept some might see as stale, recovering and modernising it for our time, rather than severing the roots.

Before turning to Barnett and his "ontological turn", let us take a brief look at an Anglo-American counterpart to the Scandinavian-German tradition of Bildung, liberal education.[9] At the core of standard conceptions of liberal education are many valuable traits and abilities connected to what we reasonably could call Bildung, such as analytic abilities, creativity, plurality of perspectives, and independence. However, we often miss a focus on the critical and emancipatory dimensions of Bildung. Academic Bildung without critical thinking and potential for resistance can soon come to fall on the side of "adaptation" rather than on the "Bildung" side of socialisation, referring to the Norwegian philosopher Jon Hellesnes' seminal distinction of what he sees as two different forms of socialisation ([1969] 1992). We also miss a focus on wonder, which is not to be confused with the phenomenon of curiosity and interest, and a focus on existential reflection. As we will see, the concepts of "wonder" and "existential reflection" can have different meanings whether these are used in an existentialistic approach or in a life and existence philosophical approach.

We also think, when working with the liberal arts and liberal education tradition, that it would be wise to distinguish between at least three different forms of liberal learning:

1   A pragmatic approach to liberal learning where the main goal of Academic Bildung is to create free democratic citizens (Dewey [1916] 2008) and self-creating the "liberal ironist" or social constructivist (Rorty 1989, 1991).
2   A conservative high culture approach to liberal learning where the main goal of Academic Bildung is to consecrate the students into higher "fine culture" and to learn the tradition and "wisdom" from the great literature, philosophy and arts (MacIntyre 1981, Bloom 1987).
3   A Socratic critical and existential approach to liberal learning where the meeting and continuing conversation with the great literature, philosophy and arts of humanity are encouraged in order to keep the human spirit open through engaging with the eternal questions (Arcilla 1995, Nussbaum 1997, Mackler 2009).

Our concept of Academic Bildung is closest to the third kind of liberal learning, although we do of course appreciate both democracy as well as learning from the tradition of the sublime arts and literature. And we do acknowledge, with the second kind of liberal learning, that the content of the culture, tradition, or knowledge that students meet is of vital importance to the kinds of Bildung that can emerge in this meeting.

The Ontological Turn in Higher Education

Ronald Barnett (2004, 2007 and 2011) has noticed an important change in the thinking of higher education research during the last two decades that seems to announce a kind of "ontological turn in higher education". We see an increasing focus on "knowledge production" in relation to the demand and request of scientific "evidence-based" knowledge. This widespread tendency at modern universities also means that the question of meaning (values, beliefs, and ethics) is increasingly relegated to a secondary status in higher education because, as also Stephanie Mackler (2009) noticed, it cannot be tested and verified methodically. "The university shifted its focus from meaning to knowledge, and liberal learning fell by the wayside" (Mackler 2009, p. 6).

So this seems in fact to indicate an "epistemological turn" in higher education, in the sense that "knowledge" came to occupy the place that previously was held by "meaning". However, because of this heavily epistemological and knowledge-oriented research approach and a university teaching that trains students to reflect on empirical facts, information gathering, and systematic knowledge analysis, it has also become still more overt that "something" is missing in the academic education of the students. Notice that the British poet T. S. Eliot's questions: "Where is the wisdom we lost in knowledge? Where is the knowledge we lost in information?" formed the key theme of an international conference in higher education research in England in 2011. Critics of the knowledge producing and still more specialised and fragmented (and utilitarianised) universities of today complain in words like: "One no longer hears administrators giving talks on 'wisdom', an old-fashioned word meaning seeing things in their widest context, including our ultimate concerns"(Sommerville 2006, p. 9). And:

> Intellectual production in the university is understood in a way which denies the full range of human transcendence and meaning making. . . . The need to make some kind of sense of the world and of our place within it is about as crude and strong as our need to eat and seek shelter.
> (Wilshire 1990, p. 124)

The critique asks ethical, aesthetical and existential questions like: What is this knowledge good for? What is the deeper meaning of creating these methods and tools? Why is this kind of technology helping us to live a more profound and wiser life? What do we mean by strengthening "life quality" and "better life"? What does "human flourishing" mean? What is the difference between knowledge and wisdom? And why do some people and not others, think that life becomes more meaningful and more beautiful, and learning becomes deeper, through these new technological innovations we see in, for instance, net-based learning? And so on. All these questions seem to live a shadow existence in the rush to find still more effective methods to "produce" more candidates and types of knowledge and skills that can satisfy the need of the financial, administrative and political interests, needs and systems.

But right in the middle of this dystopian vision of the "decline and moral collapse" (Bloom 1987, Readings 1996, Kronman 2007) of modern university society we also see other signs. Precisely because of the contemporary politicians, university leaders, and broadly speaking society's growing interest in how we can create new universities and ways of teaching that will make us more creative and innovative in the global competition, we see a growing acceptance and understanding of alternative ways of teaching and thinking. If we want to be more creative and innovative[10] might we not then learn from artists, for example, or from other alternative ways of thinking that can bring us out into "the open and unknown"? Ronald Barnett talks from this last position when he describes "the ontological turn in higher education": "Learning for an unknown future calls, in short, for an ontological turn. . . . A pedagogy of this kind will be a pedagogy that engages students as persons, not merely as knowers" (2004, p. 247); and: ". . . instead of knowing the world, being-in-the-world has to take primary place in the conceptualization that informs university teaching" (2005, p. 795).

In his book *A will to learn: Being a student in an age of uncertainty* (2007) he elaborates on this position in higher education pedagogy by making a distinction between "the voice of knowing" as the epistemological dimension, "the voice of doing" as the technological and methodological dimension, and "the voice of being" as the existential and ontological dimension. Barnett calls for a higher education pedagogy and an understanding in higher education research, which to a greater extent involves or reflects the ontological dimension. This can be done, he says, if the students learn to be more clear and conscious about who and where they themselves are in what they think, say, write, and do at the university.

Barnett has no interest in or intention of bringing a psychological or therapeutic approach into higher education pedagogy. Instead he speaks up for a concept of "authentic learning", which involves the person's more existential (and *not* purely idiosyncratic) reflections about why this subject and discipline, and this education and profession, seem meaningful to them. Thus, what Barnett is talking about is a "self-creation" learning process, rather than only a process of knowledge acquisition, skill learning, or competence development. In this self-creation learning process, focus is put on the student's own "being-in-the-world" and personal life philosophy. Without an awareness and reflection upon the students' *existential* relations to the subject, profession, and their life as such, the students and teachers will never, Barnett claims, get into a dialogue enriched by the engagement and intellectual curiosity that has to be present in order to foster deeper processes of understanding and inquiry in higher education.

Barnett also makes a distinction between two other "voices", which the student and the teacher must develop an ear for: "the pedagogical voice" and "the educational voice". The pedagogical voice is the voice that the students hear when a given subject or knowledge of a discipline, its standards, and norms are presented to them. This voice is connected to the methodological and epistemological level, that is, to the "voices of doing and knowing". The "educational voice" has to do with the student's own personal experiences of "being-in-the-world" and the construction of meaning, which the student individually can experience when engaging in his or her education or profession. This voice is connected to the existential and ontological level of higher education. As Barnett writes: "Here, the student becomes herself. If the pedagogical voice is realized through autonomy, the educational voice is realized through authenticity" (2007, p. 91-92). The teacher enables the students to get into a more deep and authentic learning process, says Barnett, when both the teacher and the students constantly try to put themselves into play and at risk, placing themselves in the open and uncertain. Barnett talks about authentic learning as a kind of shared journey of discovery, where a fusion between the teachers' and students' engagements, passions, critical reflections, wonderments and learning happens. Barnett emphasises that if *teachers* do not, in the concrete teaching or educational counselling session, experience themselves as on a real journey of discovery and in a process where they really learn something new, they will be talking only with the pedagogical voice and not the educational voice. Barnett quotes a university teacher who won the local teaching award at a university as saying:

> To me, teaching is engaging with young people who are visionaries and dreamers in vibrant spaces that resonate with the collective energies of intellectuals enriched with a wealth of prior knowledge. Teaching is a passion and a commitment that is a constant joy in my life. . . . The simple and yet complex concepts of honesty, integrity and respect are funda-mental in all my professional and personal interactions with students. The value I place on my teaching and research contributes to the passion I bring to teaching and ultimately to the successful learning by students.
>
> (ibid.)

According to Barnett one of the most important tasks of university teachers is to create room for (and themselves be a living example of) a way of being that inspires the students and the teachers themselves to think and act from a fundamental state of uncertainty ("high risk" situations), and yet flour-ish with this uncertainty and encounters with the unknown and unfamiliar. The subtitle of his book *A will to learn* (2007) is *"Being a student in an age of uncertainty"*, and by saying that, he does not only aim at teaching the students how to navigate in a hypercomplex society, but also to become change-ori-ented, flexible, etc. Barnett aims for higher education to become education *for* uncertainty, *for* the experience of what it is like to live and act and think *without* already defined learning targets, methods, best practices and well-defined problems and concepts. How, he asks, can we design new creative and innovative universities that encourage students to seek the unknown and "impossible", the not-yet-thought idea, and develop the openness to a larger kind of "inner steering" and sense of what the future seems to call for?

We are not going to go further into Barnett's thoughtful and fascinat-ing descriptions of a possible didactics of learning for the unknown future. However, we must make a critical remark on his thinking. When zooming in on precisely what he means by "the ontological" and "authenticity" as related to the "educational voice", and "the voice of being" compared to "the voice of knowing" and "voice of doing", one will discover that Barnett's concept of ontology, authenticity, education, and being is strongly influ-enced by the existentialists; that is, Jean Paul Sartre's (1905–1980) notion of the "self-creating human being". As Barnett writes:

> "In the end, authentic persons have only their own resources with which to tell their own story. . . . Ultimately, the authentic person is her own author; what authority she gains come from herself, not from those who have gone before her.
>
> (p. 45)

However, our question would be: Is the important voice of being, which Barnett helps us to discover and reflect upon in higher education research and practices, only to be understood as a striving for a will to learn through more personal and idiosyncratic preferences and activities of self-creation and meaning construction? Is the authentic person or the authentic action and way of being only to be understood as a fundamentally self-creating act, where the person essentially becomes his or her own author and resource for meaning construction? Or may authenticity and the authentic person, and perhaps also the voice of being, be understood in a fundamentally different way?

We think the latter, that we can and must think about the voice of being in another and more nuanced way. This other way will have to be an approach where Sartre's and Barnett's individual and self-creating person is also enabled and conditioned by the world in a specific way. In order to justify our critique we turn to the Scandinavian concept of Bildung and later to the German – or more specifically the philosophers Immanuel Kant's and Hans-Georg Gadamer's – understanding of Academic Bildung.

People's enlightenment and enlightenment for life – a Scandinavian concept of Bildung

To say that there is only *one* Scandinavian concept of Bildung would of course be wrong. There is today, and has been for a century, a lively and multifaceted discussion around this concept (see for example Hagtvet and Ognjenovic 2011, Steinsholt and Dobson 2011, Slagstad, Korsgaard and Løvlie 2003, Johansen 2002, Gustavsson 1996). We adhere to this diversity of ideas – as opposed to concepts like *learning, knowledge, competence, skills, self-development* or *personal growth* – because Bildung, *dannelse* or *bildning* points beyond those concepts, and because it is a normative concept. We want to unfold a very specific notion of Bildung, which is grounded in a unique Scandinavian educational tradition and philosophy called *folkeoplysning* (people's enlightenment) and *livsoplysning* (enlightenment for life).[11]

This form of education is nowadays still a very strong and progressive educational movement in Scandinavia that finds its practices especially in what is called *folkehøjskoler* (folk high schools or residential colleges). These residential colleges are mostly for young people between 18 to 25 years old, and they represent nonmandatory post-high-school education, but they are still not part of higher education. However, in order to find the source for a specifically Scandinavian understanding of the purpose of education and for Bildung in general, we need to look in this direction. Even though the ideas were coined more than 150 years ago by Grundtvig and other Danish, Norwegian, and Swedish educators and reformers, people's enlightenment and life enlightenment are still apparent in children's and adult education in today's Scandinavia.[12]

The reason why this educational idea and school culture has survived for so many years is probably that behind the concept of people's enlightenment as well as life enlightenment lies a fundamental egalitarian view on education and human life as such, which in many ways has paved the Nordic road to democracy, the welfare state, and its democratic educations. People's enlightenment focuses either on people as *ethnos* (where the aim is to enlighten people about the national culture, which was the prime concern in the nineteenth century), or people as *demos* (where the aim is to enlighten people and let them enlighten themselves about how to develop a democracy and to live as democratic citizens, which was the prime concern in the last half of the twentieth century).[13] But now the question seems to be how we can create coherence in this new pluralistic, multicultural, and cosmopolitan society and not hinder but qualify individualisation as a striving for authenticity.[14] In a report from the Association for Folk High Schools to the Danish Ministry in 2004 the authors emphasised that the new multicultural situation challenges the residential colleges and the idea of people's enlightenment to understand itself not just through the idea of a people but through the idea of humanity. Moreover it was stressed that in this cosmopolitan world we must also reinforce the fact that we no longer live in isolated monocultural islands, but in a global and geo-ecological unified whole. In fact the founder of the residential colleges, N. S. F. Grundtvig, had these ideas in mind already in the nineteenth century when he talked about a universal view of mankind and the need for life enlightenment, that is, an enlightenment about the world and life we all have in common despite our social, political and cultural differences. Therefore one of the conclusions in the report is that the overall aim of residential colleges should not in the future be guided by the idea of people's enlightenment alone, but also by the idea of enlightenment for life. As they write:

> Enlightenment for life is a more comprehensive and broader concept than people's enlightenment, encompassing universal and existential ways of presenting different problems. It is about the life relations that nobody can escape, and that make everyone equal when faced with the big questions in life. Behind the concept lies the experience that values come from life, ordinary human life, as everyone knows it through his or her own experiences. . . . There is a need to accentuate the existential character of the task of the *folkehøjskole*, which builds on the individual *højskole's* self-chosen basis of values.
>
> ("Rapport fra Højskoleudvalget",
> December 2004, p. 27, our translation)

Behind the concept of life enlightenment lies a fundamental existential and life philosophical view on education and human life as such that in a sense keeps the door open for more ontological, spiritual or metaphysical questions and experiences (experiences of transcendence or seeing life and human beings as wonderful and ungraspable mysteries – as wonders) without necessarily becoming religious, metaphysical or ideological in a more rigid way by giving well-defined answers to those big questions.

In fact, by insisting on the fundamentally enigmatic nature of human life and human phenomena (such as, for example, the lived experience of love, playfulness, humour, beauty or freedom) as deep mysteries in ordinary lives of ordinary people that we cannot get a clear, rational and scientific answer to, we also make room for a basic equal dignity between human beings. "The mysteries make us all equal", as the head of one school put it. Before the mystery of existence we are all "equally wise, equally ignorant– whether old or young, unskilled or highly trained, teacher or pupil"(Carlsen 2013, p. 12).

So we see that also in the concept of enlightenment for life do we find this egalitarian aspect, which seems so important for the Scandinavian concept of Bildung. But we also find a *life philosophical* dimension, which points towards the importance of being in an ontological relation with the world and oneself in a way that is marked by a deeply wondrous, receptive, "meaning receiving" and dialogical way of being. This way of being is not to be confused with Sartre's existentialism (or social constructivism for that matter) and his view upon the human condition as a curious, proactive, meaning making and self-creating way of being.

The elitist aspects of the concept of Bildung

The concept of Bildung is, as many will know, rooted in the Greek concept of *paideia* and the Christian concept of *bild* from Meister Eckhart (ca. 1260– 1327). These roots can also be traced back to the male aristocracy of ancient Greece, and to the Christian esoteric mystics in the Middle Ages, and later to the higher social-cultural strata of the so-called *Bildungsbürgertum* in mid-eighteenth century Germany. Jørgen Fossland (2012) points to parts of the history of Nazi Germany, and thus to dangerous and elitist aspects or developments in the conceptions of Bildung. But because we see in history that some have used the word and notion of Bildung in an elitist way, does not, in our view, make an argument for not using it today. We only have to be very conscious and critically reflective about how we use it, and where and why we want to connect to this concept.

So there is definitely a normative dimension connected to the concept of Bildung.[15] We become reflective and aware of the ethical, existential and value-based dimensions in life when we are in a Bildung process. But it is one thing to be aware of these more fundamentally ethical, existential, aesthetic and normative questions and dimensions of life, another to give finite answers and develop systems, ideologies, dogmas, rules and norms based on them. As we will later argue with Kant and Gadamer, and certainly also with the Scandinavian approach to people's enlightenment and enlightenment for life, an elitist conception of Bildung is not the issue here.[16]

To sum up: Within the Nordic folk high school tradition and its views on Bildung[17], we find a focus not only on *autonomy* (self-determination/self-expression), which is in line with the political-democratic concept of people's enlightenment and critical emancipatory pedagogy, but also *authenticity* (devotion/self-forgetfulness). It is, within this tradition, a *balance* between the striving for autonomy and authenticity that must be sought if we are not to end up becoming spiritless. A leading folk high school principal and historian of ideas, Jørgen Carlsen, (in common with Grundtvig and Kierkegaard) associates Bildung or *dannelse* to the ability to find joy and to love something:

> If one lacks the ability to rejoice over something, one is spiritless. One is spiritless if one, in short, is not present in one's own life. The lack of spirit is the total lack of personal formation – a spiritual phantom mode, a single liquidation sale, where all shelves are empty.
>
> (1999, p. 16–17, our translation)

Another folk high school manager, Hans Jørgen Vodsgaard, writes:

> A folk high school must, according to this tradition, also open students' eyes, or rather minds for life sources, which makes it extra vivid and real. The folk high school is not just about autonomy (professional or disciplinary training or state bourgeois formation), but also about authenticity (enlivening and life-disclosure).
>
> (2003, p. 54)

It is precisely this balance between a striving for autonomy and a striving for authenticity that we find to be characteristic of a relevant and updated notion of Academic Bildung. According to this public education and enlightenment tradition, which is rooted in a layman's movement consisting of adult education associations, it is particularly intellectuals and professionals (the elite) who have a tendency to become spiritless. An Academic Bildung in net-based learning inspired by the Scandinavian concept of people's enlightenment and enlightenment for life will therefore be looking for a spirited kind of learning and self-transformation process, where the academic teacher and the students meet in a living and lively dialogue and exchange of experiences and ideas that really matter to them personally as well as professionally. As such, both critical-emancipatory reflection and ethical-existential reflection constitute crucial components in this kind of Academic Bildung.

Academic Bildung – Learning from the German tradition

Now, in order to relate this double-tracked concept of Academic Bildung to the idea of the university as a research institution, and the unique educational culture that follows teaching led by real-time researchers, we have found it necessary to take a closer look at the concepts of enlightenment and Bildung as offered by the German philosopher Immanuel Kant in the eighteenth century, a mode of thinking which has had a particularly strong influence on the critical, progressive, and emancipatory pedagogy in modern times. But this is, as we have shown, only half of the story. If we are to include the other part, that is, a more existential philosophical approach to doing research and pedagogy, we also need to listen to another great philosopher of the twentieth century, Hans-Georg Gadamer.

What is Academic Bildung according to a Kantian-based understanding of the concept?

Having the courage to use your own intellect is one of the basic requirements for Bildung, as well as being a hallmark of Bildung itself. This idea goes back to Kant and his article, "An answer to the question: What is enlightenment?"

> Enlightenment is the human being's emancipation from its self-incurred immaturity. Immaturity is the inability to make use of one's own intellect without the direction of another. This immaturity is self-incurred when its cause does not lie in a lack of intellect, but rather in a lack of resolve and courage to make use of one's intellect without the direction of another. "*Sapere aude!*[18] Have the courage to make use of your own intellect!" is hence the motto of the enlightenment.
>
> ([1784] 2006, p. 17)

According to Kant, all human beings are equally equipped for using their own intellect. This provides an egalitarian basis for a concept of Bildung. To make use of one's own intellect means, according to Kant, to think for yourself. However, a notion of self-thinking built on Kant is not subjective. A Kantian notion of self-thinking should be based on his idea of *sensus communis*, and this is put in the following words in his *Critique of judgment:*

> . . . we must take *sensus communis* to mean the idea of a sense shared, i.e. a power to judge that in reflecting takes account (a priori), in our thought, of everyone else's way of presenting [something], in order as it were to compare our own judgment with human reason in general. . . . Now we do this as follows: we compare our judgment not so much with the actual as rather with the merely possible judgments of others, and [thus] put ourselves in the position of everyone else.
>
> ([1790] 1987, p. 160)

Sensus communis is here seen as a general faculty for judgment that all humans have, and the main point is that we relate our own thinking to the potential thinking of others. Thus, according to a Kantian-based notion of Bildung, one must actively engage one's own intellect without the direction of others (i.e. autonomously), and one must include the possible judgment of others in one's own judgment.[19] In order to make this a habit, one must practice together with others. This is the basis for being a skilled thinker. In order to truly think for oneself, a student at a university a person cannot start from his or her own intellect alone. One must think on the basis of the well-established knowledge in his or her discipline, and thus one needs to be acquainted with this knowledge base. One must further be able to train one's thinking skills in conjunction with one's peers and the previous and present authorities in one's field. This means that self-thinking requires a community. The lack of Bildung thus will manifest as a lack of active and independent use of one's intellect and a lack of inclusion of the possible judgment of others.

The concept of Bildung that we can extract from Kant's thinking is formal in the sense that it does not say anything about the contents of thinking or the culture in which thinking takes place. The Scandinavian universities have perhaps first and foremost been research institutions, and the core value of the education is that it should be research based. This implies that the cultures within the institutions (to various degrees) will be research cultures and also different professional cultures.[20] The core values of Academic Bildung will, if this is plausible, be the values of different research cultures – or what in general terms can be called academic values, or perhaps researcher virtues. This means that the content of the concept of Academic Bildung could be said to have common academic values at the core, and also that it needs to be seen in relation to the different research cultures actually existent in actual universities. In order for a student to be academically *dannet*, he or she will have to be initiated or socialised into a specific research community. The values and necessary academic skills will be different according to the content of the research discipline, and they will not always be conscious and explicit. We can see that this concept of Academic Bildung in some of its dimensions comes close to the concept of generic competences.

It may not be quite as easy to draw a distinction between formal requirements and contents as we have done here; even though self-thinking is a formal requirement, it is also a virtue for a successful researcher. In this Kantian-based concept of Academic Bildung the student who succeeds in his or her process will be able to develop and form his or her own rational and autonomous voice in an academic community of voices. The notion of autonomy at play in Kant's thinking is a concept of self-rule, where the individual acts from his or her own reasons (or moral law, as Kant holds), as opposed to heteronomy, where one's actions are influenced by a force outside the individual. Kant's concept is more of a moral ideal than the everyday modern use of autonomy, which is more psychologically oriented, but it is in any case about individual independence and self-determination.

What is Academic Bildung according to a Gadamerian-based understanding of the concept?

Where Kant's notion of Bildung as critical self-determination makes the rational self-reflective consciousness the centre of the Bildung process (*Verstand* driven), Gadamer ([1960] 2006) understands thinking and the Bildung process as a more intuitive and existential way of opening up to the sensual and phenomenological "being-dimension" of our life worlds. We have to transcend common sense and even the "scientific reflection" in order to get in contact and dialogue with the subject matter itself (*den Sachen Selbst*). Something is overlooked or missed, Gadamer claims, if we only look and reflect through our rational intellect and evidence-based, epistemological and methodological approaches, that is, the approach that the natural and social sciences are based on. To be a truth-seeking researcher is also to be able to see and think *beyond* what can be grasped and explained through an empirical and analytical science. Or as Gadamer writes at the very first page in the introduction to *Truth and Method*:

> They [the following investigations] are concerned to seek the experience of truth that transcends the domain of scientific method wherever that experience is to be found, and to inquire into its legitimacy. Hence the human sciences *[Geist Wissenschaft]* are connected to modes of experience that lie outside science: with the experience of philosophy, of art, and of history itself. These are all modes of experiences in which a truth is communicated that cannot be verified by the methodological means proper to science.
>
> ([1960] 2006, p. xxi)

Gadamer's philosophical hermeneutics, and the existential phenomenology and philosophy these hermeneutics are grounded in, can be seen as an increasingly developed and unfolded description of what we can understand with intuition (or phenomenological sensitivity and awareness) and it especially has to do with that which has made a deep impression on us and which we now through words and concepts and other forms of artefacts try to find expressions for.

But the existential and hermeneutical point of Gadamer is that when it comes to matters of ethical, aesthetical and existential or metaphysical/ spiritual concern, we human beings must accept the *finitude* of human rationality and discursive reflection and scientific knowledge as such. What goes on in our daily human relations – where ethical, aesthetical and existential aspects and dimensions are always at play – cannot be sufficiently described empirically, nor systematically analysed and categorised in general terms and concepts and precise and well-defined methods, which are of course the tools of empirical and analytical science (e.g. psychology, sociology, semiotics, anthropology, etc.). There are subject matters and life phenomena and human experiences of meaningfulness and actions that seem too enigmatic and too saturated with meaning to be captured by scientific language (van Manen 1990, 2002, 2014). Bildung, in the way Gadamer understands it and links it to the history of Bildung from Meister Eckhart to Wilhelm von Humboldt and the modern age, has to do with an experience of transcendence and a "speculative dimension in language", that is, a longing or quest *in* language itself to reach out for that which it cannot grasp and communicate in direct words and statements but under which it is deeply influenced.

> That is the positive implication of the "indigence of language" inherent in philosophy from its beginning. At very special moments and under very special circumstances that are not to be found in Plato or Aristotle, Meister Eckhart or Nicholas of Cusa, Fichte or Hegel, but perhaps in Aquinas, Hume, and Kant, this linguistic indigence is concealed under the smooth surface of a conceptual system, and it emerges only – but then of necessity – when we thoughtfully follow the movement of thought.
>
> ([1989] 2006, p. 566)

It is this "indigence of language" which demands a special attention, a listening and wondrous way of being in order to hear what life, or the phenomena in *this* concrete and *this* singular case, is saying as a *thou* to one as a listener. This is the form of existential and being-oriented *Bildung* which Gadamer talks about and which, at least in our view, best frames what we understand as the authenticity dimension of Academic Bildung in this article.

A last word is to be said about this kind of Academic Bildung. It is a "movement of thought", which is not, as we have already indicated, only made of a rational and conceptual form and telos. The movement of this kind of thinking is rather existential but not in a Sartrean meaning making sense, where we see the self-reflective consciousness at the centre of the world. By existential, Gadamer means our ability or musicality to be tuned in to that which *calls* us to respond. It is rather to be understood in a "meaning receiving" sense, and it happens *with* us when we engage fully in our own lives and follow what we experience as the most valuable in our human lives together. These existential moments, the existential philosopher would say, is in a way the ethical, aesthetical and existential "GPS" of our actions and judgments (the *phronesis* of the practitioner and the *Sophia* of the thinker). It is not based on common sense or scientific knowledge, nor even political and rational decisions made in the public sphere *(polis)*, when decisions are primarily based on utilitarian means-end rationality.

This more intuitive sense of the normative dimension in life is not to be confused with the norms and moral and ethical procedures that modern philosophers such as Rawls (1971) and Habermas (1984) are talking about.

It is rather to be understood along the lines of Charles Taylor (1992) when he talks about the "ethics of authenticity" and how authenticity presupposes a resonance with something (*cosmos* or existence or life as such) which is larger than ourselves and our wanting and doing in the public sphere, and which is embedded in the ontological "being-dimension" that constitutes our value structures and qualitative and normative distinctions (Taylor 1989, Raffnsøe-Møller 2007).

In this Gadamerian-based conception of Academic Bildung, the student who succeeds in his or her Bildung process will not only be able to develop and express his or her own voice into an academic community of voices in a more rational and critical way – he or she will also find his or her own intuitive and existential voice (from a kind of listening from the heart), but *only* in and through dialogue with the voice of being or the phenomena itself *(den Sachen Selbst)*. Academic Bildung in a Gadamerian sense can therefore be described as a kind of tactfulness constituted by on the one hand a phenomenological sensitivity and intuition for the phenomenon itself, and on the other hand a hermeneutic and Socratic awareness of the limitations of the intuitions and pre-understandings that are embedded in those sensitivities and intuitions (Hansen 2013).

The fourth voice when talking about the ontological dimension in higher education

Going back to Ronald Barnett's concept of "the voice of being", in short[21] what is missing in Barnett's model of the three voices of university teaching is a fourth voice: "the voice of the phenomenon or subject matter itself" *(die Sache Selbst)*. This is why Gadamer from the very start of *Truth and Method* emphasises that: "My real concern was and is philosophic: not what we do or what we ought to do, but what happens to us over and above our wanting and doing" ([1989] 2006, p. xvi).

So one could say that we must make a distinction between what Sartre and Barnett relate as "the voice of being" and what Gadamer would call "the voice of Being" with a capital *B*.[22] The latter way of being-in-the-world is one where a person is not in a "meaning making" and self-creative approach towards the world, self and others. Rather, one is in a "meaning receiving" and loving and "taken" mode, and experiences meaningfulness during self-forgetting immersion in, for instance, playing, painting, having a profound dialogue, or engaging in a caring and loving relation with what is, at a particular moment, calling for deep awareness and anticipation. In those existential moments and ontological living relations (or I-thou-relations) with the world or "the other" we are not in a state of intentional willing, wanting and doing but rather in a devotional, receptive, listening, admiring, vulnerable, contemplative and wondrous way of being-in-and-with-the-world. These are moments that Gadamer and other existential-oriented innovation, design and creativity researchers

(Scharmer 2007, Shotter 2010, Verganti and Öberg 2013) connect to the more intuitive, inspirational, evocative, and wonderment-arising moments in a researcher's work and aspirations, and therefore also attitudes and a way of being-in-and-with-the-world that our students should at least hear about and hopefully also work with.[23]

Discussion and clarifications

We want to clear up some misconceptions regarding the use of the concept of Bildung in contemporary higher education research, where it is often connected to the Humboldtian idea of a university (Kristensen et al. 2007). This idea is very often interpreted as a bit outdated, conservative, too theoretical and anti-utilitarian in its understanding of what constitutes good academic education and Bildung at a university (Käufer and Scharmer 2000). The critics of the Humboldtian tradition argue that this way of understanding higher education is locked into a "mode 1" approach to research, which is to say that the researcher becomes a solitary and narrow-minded specialist occupied only with his or her own exotic theoretical studies and proportional knowledge. Modern "mode 2" researchers (see Gibbons et al. 2004) are working in collective research environments in close contact with the world outside the university and with practical knowledge of problems and utilitarian needs of the society. This mode 2 research is in other words a more practice- and problem-based applied science, and the researcher would describe him- or herself as part of a scientific "knowledge production community" engaged in a living interchange with real life problems. We are not going to discuss this distinction between mode 1 and mode 2 research, or even if there could be a mode 3 research style (Hansen 2011, 2014). However, we do want to make the point that the Humboldtian ideal of Bildung is, in our view, neither this unworldly specialist nor this pragmatic, problem-solving innovator.

We would say that Humboldt's idea of Bildung has dimensions of both autonomy and authenticity, as well as a more general understanding of Bildung as *canon and content oriented*.[24] The teachers of Humboldt's university were not supposed to teach about certain canonical books, thinkers and artists *in order* for the students to find the "right answers". But these classical texts, that stand out as excellent readings for the students and teachers because of their admirable power to raise the big questions, might bring readers into a more open-minded, original, and self-thinking mode. Humboldt ([1841] 1988) followed Kant when Kant talked about Bildung as a path to self-determination through the use of one's own rationality, but he insisted that this self-determination should be followed and qualified by not only a rational, critical and systematic reflection and consciousness, but also a simultaneous cultivation of humanity's sensuality (*Sinnlichkeit*). So Humboldt was very keen on bringing in an *aesthetical cultivation* of the young student so that rational thinking was balanced by an aesthetic sensibility and creative imagination to form a vital unity (his notion of *Geist*/spirit). This free development of the individual's self-cultivation and self-realisation, which was an expression and result of the Bildung process, could not, Humboldt claimed, be done in isolation from the world and surrounding society and politics. Humans can, Humboldt argued, realise their potential as individuals and persons only in society.

Humboldt's successor, the German philosopher Karl Jaspers' expression "the wings of philosophising" can serve as an illustrative picture of how Humboldt saw Bildung as a two-sided process – as a creation of the student's existential unity of thinking and action:

> There are, so to speak, two wings that beat in this thinking [of "existential elucidation"], and it will succeed only if both really beat, [allowing] possible *Existenz* as well as generalized thinking. If one wing fails, the soaring elucidation will plummet to the ground. It is in this elucidation that the universal and I myself coincide [that I see] as the wings of philosophizing.
>
> (Jaspers [1932] 1971, p. 12)

In other words, the balance between the autonomy and authenticity dimensions of Bildung has to do both with a generalised conceptual, critical and Socratic thinking as well as an opening towards being or "possible Existenz" itself, which is often described as an intuition or lyrical sense of "that which speaks to me". The autonomy side of Academic Bildung is characterised by its formal orientation towards common human cognitive abilities, while the authenticity side of Academic Bildung is characterised by its substantial orientation towards the meaningfulness in the life of each individual person. The substantiality is not, as one might easily think, connected to a rigid description of a specific content and answers to the big questions. But the content level (the meeting with grand literature, art and philosophy of humanity with all their open-ended existential topics and questions) is important in order to have a medium through which the big questions can be raised and dwelled upon. This might lead to a high culture and elitist approach to the understanding of Bildung, but not necessarily.

In our view, neither the Kantian nor the Gadamerian way of understanding Bildung can be seen as elitist or as an education for a social stratum in line with a *Bildungsbürgertum*, although Gadamer certainly would be critical of the current widespread and comprehensive tendency in modern society and higher education to become increasingly utilitarian.[25] But we do not see, as Jørgen Fossland seems to be indicating, that a critical scepticism towards utilitarianism will necessary lead to an aristocratic elitism and anti-humanistic or anti-democratic worldview (2012). On the contrary, this means that neither of the two concepts require *specific* forms of content. However, at the same time we say – in line with Humboldt – that working with art, philosophy and literature that raise the big questions (but do not necessarily give big answers) can be a good way of keeping the student (and teachers) alert and "in shape" in their own critical and existential reflections and Socratic dialogues.

Academic Bildung is a question of moving beyond learning

If we now, as a final and concluding remark, turn to our notions of an autonomy- and authenticity-oriented concept of Academic Bildung, we would say that knowledge-oriented thinking is more connected to the autonomy dimension of Academic Bildung. Here we are working with Academic Bildung in different, but indeed important and necessary, ways in an epistemological and learning-oriented "grip" of the world and our lives, in order better to master our lives. But as we have discussed in this article, through Gadamer's notion of Bildung, the Nordic folk high school tradition and its view on Bildung, and through Barnett's description of the "ontological turn in higher education" – there is also another important "second wing" (cf. Karl Japers) in the notion of Academic Bildung, which is concerned with the ethical-existential and ontological being-dimension of the Bildung process and concept. And this has to do with the Academic Bildung ideal of authenticity.

To be in a knowing position and to be in a wondrous and fundamental not-knowing position (to be in the field of "that, which I do not know that I do not know – but that I am or I am becoming to be") are of course two different positions that at the same time are necessarily interwoven. It is like the Socratic dictum: The only thing I know is that I do not know. It is this kind of Socratic *docta ignorantia* (scholarly not-knowing wonderment) and the openness and humbleness that follows that is indeed a part of what we would describe as good Academic Bildung. In these "fields of wonder" we move beyond learning and touch upon an ontological dimension in higher education which requires another subtle attitude of *not* being in a pro-acting, coping, constructing, and mastering attitude but rather in a receptive, listening, reluctant, devoted and wondrously open attitude towards the calling of the phenomenon we wish to understand better. Our concept of Academic Bildung, as we have developed it in this chapter, is indeed two-dimensional. If one dimension is lacking, we would say that it is no longer a Scandinavian conception of Academic Bildung.

Notes

1 Grundtvig, and the movement of folk high schools that he inspired, had a noticeable influence on Nordic educational ideas of adult education as such. The people's enlightenment tradition from Grundtvig moreover influenced a democratic and egalitarian educational policy in the Nordic countries on a general basis, and an educational policy that at its best also held the existential and life-quality-oriented dimensions in view.

2 See page 42–43 in this chapter for a more nuanced introduction to the notion of autonomy.

3 Our specific understanding of authenticity will be elaborated throughout our description of Ronald Barnett's concept of authenticity as well as our critical comments to Barnett's existentialist view on authenticity.

4 See Solberg (2011) for a discussion of how the technology of synchronous web meetings can give good opportunities for facilitating Bildung processes between teachers and students in net-based studies.

5 Richard Rorty has been somewhat more inventive, with the introduction of the notion of "edification" (1979, see chapter viii).

6 However, Bildung is not exclusively a concept of formal education. Reinhart Koselleck, in his *The practice of conceptual history: Timing history, spacing concepts*, presents Bildung as " . . . neither formal education *(Ausbildung)* nor imagination *(Einbildung)*. . . . Bildung can neither be reduced to its institutional presuppositions – the mere result of formal education, nor can Bildung be dissolved into the terms of a psychological or ideological critique – the mere imagination of those who take themselves for educated *(Gebildet)*" (2002, pp. 170).

7 This situation, that there exist several different conceptions of Bildung, is in a sense not new. There have been a number of conceptions and theories about Bildung around for a very long time. A theory of particular interest in a didactic connection like ours is the German educator Wolfgang Klafki's theory of categorical Bildung. Unfortunately, we could not find room for a comparison with our theory in this chapter.

8 For an introduction to a history of the philosophy of Bildung, see Straume (ed., 2013). We recommend in particular the first introductory chapter by the editor.

9 For a more thorough introduction to the differences between these two traditions, we recommend Lars Løvlie and Paul Standish's "Introduction: Bildung and the idea of a liberal education" in Løvlie et al. (eds., 2003).

10 See for example Scharmer (2007) and Hansen (2013) for a more existential and being-oriented approach to the development of creativity and innovation in higher education and professional development.

11 For an Anglo-American view on and good introduction to the Nordic concepts of people's enlightenment and enlightenment for life, see Stephen M. Borish (1991, p. 164–78).

12 For an inspiring description of what a folk high school is, and the main educational ideas behind the folk high school, please see: http://danishfolkhighschools.com/media/247068/the-danish-folkeh_jskole-web.pdf

13 For elaborated descriptions and discussion of these two understandings of *folkeoplysning*, see Korsgaard (1997, 2004).

14 For the qualification of the concept of individualisation see Taylor (1992), and for coherence and democracy in a pluralistic and cosmopolitan world see Nussbaum (1997) and Villa (2001).

15 This insight is the basis for the Norwegian philosopher Hans Skjervheim's (1926–99) seminal article from 1976 "Eit grunnproblem i pedagogisk filosofi" (reissued 1996), a major influence in Scandinavian pedagogy.

16 For a late modern elaboration of how the concept of authenticity is important for the development of a non-elitist democracy and society, see Jensen and Lübker (2006) and especially Hansen (2006).

17 For further descriptions and elaboration of the educational philosophy behind the Nordic folk high school see Rosendahl (1961), Slumstrup et al. (1983), Zøllner (1993), Korsgaard (1997), Hansen (2000, 2002, 2008, and 2010), and Vodsgaard (2003).

18 *Sapere aude* means, more directly translated into English, "dare to know", and the phrase is said to stem from Horace.

19 See Solberg (2010) for a development of a Kantian notion of Bildung, based on an elaboration of Kant's *sensus communis* and his principle of enlightenment, and Søndenå and Solberg (2013) for application of this notion in a setting of tutoring in teacher education.

20 See for instance Mangseth (2010) and Slagstad (2003, p. 253).

21 For further development of this argument please read Hansen (2010a, 2011, and 2013).

22 This is comparable with the distinction that late Heidegger makes between *Dasein* and *Sein* (Heidegger [1954] 2004), and with Arendt (1978) and Marcel (1950).

23 For an elaboration of a higher education pedagogy, which is led by this kind of wonder-based and "four-voiced Bildung pedagogy" please read Hansen (2008c, 2014). See also Chapters 9 and 11 of this book for employment of the "four-voiced Bildung pedagogy".

24 For a profound introduction to the thoughts of Wilhelm von Humboldt and his views on education and Bildung, see: http://plato.stanford.edu/entries/wilhelm-humboldt

25 See Solberg and Fossland (2013) for a further discussion of elitism and Academic Bildung.

References

Arcilla, R. V. (1995), *For the love of perfection: Richard Rorty and liberal education*. Routledge: New York.

Arendt, H. (1978), *Life of the mind*. Harcourt: London.

Barnett, R. (2004), "Learning for an unknown future". *Higher Education Research and Development*, vol. 23, no. 3, pp. 247–60.

Barnett, R. (2005), "Recapturing the universal in the university". *Educational Philosophy and Theory*, vol. 37, no. 6, pp. 785–97.

Barnett, R. (2007), *A will to learn: Being a student in an age of uncertainty*. Open University Press/McGraw Hill: Berkshire, UK.

Barnett, R. (2011), *Being a university*. Routledge: London.

Bloom, A. (1987), *Closing of the American mind*. Simon & Schuster: New York.

Borish, S. (1991), *The land of the living: The Danish folk high schools and Denmark's nonviolent path to modernization*. Blue Dolphin: Nevada City, CA.

Buber, M. ([1923] 2004), *I and Thou*, tr. Smith, R. G., Insel-Verlag: Leipzig, DE.

Carlsen, J. (1999), "'Vi er her allerede!' Om folkehøjskolen som moderne dannelses-institution". *Uddannelse*, vol. 8, Undervisningsministeriet: Copenhagen.

Carlsen, J. (2013), "The Danish 'folkehøjskole'". Royal Danish Ministry of Foreign Affairs, Copenhagen. Available online at http://danishfolkhighschools.com/media/812419/the-danish-folkeh_jskole-web.pdf

Carlsen, A. and Sandelands, M. (2011), "Living ideas at work", In: Pitsis, T., Simpson, A. and Dehlin, E., eds., *Handbook of organizational and managerial innovation*. Edward Elgar Publishing: Cheltenham, UK.

52   *Mariann Solberg and Finn Thorbjørn Hansen*

Dewey, J. ([1916] 2008), *Democracy and education*. Wilder Publications: Radford, VA.

Fossland, J. (2012), "Nazisme og dannelse", *Norsk filosofisk tidsskrift*, March, 2012, pp. 155–67.

Frisch, M. ([1957] 1994), *Homo faber*. Mariner Books: Boston.

Gadamer, H. G. ([1960] 2006), *Truth and method*. Continuum: New York.

Gibbons, M. L., Limoges, C., Nowotny, H., Schwartzman, S., Scott, P., and Trow, M. (1994), *New production of knowledge: The dynamics of science and research in contemporary societies*. Sage Publications: London.

Gustavsson, B. (1996), *Bildning I vår tid. Om bildningens möjligheter och villkor i det moderna samhället*. Wahlström and Widstrand: Stockholm.

Habermas, J. (1984), *The theory of communicative action*. Beacon Press: Boston.

Hagtvet, B. and Ognjenovic, G., eds. (2011), *Dannelse. Tenkning, modning, refleksjon*. Dreyers Forlag: Oslo.

Hansen, F. T. (2000), *Den sokratiske dialoggruppe*. Gyldendal: Copenhagen.

Hansen, F. T. (2002), *Det filosofiske liv. Et dannelsesideal for eksistenspædagogikken*. Gyldendal: Copenhagen.

Hansen, F. T. (2006), "Er stræben efter autenticitet elitært?" In: Jensen, R. and Lübker, H., eds., *Elite og samfund – En antologi*. GPO Forlag: Odense, DK.

Hansen, F. T. (2008a), *Det var, som om de havde en slags kærlighed til det, de gjorde. Om den eksistentielle dimesion i højskolens uddannelses – og erhvervsvejledning*. Folkehøjskolernes Forening i Danmark: Copenhagen.

Hansen, F. T. (2008b), *At stå i det åbne. Dannelse gennem filosofisk undren og nærvær*. Hans Reitzel: Copenhagen.

Hansen, F. T. (2008c), "Demokrati med og uden ånd". In: Kjær, R., ed., *Højskolens kerne. Demokratisk dannelse, folkelig oplysning og livsoplysning*. E-book available from Folkehøjskolernes Forening i Danmark: Copenhagen.

Hansen, F. T. (2010a), "The phenomenology of wonder in higher education". In: Brinkmann, M., ed., *Erziehung. Phänomenologische perspektiven*. Königshausen & Neumann: Würzburg, DE.

Hansen, F. T. (2010b), "Demokrati – Med og uden ånd". In: Kjær, R., ed., *Højskolens kerne: Demokratisk dannelse, folkelig oplysning, livsoplysning*. E-book available from Folkehøjskolernes Forening i Danmark: Copenhagen.

Hansen, F. T. (2011,) "Universitetets overordnede mål bør være at skabe frihed for 'åndens liv'". In: Feldt, J. E. and Dohn, N. B., eds., *Universitetsundervisning i det 21. Århundrede. Læring, dannelse, marked*. Syddansk Universitetsforlag: Odense, DK.

Hansen, F. T. (2012), "One step further: The dance between poetic dwelling and Socratic wonder in phenomenological research". *Indo-Pacific Journal of Phenomenology*, July 2012, pp. 1–20.

Hansen, F. T. (2013), "Dannelse forstået som taktfuldhed over for 'det sande og gådefulde' i tilværelsen". In: Pahuus, M., ed., *Dannelse i en læringstid*. Aalborg Universitetsforlag: Aalborg, DK.

Hansen, F. T. (2014), *Kan man undre sig uden ord? Design- og universitetspædagogik på kreative videregående uddannelser*. Aalborg Universitetsforlag: Aalborg, DK.

Heidegger, M. ([1954] 2004), *What is called thinking?* HarperCollins: New York.

Hellesnes, J. (1992), "Ein utdana mann og eit dana menneske". In: Dale, E. L., ed., *Pedagogisk filosofi*. Ad Notam Gyldedal: Oslo.

Jaspers, K. ([1932] 1971), *Philosophy*, vol. 2. Chicago University Press: Chicago.

Jensen, R. and Lübker, H., eds. (2007), *Elite og samfund – en antologi*. GPO Forlag: Odense, DK.

Kant, I. ([1790] 1987), *Critique of judgment*, tr. Pluhar, W. S. Hackett: Indianapolis, IN.

Kant, I. ([1784] 2006), "An answer to the question: What is enlightenment", In: Kleingeld, P., ed., *Toward perpetual peace and other writings on politics, peace, and history / Immanuel Kant*, tr. Colclasure, D. L. Yale University Press: New Haven, CT.

Kaüfer, K. and Scharmer, C. O. (2007), "Universitetet som udsigtspunkt for det iværksættende menneske". In: Kristensen, J. E., et al., *Ideer om et universitet*. Aarhus Universitetsforlag: Aarhus, DK.

Korsgaard, O. (1997), *Kampen om lyset*. Gyldendal: Copenhagen.

Korsgaard, O. (2004), *Kampen om folket*. Gyldendal: Copenhagen.

Kristensen, J. E., Elstrøm, K., Nielsen, J. V., Pedersen, M., Sørensen, B. V. and Sørensen, H. (2007), *Ideer om et universitet*. Aarhus Universitetsforlag: Aarhus, DK.

Kronman, A. (2007), *Education's end: Why our colleges and universities have given up on the meaning of life*. Yale University Press: New Haven, CT.

Løvlie, L. (2003), "Teknokulturell danning". In: Slagstad, R., Korsgaard, O. and Løvlie, L., eds., *Dannelsens forvandlinger*. Pax Forlag: Oslo.

Løvlie, L. and Standish, P. (2003), "Introduction: Bildung and the idea of a liberal education". In: Løvlie, L., Mortensen, K. P. and Nordenbo, S. E., eds., *Educating humanity: Bildung in postmodernity*. Blackwell: Oxford.

MacIntyre, A. (1981), *After virtue*. University of Notre Dame Press: Notre Dame, IN.

Mackler, S. (2009), *Learning for meaning's sake: Toward the hermeneutic university*. Sense Publishers: Rotterdam, NL.

Mangset, M. (2010), "Blir studentene bedre mennesker i utlandet?" *Nytt Norsk tidsskrift* vol. 1-2, pp. 105–14.

Marcel, G. (1950), *Mystery of being*, 2 vols. Gateway Editions: South Bend,IN.

Nussbaum, M. (1997), *Cultivating humanity: A classical defense of reform in liberal education*. Harvard University Press: Cambridge, MA.

Postman, N. (1993), *Technopoly: The surrender of the culture to technology*. Vintage Books: New York.

Raffnsøe-Møller, M. (2007), "Taylors politiske filosofi. Ontologisk politik og hermeneutisk retfærdighed". *Slagmark* vol. 49, pp. 61–82.

Rawls, J. (1971), *A theory of justice*. Harvard University Press: Cambridge, MA.

Readings, B. (1996), *The university in ruins*. Harvard University Press: Cambridge, MA.

Rorty, R. (1979), *Philosophy and the Mirror of Nature*. Princeton University Press: Princeton, New Jersey.

Rorty, R. (1989), *Contingency, irony, and solidarity*. Cambridge University Press: New York.

Rorty, R. (1991), "Uddannelse, socialisation og individuation", In: Hauge, H. and Tøjner, P. E., eds., *Kritik*, vol. 95, Gyldendal: Copenhagen.

Rosendahl, J., ed. (1961), *Højskolen til debat*. Gyldendal: Copenhagen.

Sandel, M. (1998), *Liberalism and the limits of justice*, 2nd edn. Cambridge University Press: Cambridge, UK.

Scharmer, C. O. (2007), *Theory U: Leading from the future as it emerges*. Society for Organizational Learning: Boston.

Shotter, J. (2010), *Social construction on the edge: "Withness", thinking and embodiment*. Taos Institute Publications: Chagrin Falls, OH.

Skjervheim, H. ([1976] 1996), "Eit grunnproblem i pedagogisk filosofi". In: *Deltakar og tilskodar og andre essays*. Aschehoug Forlag: Oslo.

Slagstad, R. (2003), "Universitetet som dannelsesinstitusjon". In: Slagstad, R., Korsgaard, O., and Løvlie, L., eds., *Dannelsens forvandlinger*, pp. 246–55. Pax Forlag: Oslo.

Slumstrup, F., Akelie, O., Terning, P. and Björkstrand, G., eds. (1983), *Grundtvigs oplysningstanker og vor tid.* Nordisk Folkehøjskoleråd: Jelling, DK.

Solberg, M. (2010), "Om akademisk danning med utgangspunkt i Kants sensus communis og 'Hva er opplysning?'" In: Nilsen, F. and Dybdal, L., eds., *Festskrift til Hjördis Nerheim i anledning 70-årsdagen,* pp. 51–68. Unipub Forlag: Oslo.

Solberg, M. (2011), "Educating the citizen of academia online?" *International Review of Research in Open and Distance Learning,* vol. 12, no. 4, pp. 77–87.

Solberg, M. and Fossland, T. (2013), "Akademisk danning – Et mulig prosjekt for voksne studenter i fleksible studier?", pp. 46–62. Gyldendal Akademisk: Oslo.

Sommerville, C. J. (2006), *The decline of the secular university.* Oxford University Press: London.

Søndenå, K. and Solberg, M. (2013), "Danningsfundert rettleiing – Utvida tenking og kraftfulle refleksjonar", pp. 42–53. Gyldendal Akademisk: Oslo.

Spinosa, C., Flores, F. and Dreyfus, H. L. (1997), *Disclosing new worlds: Entrepreneurship, democratic action, and the cultivation of solidarity.* MIT Press: Boston.

Steinsholt, K. and Dobson, S. (2011), *Dannelse. Introduksjon til et ullent pedagogisk landskap.* Tapir: Trondheim, NO.

Straume, I. S. (2013), "Danningens filosofihistorie: En innføring". In: *Danningens filosofihistorie.* Gyldendal Akademisk: Oslo.

Taylor, C. (1989), *Sources of the self.* Cambridge University Press: New York.

Taylor, C. (1992), *The ethics of authenticity.* Harvard University Press: Cambridge, MA.

Universitets og høgskolerådet. (2011), *Dannelsesaspekter i utdanning. Rapport fra en arbeidsgruppe nedsatt av UHRs utdanningsutvalg.* Available online athttp://www. uhr.no/aktuelt_fra_uhr/dannelsesaspekter_i_utdanning van Manen, M. (1990), *Researching lived experience: Human science for an action sensitive pedagogy.* Althouse Press: Ontario.

van Manen, M. (2002), *Writing in the dark: Phenomenological studies in interpretive inquiry.*Althouse Press: Ontario.

van Manen, M. (2007), "Phenomenology of practice", *Phenomenology & Practice,* vol. 1, pp. 11–30.

van Manen, M. (2014), *Phenomenology of practice: Meaning-giving methods in phenomenological research and writing.* Left Coast Press: Walnut Creek, CA.

Verganti, R. and Öberg, Å. (2013), "Interpreting and envisioning. A hermeneutic framework to look at radical innovation of meanings". *Industrial Marketing Management,* vol. 42, pp. 86–95.

Villa, D. (2001), *Socratic citizenship.* Princeton University Press: Princeton, NJ.

Vodsgaard, H. J. (2003), *Højskole til tiden.* Foreningen for Folkehøjskoler i Danmark: Copenhagen.

von Humboldt, W. ([1841] 1988), *Gesammelte werke,* vol. 1, Brandes, C., ed. De Gruyer: Berlin.

Wilshire, B. (1990), *The moral collapse of the university: Professionalism, purity, and alienation.* State University of New York Press: Albany, NY.

Zøllner, L., ed. (1993), *Almen dannelse, folkelig dannelse, folkelig livsoplysning.* Kroghs Forlag: Vejle, DK.

4 Strategies for net-based education in Scandinavian universities

Frank Holen

Introduction

Higher education institutions have increasingly embraced net-based education, and the number of students enrolled in such programmes is rising at colleges and universities in Scandinavia and throughout the world. In response to these changes in enrolment demands, many institutions, and organisations have been working on strategic plans or goals to implement net-based education (Salmon 2005). This takes place at the same time as European universities face demands for urgent and radical reform. A standard claim is that environments are changing rapidly and that universities are not able or willing to respond adequately. It is claimed that it is necessary to rethink and reshape their internal order and role in society simply because European universities do not learn, adapt and reform themselves fast enough (Olsen and Maassen 2006; Maassen et al. 2007). Typically, this has focused attention on managerialism marked by "a new kind of executive power, characterised by a will to manage; often in combination with adoption of business methods and the creation of quasi-markets and, in some respects, a freedom to act greater than what was once the case" (Marginson and Considine 2000, p. 9; also see Ferlie 1996). All these trends are invoked in the context for both the discussions and cases in this book; there is no sign of the Scandinavian countries steering clear of this controversy.

Evidently there are demanding complexities in higher education with misconceptions and myths related to the potential and difficulty of teaching and learning in a digital environment – both the pedagogic and technological knowledge is in development. The combination of new public management (NPM) making its way in higher education and an immature field of research creates challenges for the institutions (Fairweather and Gibbons 2000). How do they respond to this through vision statements and planning documents, strategies and such? Is net-based education featured in strategies at the institutions?

The primary focus in this chapter is strategies for, and organisation of, net-based higher education with examples from three universities. What are the ideals manifested in these strategies and practices, and what are the educational consequences? More specifically I ask: How do the potential and actual strategies, organisation and processes in higher educational institutions regarding net-based education affect the space for Academic Bildung?

The first part is twofold. It is concerned with how, and to what extent, net-based education is present in strategic documents in the universities and how it is argued. The other aspect is about manoeuvrability and future development. Given technological, societal and political forces, what strategies might unfold and influence the terms for Academic Bildung?

The second part of the problem is concerned with how institutional arrangements influence how net-based education is understood and practiced in the universities, and hence the space and drive for Academic Bildung, both at a general level and in net-based education. Academic Bildung in an educational context is "about acquiring a certain amount of knowledge and skills, in depth and width, that one gains through independent processing and consideration" (Solberg and Fossland 2013, my translation). It is not a process that takes places out of context though; it happens throughout an academic community, as Solberg and Hansen write in Chapter 3:

> One must think on the basis of the well-established knowledge in his or her discipline, and thus one needs to be acquainted with this knowledge base. One must further be able to train one's thinking skills in conjunction with one's peers and the previous and present authorities in one's field. This means that self-thinking requires a community. The lack of Bildung thus will manifest as a lack of active and independent use of one's intellect and a lack of inclusion of the possible judgment of others.
>
> (p. 43)

In line with such arguments it is obvious that Bildung depends on the individual, the institutional framework (ie. curriculum, didactics, teacher and fellow students), and society at large. The goals and organisation of education will affect the students both when they are still enrolled in the university courses and programmes and after their graduation. Whether strategies emphasise knowledge production in terms of a demand and request for scientific "evidence-based" knowledge, or the question of meaning (values, beliefs, ethics) (Mackler 2009, p. 6), they have potential impact on the outcome of the learning process.

Net-based education has obviously become an integral part of higher education, but the institutions' strategies and goals concerning the subject are seemingly vague and implicit. When the problem relates to both the potential and actual goals and strategies, it does so in order to highlight the potential consequences for Academic Bildung. Consequently, this chapter will be both a discussion of the actual strategies on net-based education and a meta-discussion on the relation between potential strategies and Academic Bildung.

In this chapter, I will start by elaborating on arguments and strategies for net-based education. I am relating to both the present and historical context. The enlightenment tradition is deeply rooted in Scandinavia as well as in distance education in general. These and other arguments and influences are discussed here and illustrated with examples related to Academic Bildung from the universities in Tromsø, Norway, Aarhus, Denmark, and Umeå, Sweden. Are the potential or actual strategies formed in a way that stimulates or hinders Academic Bildung?

The next part looks into essential aspects of organising and developing net-based education as a new and promising field in the universities. How are the infrastructure (competence, incentives, measures and the like) and responsibilities organised within the universities to ensure the realisation of intentions (goals and strategies)? Furthermore, this infrastructure might represent hindrances or possibilities for Academic Bildung.

Net-based education is obviously an area of attention at the institutions in focus here. At the same time, it is difficult to identity explicit strategies on the subject, let alone analytical or theoretic strategies existing in the field. In order to get a grip on the matter it is necessary to identify analytical categories and the context for net-based education. These are necessary in order to place the initiatives at the universities and relate them to Bildung. Being an immature field in development it is not one with abundant empirical material.

The strategies are incremental, evolving over time, but are not very evident and explicit. Hence, it has been difficult to find empirical material for specific strategies in the institutions. Consequently this chapter will be concerned with identifying and developing the strategies or strategic leeway here, and trying to relate experiences from the institutions to it.

Strategies for net-based education

Net-based education is a term that contains different perspectives and arguments. The nature of the arguments depends on what dimensions related to net-based education they emphasise. In a global perspective, the driving force for many institutions is the idea of staying competitive in the "e-hype" with a substantial share of the huge revenues promised in the new economy. Predictions were that in the US alone the net-based learning market would make $6 billion in 2002 (according to an IDC report, 1998) – and everyone wanted their share (Gerhard and Mayr 2002). This line of thinking has obviously influenced Scandinavian universities, but is often combined with other reasons ranging from the economic, as above, to more ideological ones. The next sections map out different strategies that have been made more or less explicit both from institutions and in the literature.

Effectiveness and efficiency approach

Universities today are heavily influenced by ideas that promote effectiveness and efficiency. This is not necessarily a cohesive and well-established perspective that management or others argue explicitly for. Still, it is an underlying theme in arguments for standardisation and low cost productions. Systems for automatic recordings of lectures is one such example where costs are low, the potential for re-use of lectures is high, and the availability for students is high. Put in economic terms the cost per unit becomes lower, and once digital material and recorded lectures are produced, the amount of necessary teaching resources might be lowered. In essence this is a matter of taking the promises of technology into the production and rationalisation of education. However, this is often a more implicit part of other strategies. Bates' (2005, p. 10) answer as to why higher education institutions consider technology-based learning exemplifies this:

- The need to do more with less
- The changing learning needs of society
- The impact of new technologies on teaching and learning

This often rests on e-learning having the potential to result in significant cost savings. Gibbons and Fairwhether (2000) estimate the reduction as sometimes being as much as 50 per cent compared with traditional instructor-led learning. The estimation of expected savings differ, but in the instructional domain this is a very dominant understanding (Kulik and Kulik, 1991).

Economical and marketing approach

Through increased reach, students can take part in courses and programmes independent of time and place, which, because it gives opportunities to new groups or segments, makes the potential market for students larger, both regionally and globally. The example from Stanford where the online computer science subject CS 2143 recruited over 100,000 students both from the US and other countries all over the globe, illustrates such possibilities. However, there are institutions that have failed or wasted large amounts of money because they were taken by surprise by the low conversion rate of potential markets into actual registrations. The difficulty in reaching a global market through advertising or agents, the requirements of higher levels of resources, and the slow time required to arrive at market are among the challenges faced by the higher education institutions (Salmon 2005).

Another evident but implicit dimension within a marketing domain relates to the use of modern technology to attract students. Using modern technology, and supposedly modern forms of teaching and learning, may display the institution as more attractive for the students. Hence flexibility and modern technology can be seen as both a marketing instrument and a contribution to a positive reputation for the institution. Looking at many of the initiatives at the universities, one could easily suspect such motives. Initiatives on massive open online courses (MOOC) can be understood on the basis of such a rationale – at present MIT has a total of 26 courses available on the MOOC platform edX. Relative to their total portfolio of courses and programmes these are very few. But their presence garners a lot of media coverage and promotes a positive image of MIT. Conscious strategy or not, their presence serves to market a proactive and modern university.

In an environment where universities compete for students, flexibility and digital learning material may be a deed of necessity. Not doing it might not be an option. I have yet to see this argument in any discussions regarding net-based education, but it is natural to think that it would be difficult for institutions not to "go online". This is a quite normal dynamics for markets.

Quality approach

Part of the argument for net-based education, especially in the strategic and practical domains, is that it could enhance quality for students. This is more of a general argument. We seldom find it substantiated by thorough argumentation –seemingly it is an understanding taken for granted that technology and flexibility are experienced as a quality enhancement. Typically the "argument" is that additional digital material contributes to the quality of the teaching material, and a larger repertoire of forms of teaching and learning.

Another dimension to this is answering the students' quest for flexibility in their use of technology. Younger students find it both old-fashioned and strange that exams are to be done by pen and paper – an almost unfamiliar way of writing for most nineteen- and twenty-year-olds. Meeting the needs for the distribution and organisation of education among students will also be seen as an enhancement of its quality, or at least it will satisfy their perceived need. For students with a positive perception of technology, Drennan and colleagues (2005) document how digital resources are perceived as positive contributions to the learning environment. Learners' satisfaction rates typically increase along with perceived ease of use and access, navigation, interactivity and user-friendly interface design (Fairweather and Gibbons 2000; Chumley-Jones et al. 2002).

Traditionally flexibility has been a concern for off-campus students, but this is changing. The change emerges partly because students spend less time on campus. The full time student is no longer predominant in Scandinavian universities. There are several explanations for this development, most simply the development among students in these countries that they spend an increasing part of their time working. Among the 220,000-some students in Norway with an ongoing university education, about 93 per cent have registered earned income on their tax report. The percentage of students with an income over $10,500 (USD) was 54 per cent, or about 80,000 students in 2008. Of these, 34 per cent had an income over $21,000 (USD). This obviously changes demographics and needs among students. The needs of more affluent students are complex and differentiated, and challenge higher educational institutions on the issues of availability and flexibility, as discussed in the next section.

Equality and availability approach

Strategies based on arguments of equality and availability relate to the idea that net-based education will make education more accessible and thereby represents a contribution to enlightenment. In Bertrand Russell's words, the goals of education is:

> to give a sense of the value of things other than domination, to help create wise citizens of a free community, to encourage a combination of citizenship with liberty, individual creativeness, which means that we regard a child as a gardener regards a young tree, as something with an intrinsic nature which will develop into an admirable form given proper soil and air and light.
>
> (Russell, in Chomsky 2003, p. 26)

As such, education can contribute to enlightening the citizens of a country. Both Dewey (in Archambault 1964) and Russell shared the understanding that these leading ideas of the Enlightenment and classical liberalism had a revolutionary character, which was retained right at the time they were writing about it. If implemented, these ideas could produce free human beings, whose values were not accumulation and domination, but rather free association in terms of equality, sharing and cooperation, participation on equal terms to achieve common goals, which were democratically conceived.

Besides being an argument for democracy, there is also an argument for education being a right. Public educational institutions should be open on equal terms to all those who are qualified. Although there are good financial arrangements for students in the Scandinavian countries, there are parts of the population that for several reasons are unable to attend classes on campus. Typically they live, work or have family in places other than where there are educational institutions. Hence net-based education often represents the only real alternative for these people to take part in a programme or subject at the university (Grepperud 2005, p. 193).

Liberalistic arguments

With resemblance to the arguments advanced in the democratic approach Rumble (1990) and Lewis (1990) argue for open learning. For them, open learning is essentially an ideology or philosophy of learning and the learning process. Emphasis is on the situation and optimal conditions for the learners – in contrast to optimising the educational institution's production-oriented mode. Grepperud (2005) argues that a common denominator in this view is to reduce as many obstacles as possible in order to give the individual ideal conditions for learning. This approach, with its clear normative suggestions, presents a moral argument: allowing free access to education and learning will lead to greater social justice by enabling more people to gain qualifications, which, in turn, leads to wealth redistribution. Related arguments are found with reference to the individual's capabilities and needs (Cooper 2007; Rumble 2007).

Work life applicability and social responsibility

Over the years, universities have received massive criticism for being institutions disconnected or distant from society. The critique concerns both research and organisational culture, which is said to be introverted and not contribute to societal development, while the knowledge produced does not solve practical or important problems in society.

There is no doubt that the operational environment of universities has changed, and probably continues to change. Universities are expected to innovate and to produce tangible results in terms of fostering economic growth, student employment and business opportunities, and to offer solutions to ecological problems. Simple and quick solutions are expected, but universities tend to provide complex and long-term answers. As Clark (1998) notes, there is a widening asymmetry between environmental demand and institutional capacity to respond. Still we find that institutions in higher education are changing, but more often through incremental processes than revolutionary. This is also evident in the examples in this chapter. There is no revolution taking place in Scandinavian institutions, but there are changes.

How do the three universities approach net-based education?

Analysing the management perspective in the three institutions, there are varying degrees of explicit ambitions on behalf of and within net-based education. The change strategies are best characterised as moderate, which involves cautiously enhancing existing practice through introducing well-rehearsed and easy-to-use technologies. This is in contrast to a radical approach changing the over-all structures (Johnston 2001). Although technology changes rapidly, the processes at the three universities are best characterised as incremental and slow, not as large-scale centralisation with noteworthy impact on organisational structures. Naturally, ideas and examples of use of more innovative technology can be found, but not in any large scale. Mostly it can be seen as a moderate adaptation within a context of growing impact of technology in education and learning. At the universities in Tromsø, Umeå and Aarhus there are projects and initiatives that are innovative and radical, but they do not add up to a massive wave of change at the institutional level.

Based on the attention net-based education has received both in Scandinavia and the world at large, it could be expected that this is a field where explicit strategies and goals were formulated at all institutions within higher education; however, this does not seem to be the case. Looking at the strategies at the three institutions used as examples in this chapter, the most explicit and elaborated strategies are at Aarhus University. Aarhus underlines what they call "educational IT" as a plan for quality. As their web site says about the vision:

> It is the vision that educational IT supports the relationship between students and teachers and the academic content of the lectures, and creates the best conditions for:
>
> • Lecturers' planning, conducting, and evaluation of lectures
> • Students' opportunities to work and learn what is required
> • Interaction between students, and between students and lecturers
> ("Den faglige utviklingsproces Aarhus universitet 2014",
> p. 65, my translation)

Additionally, Aarhus's materials say that educational IT shall open a wide range of learning resources that can give the students differentiated learning possibilities in reaching their competence goals.

As with the other institutions, the main approach here is for ICT to enhance quality for the students in some way. Net-based education is supposed to enhance quality with an underlying rationale that attractive learning environments will attract students. Both UiT The Arctic University of Norway and Umeå University argue for enhancing the quality of the experience, although the strategies here are even more vaguely formulated. In the latest strategy plan at UiT The Arctic University of Norway one finds this exemplified through formulations such as: "UiT shall develop good and new tools to create outstanding educational and teaching quality" ("Drivkraft i nord: Strategi for UiT mot 2020", my translation).

Umeå University though is somewhat different in its approach since it is the only one of the three that argues for the use of net-based education in relation to life-long-learning, and makes the important point that on-line courses enable all to take part in education. In this respect Umeå argues for equality and availability strategies. Umeå, with over 200 courses available that are net-based and off-campus, is now reducing the number of online courses due to (Swedish) prescriptions on future enrolments at the universities that predict student numbers will drop.

Judging from the strategies, there are few signals of a weakening of the Academic Bildung dimension as such. In the case of Umeå it could well be that the school is strengthening this dimension through educating people who otherwise would not attend university courses – net-based instruction enhances the availability of higher education. As such, it has an important role in the enlightenment of society. It most certainly has the transformative potential that Deimann and Farrow (2013) argue for in relation to Bildung – as "*the structures of assumptions through which we understand our experiences to selectively shape cognitive, conative, and emotional processes*" (p. 350). Still, the question will always be to what extent this will be an effect of education itself, net-based or not.

As for the other strategies, it is difficult to say how they affect the concept of Academic Bildung. Quality in itself does not necessarily affect Bildung as it can include many variables that might not be of relevance here. Deiman and Farrow (2013) refer to the distinct difference between knowledge of how things can be better produced more efficiently (*Verfügungswissen*) and knowledge of why or for what reason things are done or produced (*Orientierungswissen*). Measures to improve marks might be seen to enhance quality, but they do not necessarily stimulate Academic Bildung. Values like autonomy, authenticity and critical reflection in learning and education can be stimulated through different didactics and methods for evaluation, but the strategies do not say anything about that. The same goes for the availability of education that has been central at Umeå University. Scale and availability does not in itself create learning activities that emphasise curiosity, imagination, passion and creativity in order to encourage authentic and personal forms of learning. Still the strategies that are central to the universities examined here do not represent a hindrance to Bildung as such. At the same time they are vague, and hence open for discussion and/or use of power. The strategies include some elements of choice, but the execution of them are, in my view, both in need of and open for discussion and definition. Based on the more general discussions concerning the educational sector it might well be that the strategies to influence the effectiveness and efficiency of online courses might become more central. If that were the case, the conditions for Academic Bildung might be different.

From the different approaches to net-based education, existing practice is not focused on strategies to move the institutions towards a production mode where the essential question is how things can be better produced, more efficiently (*Verfügungswissen*), with the potential to hinder Academic Bildung.

At the same time there are strong forces influencing higher education, and it might be that these will move higher education more towards a production mode in the future. Both the arguments from media and technology companies on the one side, and from policy institutions and society on the other, represent a push towards transfer and acquisition of knowledge and skills in university programmes (Olsen and Maassen 2007).

Furthermore strategies are not lived realities but plans, often not implemented, as Collins (2001) has documented thoroughly. The majority of initiatives related to net-based learning find their way through other arrangements and processes. These are not a result of explicit strategies, but can at the same time be understood as responses to both student demands and context (market). At the selected institutions, the initiatives differ in scope, time and goals. At UiT The Arctic University of Norway there has been a four-year project on net-based education where the arguments for establishment have been to increase access to education, recruitment, re-use of learning resources, quality, increased repertoire of teaching methods and adaptation to working life and society. Three million Norwegian kroner have been allocated to this initiative each year. Here the different actors could apply for funding for projects on net-based education. Those projects granted funding have had a wide range of aims and reflect the wide ambitions with the overall project. In light of how the funds have been distributed, there seemingly has been a desire to engage as many of the departments as possible in net-based education, widening the interest and experience in the field.

In relation to such initiatives it is interesting to look at how net-based education is manifested in practice through the organising and processes surrounding it. Who has the power to define "how and what" within the teaching and learning processes? Thus far we have not seen much of the effectiveness and efficiency approach that, if present, might make Academic Bildung a difficult ideal to seek. As I will point out in the next section, there are institutional structures that potentially challenge an Academic Bildung perspective.

Organising and processes

Innovations in the democratic and conservative decision-making structures of universities have always had somewhat of a hard time. Universities are political coalitions of interests and demands emanating from within and outside the organisation (Thompson 1967). Different interests and demands arise because organisations are loosely coupled systems (Weick 1976), information bound (Simon 1947), resource constrained (Salancik et al. 1978), and are characterised by unclear technologies (Cohen et al. 1972). Net-based education creates further pointed tensions in these political processes due to the pace of change, the investments required, and the need for involvement of more staff and stakeholders (Whitworth 2005; Salmon 2005). The picture is further complicated by net-based education being an immature field (of research and development), as well as an interdisciplinary field (technology, pedagogy and the various disciplines), and in these instances also contains vague strategies.

As a consequence of this complexity we find a multitude of discussions, initiatives and decisions at all levels in the institutions. Typically there are several actors trying to define what would benefit the development of net-based education, what technology and pedagogy would contribute to the quality of courses or programmes and so on. This bewildering situation resembles what Charles Lindblom discussed in his classic article "The Science of Muddling Through" (1959) where he outlined his view that the US executive bureaucracy uses limited policy analysis, bounded rationality,[1] and limited or no theory at all in formulating policy.

Lindblom took issue with the so-called "rational-comprehensive" approach that had dominated research and teaching in public administration, and still is often presented as the ideal method for developing public policy. According to this approach policy makers begin addressing a particular policy issue by ranking values and objectives. Next they identify and comprehensively analyse all alternative solutions, making sure to account for all potential factors. In the third and final step, administrators choose the alternative that is evaluated as the most effective in delivering the highest value in terms of satisfying the objectives identified in the first step. This approach seems to make perfect sense. But bureaucrats and administrators do not work this way in the real world, according to Lindblom, and probably not in the context of education either.

First, defining values and objectives is very difficult. There are always trade-offs in university policy. It is difficult to say with certainty, for example, that it is better to spend more on podcasts in order to balance the budget (more students passing their exam). Or that introducing more technology is a better way to enhance the reflection among students than more teaching hours. Or vice versa.

Second, separating means from ends (policy recommendations from the objectives of those policies) is impossible. Instead the policy solution is always bound up with the objectives. The problem of enhancing throughput could involve more of either digital resources or lectures in the classroom. But for many interested parties each of these potential "solutions" to the problem of congestion is likely to be a policy goal in its own right.

Third, it is impossible to aggregate the values and objectives of the various constituencies of the executive bureaucracy, citizens, private organisations, legislators and appointed officials, among others, to determine exactly which preferences are of most importance. The virtue of a policy is indicated by its ability to achieve broad support, not by some assessment that it is most efficient according to some abstract criteria.

Finally, it is inefficient to identify and analyse every policy option. For all but the most narrow policy choices it takes too much time and too many resources. Administrators are very busy and the volumes of detail on even relatively simple issues would be overly burdensome to analyse.

It is fair to say that many initiatives are bottom-up, and supported by the management of the university. At the same time this path is evidently complicated by a "muddling through" logic. I characterize the process as bottom-up because the implementation strategies are vague, and muddling through because of the many actors in the arena making arguments, defining and deciding matters based on vague goals, and unclear organisational structures.

More so than many other areas of policy within the universities, net-based education is open to discussion. The research within the field is scarce and the authoritative institutions within research and education are very few. Hence, the field is open for discussion, conflict and gatekeepers. Without authoritative scientific actors, net-based education is susceptible to struggles for power and policy direction, and all three universities have had problems in establishing responsibilities for the development regarding this subject. At all three universities included in this project, the departments working on net-based education have been subject to several reorganisations and their status has been shifting. Today none of them have any role in defining or developing policy, or in bringing explicit knowledge into such processes. With small differences these departments now provide services for the university staff and conduct research and developmental work within the field. They do not hold any defining role over strategies, policies or decisions. In many respects one could assume that this has to do with the nature of their task. In all cases the departments are interdisciplinary, typically with a mix of technical, pedagogical and subject-specific competence reflecting the different parts comprising net-based education. All three departments have been a mix of research and developmental organisations, and up until now probably more practice based than research based. Whatever the explanations might be for the present status concerning the organisation and responsibilities on net-based education, the field is open for a wide range of influences.

A recent example taken from UiT The Arctic University of Norway illustrates how such lack of status might unfold in practice. In the process of putting up a new building for the natural sciences at the university there was an enormous investment in educational IT (smartboards, computers, projectors etc.). The processes and decisions regarding this were done by a committee headed by the IT department, without any involvement from the department working on net-based education. After the decisions on investments were made, there was an inquiry to the department involved with net-based education on how to make use of the ICT infrastructure. Without an authoritative position or role for an actor knowledgeable on ICT in education, as this exemplifies, it might be easier to decide in favour of production and distribution of knowledge rather than Academic Bildung.

At the same time the concept of Academic Bildung is mainly rooted in the academic staff; the disciplinary subjects (and knowledge regarding it) and the pedagogy have thus far been their domain to decide. Normally, decisions about going online, use of digital resources and such are made by the academic staff themselves. But their autonomy in this respect is under pressure at a general level, and the outcome will probably affect questions regarding net-based issues. As long as initiatives on net-based education are created bottom-up without extensive need for infrastructure and/or investments they still have the autonomy. But if not, and it becomes policy, the situation might be different. Then net-based education might easily become subject to the limitations of a more production-oriented approach.

Conclusions

Although encountering challenges, the field of net-based education has thus far largely maintained academic integrity as it has developed. As will be evident in the case studies, no institutional structures represent a hindrance to Academic Bildung. At the same time the scarce knowledge base and vague strategies open up the field of net-based education to arguments or rationales other than subject (disciplinary-based) values and pedagogy. It will not come as a surprise if more financially-based arguments will be weighted in the future. We already see this in discussions regarding automatisation of lecture recordings. Here an argument of the efficiency of automated recordings is fronted, often without any reference to pedagogy or how such recordings add explicit value to a subject or programme. It might add value, but in what way? In itself it is an interesting question, but so is the question regarding whose premises and arguments are taken into account. Here extensive knowledge development is needed as well as discussions on the values appreciated and built upon.

The presence of Academic Bildung in the Scandinavian universities is, according to Solberg and Hansen (Chapter 3), related to their being research institutions, and that research is a core value of education. This implies that the cultures within the institutions (perhaps to various degrees) will be research cultures, as Solberg and Hansen state. Their argument is that: "The core values of Academic Bildung [in a Scandinavian setting] will . . . be the values of different research cultures – or what in general terms can be called academic values, or perhaps researcher virtues" (p. 43).

If the strategies, processes and concepts of education evolve through policy discussions the academic staff might have less influence over the content and results. Through the language and action emphasising "modernisation" and necessary adaptations to economic and technological change it might be that net-based education as a bottom-up "movement" in Scandinavia will be threatened. There is a growing organisational isomorphism[2] where higher education institutions develop the same organisational forms (Powell and DiMaggio 1983). Structures, goals, strategies and ideals among the institutions are starting to become very much alike (Olsen 2007). Traditionally such overreaching isomorphism provides leeway and opportunities for "business as usual" at lower levels regarding subjects and programmes. Here the key to pursuing Academic Bildung as an ideal is likely to be in the hands of the teacher. We might see traces of new public management, but one plausible hypothesis would be that variables such as incentive systems and major investments in infrastructure are what really would be a driving force towards a production-oriented mode rather than a Bildung-oriented mode. Large investments in, for example, technological infrastructure would create expectations of cost savings on other items of expenditure, efficiency and effectiveness.

Notes

1 Bounded rationality is the idea that in decision making, rationality of individuals is limited by the information they have, the cognitive limitations of their minds, and the finite amount of time they have to make a decision.
2 Powell and DiMaggio (1983) elaborate three forms of isomorphism: (1) mimetic isomorphism, (2) coercive isomorphism and (3) normative isomorphism. Mimetic isomorphism refers to the tendency of an organisation to imitate another organisation's structure because of the belief that the structure of the latter organisation is beneficial. Mimetic isomorphism is in contrast to coercive isomorphism, where organisations are forced to change by external forces, or normative isomorphism, where professional standards or networks influence change.

References

Archambault, R. D., ed. (1964), *John Dewey on education*. University of Chicago Press: London.

Bates, T. (2005), *Technology, e-learning, and distance education*. RoutledgeFalmer: London.

Chomsky, N. (2003). *Chomsky on democracy and education*. RoutledgeFalmer: London.

Chumley-Jones, H. S., Dobbie, A. and Alford, C. L. (2002), "Web-based learning: Sound educational method or hype? A review of the evaluation literature". *Academic Medicine*, vol. 77, pp. 86–93.

Clark, B. R. and Pergamon, B. R. (1998), *Creating entrepreneurial universities: Organizational pathways of transformation*. Emerald Group Publishing: Bingley, UK.

Cohen, M. D., March, J. G. and Olsen, J. P. (1972), "Garbage Can Model of Organizational Choice". *Administrative Science Quarterly*, vol. 17, pp. 1–25.

Collins, J. (2001), *Good to great: Why some companies make the leap . . . and others don't*. Random House: London.

Cooper, J. E. (2007), "Strengthening the case for community-based learning in teacher education". *Journal of Teacher Education*, vol. 58, pp. 245–55.

Deimann, M. and Farrow, R. (2013), "Rethinking OERs and their use: Open education as Bildung". *International Review of Research in Open and Distance Learning*, vol. 14, pp. 344–60.

"Den faglige utviklingsproces Aarhus universitet" (2014). Available from: http://medarbejdere.au.dk/fileadmin/res/fau/dok/fau_bilag_oevrige_bilag_090311.pdf (accessed 25 Oct. 2014).

"Drivkraft i nord: Strategi for UiT mot 2020" (2014). Available from: http://uit.no/om/art?p_document_id=355830&dim=179033 (accessed 25 Oct. 2014).

Drennan, J., Kennedy, J. and Pisarski, A. (2005), "Factors affecting student attitudes toward flexible online learning in management education". *Journal of Educational Research*, vol. 98, pp. 331–38.

Fairweather, P. G. and Gibbons, A. S. (2000), "Distributed learning: Two steps forward, one back? One forward, two back?" *IEEE Concurrency*, vol. 8, pp. 8–9.

Ferlie, E. (1996), *The new public management in action*. Oxford University Press: Oxford.

Gerhard, J. and Mayr, P. (2002), "Competing in the e-learning environment: Strategies for universities". *System Sciences, HICSS. Proceedings of the 35th Annual Hawaii International Conference*, Jan. 2002, pp. 3270–79.

Grepperud, G. (2005), *Fleksibel utdanning på* universitets- og høgskolenivå: *forventninger, praksis og utfordringer.* Universitetet i Tromsø: Tromsø, NO.

Johnston, K. M. C. (2001), "Why e-business must evolve beyond market orientation: Applying human interaction models to computer-mediated corporate communications". *Internet Research: Electronic Networking Applications and Policy,* vol. 11, pp. 213–25.

Kulik, C. L. C. and Kulik, J. A. (1991), "Effectiveness of computer-based instruction: An updated analysis". *Computers in Human Behavior,* vol. 7, pp. 75–94.

Lindblom, C. E. (1959), "The science of muddling through". *Public Administration Review,* vol. 19, pp. 79–88.

Maassen, P., Olsen, J. P., eds. (2007), *University dynamics and European integration.* Springerlink: Dordrecht, NL.

Mackler, S. (2009), *Learning for meaning's sake: Toward the hermeneutic university.* Sense Publishers: Rotterdam, NL.

Marginson, S. and Considine, M. (2000), *The enterprise university: Power, governance and reinvention in Australia.* Cambridge University Press: Cambridge.

Olsen, J. P. and Maassen, P. (2007), "European debates on the knowledge institution: The modernization of the university at the European level". In: Olsen, J. P. and Maassen, P., eds., *University dynamics and European integration.* Springer: Dordrecht, NL.

Rumble, G. (2007), "Social justice, economics and distance education". *Open Learning: The Journal of Open, Distance and e-Learning,* vol. 22, pp. 167–76.

Russell, B. (1926), *On education, especially in early childhood.* George Allen and Unwin Ltd.: London.

Salancik, G. R., Pfeffer, J. and Kelly, J. P. (1978), "Contingency model of influence in organizational decision-making". *Pacific Sociological Review,* vol. 21, pp. 239–56.

Salmon, G. (2005), "Flying not flapping: A strategic framework for e-learning and pedagogical innovation in higher education institutions". *Research in Learning Technology,* vol. 13, no. 3, pp. 201–18.

Simon, H. A. (1947), "Effects of increased productivity upon the ratio of urban to rural population". *Econometrica,* vol. 15, pp. 31–42.

Solberg, M. and Fossland, T. (2013), "Akademisk danning – Et mulig prosjekt for voksne studenter i fleksible studier?" In: Arbo, P., ed., *Utdanningssamfunnet og livslang læring: Festskrift til Gunnar Grepperud.* Gyldendal Akademisk: Oslo.

Thompson, J. D. (1967), *Approaches to organizational design.* University of Pittsburgh Press: Pittsburgh, PA.

Weick, K. E. (1976), "Educational organizations as loosely coupled systems". *Administrative Science Quarterly,* vol. 21, pp. 1–19.

Whitworth, A. (2005), "The politics of virtual learning environments: Environmental change, conflict, and e-learning". *British Journal of Educational Technology,* vol. 36, pp. 685–91.

Part II
Case studies

5 Philosophical orientations of teaching and technology

A Scandinavian case study

Heather Kanuka

Introduction

As net-based technologies have become more pervasive, expressions of uncertainty, concern and scepticism – alongside intemperate enthusiasm for new and emerging technological innovations – have also become more pervasive (see for examples past issues of *The Chronicle of Higher Education* http://chronicle.com/section/Home/5 and *Wired*). When these kinds of extreme and polarized views on teaching with technology arise, it can be useful to step back, reflect, and consider the nature of what is being said. If we reflect on our own, as well as others', opinions about technology and teaching through a reflective lens it is possible to become cognizant of the differences in opinions, which can be bridged with perspectives on tacitly held beliefs. Draper (1993) asserts that an examination of our opinion, conceptions, attitudes – or our philosophical orientations – is more than an academic exercise. Our beliefs determine how we perceive and deal with our preferred teaching methods including how (or if) we choose to use technologies.

Embedded into the fabric of our core beliefs about teaching and learning with technology are our cultural underpinnings. The ways in which we communicate and objectify our ideas and thoughts in our everyday lives, including our classroom activities, are culturally embedded. It follows that our use of net-based technologies originate from our cultural norms, values and beliefs. This case study examines how Scandinavian academics articulate their philosophical orientations on teaching and technology.

Background to the study

In previous studies (Kanuka and Kelland 2008; Kelland and Kanuka 2008; Kanuka, Smith and Kelland 2013), we brought together Canadian e-learning administrators and researchers to discuss effective uses of technologies in the higher education sector. Three conclusions emerged from this prior research: (1) perspectives of educational technology are many and varied, if not polarized; (2) policymakers and administrators concerned with implementing technologies should carefully consider each position for effective administration and policy making; and (3) it is unlikely that educational technology experts will ever reach consensus on the influence and purpose of information and communication technologies within institutions of higher education.

While most educational technologists would agree that knowing our philosophical orientations is important, can we identify our teaching and technology philosophical orientations? Is this prior research generalizable beyond the Canadian context? I sought to answer this question by exploring how educational technologists self-identify their philosophical orientations. Elias and Merriam's (1995, 2001) teaching philosophy framework and Dahlberg's (2004) technology philosophy framework were used to guide this study.

Philosophies of teaching and technology are defined in this study as a conceptual framing that embodies our values and beliefs from which we view the many aspects of education (Zinn 1990), including the field of educational technology. Such philosophies are necessary to avoid focusing on "what to do with" technologies in the classroom without examining sufficiently "why" we should do it.

Research design and methods

The method used in this study to collect data was a closed interview, using repertory grid techniques (Kelly 1995). The study was designed using the "laddering" techniques of repertory grids. Rather than "laddering up" from elements (concrete activities) to constructs (beliefs underpinning concrete activities), this study "laddered down", moving from constructs (philosophical frameworks of teaching and technology) to elements.

Participants for this study were academics whose area of research and teaching experience is in educational technology, purposefully selected from Australia, Norway, Sweden, Denmark, Canada, United States and United Kingdom (n=75; 15 participants from each country). The data presented in this chapter focuses on the Scandinavian participants (Norway, Sweden, Denmark; n=15).

The interviews opened with statements based on six of Elias and Merriam's (2001) teaching philosophical orientations, followed by names of theorists commonly associated with each orientation (Appendix A). The first part of the structured interview was designed to laconically capture the essence of each of Elias and Merriam's teaching orientations. As the participants were academics within the field of education, it was assumed that participants would be able to recognize and identify their philosophical orientations based on the statements provided and associated theorists. For those for whom this information was not sufficient, supplementary information was provided on each philosophical orientation to assist in the participant's own identification, again drawn from

Elias and Merriam's work. Participants were also asked to think about their teaching orientations within the context of a senior undergraduate course (preferred) or early graduate course (for those participants who did not teach in undergraduate programs). The rationale for this was that at this point in (most) students' programmes of study, students would or should have acquired, and are using, high levels of critical, creative and complex thinking skills. Participants were also asked if there was anything in the opening statement of their preferred orientation that they would edit, add or delete.

Once the participants selected the philosophical orientation they most closely aligned themselves with (Appendix A, Part 1), they were then provided with a second set of statements related to their preferred teaching orientation, based on Elias and Merriam's (1995, 2001) teaching philosophy framework (Appendix A, Part 2). As with the first part, participants were asked, as they reviewed the elements associated with the constructs (the teaching philosophical orientations), to edit, add or delete the statements to fit with their beliefs.

The final part of the interview focused on philosophical orientations of technologies based on Dahlberg's framework (Appendix A, Part 3). Again, the participants were provided with statements based on Dahlberg's four technological orientations, followed by associated beliefs on teaching with technology. The interviews were conducted in person, spanning in duration from approximately 30 to 90 minutes. The data were inductively analysed using constant comparison techniques (Strauss and Corbin 1998), eventually divided into units and grouped into categories for patterns to emerge.

Findings

Part 1: Responses on the aim of a university education

All participants from the Scandinavian countries selected the Progressive orientation (see Appendix A, Part 1) as being most closely aligned with their teaching philosophical orientations, though three participants also said that the Radical orientation had aspects that reflect their teaching beliefs. Within the Radical orientation, aspects related to change and society – in particular Paulo Freire's views (1973) – were noted as relevant. On this front, both the Progressive and Radical philosophical orientations perceive education and society to be interconnected. One participant also noted that it should be no surprise that Scandinavian teaching orientations fall into the Progressive orientation, stating that "this is the culture . . . the way they teach us here really goes for the group [society] in staff development programs".

Several comments were also made by participants revolving around "personal growth" as being paramount and that in a university one must also account for student development, hence, there were aspects of other orientations, such as the Behavioural and Humanistic, that cannot be discounted. In the second part of the interview, the comments relating to this were more clearly highlighted and described. The second part of the interview asked participants about the specific constructs and elements of each orientation. While all participants aligned themselves with the Progressive orientation, additional insights and qualifications to the constructs were expressed. Below is a fuller description of each of the six constructs by the participants.

Part 2: Responses to the constructs and elements

Most preferred instructional strategies

While generally participants agreed with the instructional strategies listed (experimental/inquiry-based, problem-solving and/or situational approaches to learning, which is organized to relate to experiences of the learners), most also noted that the aims and objectives need to match the instructional strategies. Hence, instructional methods can be situational. One participant, for example, noted that problem-solving strategies " . . . can be used to identify troublesome areas . . . we all need to face the problem and invest in the work . . . we all go through misunderstandings."

It was also expressed by a number of participants that knowledge creation precipitated by challenging activities should be a primary aim, resulting in students acting and then reflecting on their actions. On this point, one participant noted, "I have the students engage in the literature, but the main point is active reflection. . . . The methods need to build on the experiences of the learners to achieve knowledge construction."

The focus of the learning

At a basic level, participants agreed that the focus of the learning activities should be toward democratic cooperation, personal growth and insights, though some participants expressed certain caveats. One participant, for example, noted that "extremes are problematic . . . this statement overlooks the need to have basic knowledge as well." A number of participants also stated that the meaning of democracy is unclear, with one participant succinctly stating what others expressed: "Democratic cooperation has a collective aspect but learning involves personal growth . . . changing as a learner and growing as a person. The challenge is providing 'personal' growth versus providing for the group. Students are different, with different growth potentials but the 'collective' aspect of democracy is also important. Both are important but are not one element as is stated here." Hence, with respect to "personal growth" participants agreed that while individual growth is important, it is important that this connect to the social systems.

The role of content

Participants had difficulty agreeing, entirely, on the view that the content is secondary to the method. For example, one participant noted that "the construct of methods is difficult and has to be related to context and content. It is relational . . . one cannot make a hierarchy of the content and method." Another participant changed the word "secondary" to "parallel" and noted that theory is an important aspect and both process and product need equal focus. Another participant changed the word "secondary" to "connected" and noted that "in practice, the cognitive aspect needs to be emphasized." While another participant asserted that "in higher education, we must have core content, as it provides ways into personal growth. We use the content to teach the students that it [the process aspect] has to be challenged . . . the content is the source of reflection for students." The belief that there must be a "core content" was shared by most participants – as the relevance of higher education comes from the curriculum and/or the course content. However it was also noted that the content does not, necessarily, have to play a singular role of being practical, pragmatic and utilitarian; nor does it necessarily have to relate to the students' social context. Overall, the sentiment was that process is not enough; a product (content) is key as well.

Participants did, however, agree that cognitive, affective and skill developments should be stressed equally as they relate to a student's social context – though many participants had additional comments. For example, one participant added that "skill development is important, as is the cognitive development, but there are many ways to achieve this, with the most important being developing students who are self-directed, autonomous and critical thinkers." Although relating to the students' social context was agreed to be important, some also acknowledged, "we are not very good at it."

Role of the teacher

All participants agreed that the role of the teacher is to organize, stimulate, instigate and evaluate the highly complex processes of education – with many additional comments. One participant, for example, continued, "while being important, it can be painful, but is very important with respect to initiating a transformative experience for students." Another participant added that the teacher's role is to be "a critical friend who poses questions and challenges students' understanding; to be critical, not criticize."

As for the teacher's role as a helper/consultant, and being a learner as well as a teacher, many participants expressed disagreement, or at least discomfort in agreeing without qualifying comments. The comments were varied, with participants explaining that in a credentialed environment, although "facilitator" may be an ideal, the (1) student-teacher relationship cannot be construed as a "partnership", and (2) academics have expertise and authority in their disciplines, hence are not learners as well as teachers. As one participant noted, "these constructs raise the issue of symmetry, which is not possible in a university; role differences [between students and instructors] are clear . . . equality [between student and teacher] is not possible [in a credentialed environment]." Another participant noted that this kind of language (facilitator, partner, co-learner) allows faculty to abdicate their responsibilities.

Role of the university in relationship with society

Participants by and large agreed that the relationship between society and the university is symbiotic, though some participants noted that the word "symbiotic" might in some ways be troublesome and learning can, in fact, be separated from society. On the latter point one participant stated, "this element needs to make clear that the education system is not 'the' society." Another participant noted that this "symbiotic relationship" can be a challenge to link. This participant explained, "Many students will be joining a profession in society so it is important to understand they are part of a collective, like a football team . . . we need to solve society issues together but it can be a challenge to make these links in reality."

Many participants also mentioned that the notion of "symbiotic" is not enough. As one participant stated, "We need to question what is going on in society, with the aim of further development of society." Another participant added that "It is important to produce graduates that can frame and solve societal problems." Another aspect offered on the word "symbiotic" is that "this must have boundaries and cannot be driven by political agendas . . . it is important that academia is autonomous [from the politics of society] but it is also important [that education] gives back to society; [this relationship] is easy to be misused."

Beliefs about learning

Participants generally agreed that learning is something that students do for themselves, and involves experience that is reflected and acted upon. The result is knowledge that is inseparable from the ever-changing experiences. Participants agreed that this is important as it connects to the construct of self-directed learning, though it was also noted by a few participants that not all students are strong enough to direct their own learning. One participant provided Vygotsky's zone of proximal development as an example of the need for teachers to challenge and stretch students to a new, higher level but students must be at a state of readiness.

Some participants also expressed the key importance of the need to connect theory to practice, as well as experience and reflection. Though, as one participant noted, "these are relevant to Nordic culture as we are shaped by how we are taught . . . there is still a foothold of traditionalism with respect to learning . . . like *folkehøgskole* [folk high schools] and Bildung." Another participant noted that "this is only part of it; knowledge construction and applying to it to new contexts is also important."

It should also be noted that, while not disagreeing that students should act as a consequence of their learning, some participants said that not all knowledge results in action. As one participant stated, "higher education, ultimately, rests on abstractions."

Beliefs about education

On this construct, most participants had a lot to say. The key words participants used were "democracy", "social reconstruction" and "a better society". One participant stated, "These are the key issues since World War II. I am comfortable trying to combine these three and this should be the ideal. There is a German word that we use to say this, and does not have an English translation – it is Bildung." Another participant added, in respect to social reconstruction, it is important that students "be so informed that they can act upon it." Another participant stated that "social reconstruction is a trap . . . we can't define it but it can be normative . . . so it depends."

On the element of democracy, it was expressed by all participants that the word "democracy" can be problematic. One participant noted, " . . . it is so imperfect in reality, at times problematic and often depends on the situation." This same participant added that a more accurate description is that "we need to educate our students for the formation of knowledge." With respect to democracy, another participant stated that "[democracy] is not a problem, but what are we talking about? Denmark is a democracy – education is free so it is different . . . so not a main issue." This same participant also stated that with respect to the element on "what society requires" – this too is not a main issue. The main issue is that students have a meaningful life and acquire socially responsible ways of thinking. Another participant explained that there are two levels to consider in this construct: "The first level is personal growth. We achieve this through giving our students challenges, taking a critical stance and reflecting. The second level is social democracy. This level is concerned with being literate. What does this mean? The best way I know how to say this is by using the word Bildung. I interpret this as twenty-first century skills and competencies. This also includes digital literacy."

On the element of promoting a better society, participants agreed this was important. Perhaps this comment from one participant captured the sentiment: "Yes, whatever we think this [better society] is."

Summary of orientations of teaching

The data from the Scandinavian participants on teaching philosophical orientations align closely with the double-tracked definition of Academic

Bildung described in this book. In particular, there is remarkable consistency by participants regarding knowledge creation through challenging activities followed by reflection, and in a manner that follows the constructs of authenticity and autonomy described by Solberg and Hansen in Chapter 3. Another noteworthy thread running consistently through the Academic Bildung constructs by the Scandinavian participants is the notion of democratic cooperation as a collective, but also a focus on the individual with respect to personal growth – with personal growth viewed as connecting to the social systems. The primary aim expressed by participants was through the students' learning, with the aim of achieving a meaningful life and acquiring socially responsible ways of thinking. Although participants from other countries were also inclined to select the progressive orientation, none of the countries were as consistent in their orientation as the participants from Scandinavia.

Part 3: Responses to orientations to technology

The third part of the interview asked participants about the constructs and elements of each technological orientation. The Dahlberg (2004) framework has a different structure from the Elias and Merriam framework (2001), as reflected by the structured interview. In particular, the opening constructs and elements are integrated, with two question-sets. Both are described further below.

The majority of participants described net-based technologies as a necessity to meet the teaching needs of teachers and learning needs of students; though, many also noted that understanding technology as a tool is also important. As one participant queried, "How can you enhance learning by using technology? [This can be achieved] both as a tool and as a media." Similarly, another participant asserted that "we need to look at how our society reflects us. Our teaching needs to reflect this and we need to be careful. For example, tech-freaks really need to think about what works in that context . . . a little bit of everything is the answer. . . . We need to be focused on the objectives – they need to be tenderly attended to, as well as more historically oriented. . . . It is so complex."

The importance of using net-based technologies to meet the needs of teachers and students was explained further by participants as an explicit need to look at students carefully and determine their requirements. It was also noted by some participants that certain technologies meet the students' needs better than others, for example, wikis as a collaborative product (versus LMS, learning management systems, where students come with input). One participant commented further that a wiki "fits better with my philosophy. . . . Students can reflect on how we arrived here, making it a second order reflection."

Many participants also shared that technology has not been without its challenges. One participant stated, "In Norway, at the end of the '90s, there were two phrases: (1) use ICT in learning and (2) you should learn to use the tools . . . but combining these, well this is difficult. . . . There is very little room for teaching how to use ICT for learning. You can't ask [teachers] to come up with ICT tools that they can't apply. It has been a very slow process and difficult to initiate."

The majority of participants saw net-based artefactsas a mutual shaping process between the context, the technology and its users. One participant's belief captures what most participants expressed: "There is no one way of dealing with technology, or researching technology. We need to reflect on the different technologies. Technology is a resource that gives affordances but it depends on how technology is framed. Technology also has structures. For example, LMS created tensions. . . . Affordances in some ways . . . forces us into working in certain ways, such as organizing course materials and assignments. But LMS is bad for reflecting together. . . . Technologies are not static; humans develop them further. So there is an interconnection between technologies and humans. As humans we have an urge to explore, create tools and see the world in different ways." Capping this insight, another participant commented, "The hallmark of higher education is to take and hold another point of view; this is what a progressive and a liberal education is all about" and concluded by restating the opening question: "When teaching with technology, technological tools should be viewed as aligning with the aims, asking ourselves what should a higher education provide?"

There was also fairly good consensus that net-based tools are not neutral artefacts. On this orientation, one participant noted that "this is the most interesting but we are not in tune enough to know, so it is difficult. There is a word for this [neutral artefacts], 'domestication'; to be neutral, technology would need to be a part of regular life." Another participant stated, "We should not let technology take command . . . social structures develop over time. When technologies are institutionalized then they become something else . . . when institutionalized, it [technologies] becomes difficult as a teacher." Many participants were clear in explaining that there is no such thing as a "neutral" artefact.

Summary of orientations of technology

On the aspect of philosophical orientations of technology, there was also good consistency in responses from the Scandinavian participants, though not as consistent as the philosophical orientations of teaching. Participants were clear in articulating the necessity for net-based technologies to meet the stated and/or desired teaching and learning outcomes, and the view that technologies are non-neutral, though most participants acknowledged that there is a recursive effect between net-based tools and their uses. All participants were of the opinion that when teaching with technology, the uses of technologythat we choose must align with the aims of a higher education, described in the teaching orientations as the core tenets of Academic Bildung.

Discussion and conclusions

The findings of this case study reveal that the Scandinavian philosophical orientation of teaching is remarkably consistent, with all participants identifying with the progressive philosophical orientation (Elias and Merriam 2001) and most (76 per cent) participants falling in the "uses determinism" technological orientation (see Appendix B for definition).

Perhaps as important, the data reveal that Scandinavian academics who participated in this study hold a decidedly distinct view of how knowledge is constructed, which is that it is tightly connected to society. Specifically, the data reveals that Scandinavian academics have a proclivity to approach learning activities with a belief that knowledge is a social process (e.g., through conversations and didactics) together with a primary aim of supporting their students' personal growth with a critical stance. Consistent with these beliefs, orientations and uses of teaching with technologies is supported in their teaching orientations. As the data illustrate, participants believe that net-based technologies should be used to meet the needs of teachers (the content and curriculum)and learning needs of students (personal growth) – but also includes an important connection to the broader societal needs.

It is rather striking that all the Scandinavian participants were consistent in their teaching philosophy, selecting the progressive orientation accompanied by comments revolving around their students' personal growth, and the connection to social systems. Alongside a common view that knowledge is constructed as a social process (aimed to support personal growth with a critical stance), this study indicates that the Scandinavian academics have a solid consistency with the most central assumptions underlying this anthology and the core concepts of Academic Bildung. In particular, the data reveal a specific and shared view on the orientation of higher education in Scandinavia. This view involves a close connection between the individual, society and growth – or what is referred to by Scandinavians as life enlightenment and critical thinking. As importantly, these data are consistent with the double-tracked Bildung concept and pedagogy described in Chapter 3. Double-tracked Bildung has a dimension of critical, emancipatory and society-oriented reflection, as well as a dimension of ethical-existential and being-oriented reflection.

Also revealed by the data in this study with respect to net-based technologies is a recognition that within the learning process technologies have recursive effects that occur between the users, the technology and the context. The majority of Scandinavian participants (9/15) stated that the aim of teaching with technology should be to meet the teaching and learning needs of teachers and students (versus, for example, the US where 3/10 stated this as an aim) and that such uses include the ability of individuals to manipulate technological tools for educational purposes to meet needs with respect to motives, interests, and/or attitudes. However, the Scandinavian participants also acknowledged a recursive effect of the media they use. In particular, all Scandinavian participants also acknowledged there is a mutual shaping process between the context, the technology and its users.

Returning to the question guiding this book, "How can we educate students through net-based education and at the same time facilitate Academic Bildung?" the data from this study reveal that academics whose area of expertise is teaching with technology believe that net-based technologies should be used in alignment with the aims of the progressive philosophical orientation. Participants in this study agreed that the aim of higher education is the promotion of personal growth and maintenance, as well as a better society. In a more specific sense, the data confirm this aim is seen through the constructs of the double-track Academic Bildung (autonomy and authenticity) and achieved through the provision of experiences of meaningfulness and personal growth.

It may also be of interest to readers to know the similarities and differences between other jurisdictions participating in this study. As the themes and topics emerged throughout the data analysis, it became apparent there are certain areas where similarities and differences can be demarcated. Specifically, there are distinct views regarding (1) the learning process versus content, and (2) whether students construct their knowledge socially or individually. On these views, the Scandinavian participants were inclined to state that they believe the learning process is negotiated through conversation/didactics and this, in turn, results in the construction of a real and shared reality – or more precisely, an "authentic" shared reality. Participants in the UK and US are aligned in their beliefs with Scandinavians in that there is an inclination to also emphasize knowledge as an external and shared reality. Unlike the Scandinavian participants, however, teachers in the US and UK believe that knowledge is constructed through internal conflicts within each learner, with knowledge construction being an individual process, rather than socially shared. Alternatively, the antithesis of Scandinavian beliefs on knowledge construction occurs with academics from Australia, who tend to view knowledge as being constructed individually based on a person's unique experiences, with no one objective reality. Canada is similar to the Scandinavian countries with respect to the belief that learning has social/society/group aspects of knowledge construction but depart with respect to the belief that there are multiple realities, rather than one shared reality.

With respect to philosophical orientations on teaching with net-based tools, (as mentioned prior) the US participants have decidedly distinct views. With few exceptions, all participants from Scandinavia, Canada, Australia and the UK believe that "uses determinism" is a close representation of their beliefs (respectively: 9/15, 9/15, 9/15, 8/15) acknowledging that we are in many ways also shaped by tools. Alternatively, most US participants (10/15) identify themselves with the technical determinism orientation.

Précis

This study was initiated based my own experiences conducting research on net-based technologies within the higher education sector in the Canadian context. Much of the research that has been, and continues to be, conducted within the field of educational technology (including my own) has begun at the basic level of assumptions by both participants and researchers with undeclared understandings that the phenomenon of technology enters into an inquiry of the praxis of technology. Initiating research without examining and articulating our philosophical orientations on both teaching and technology bypasses the need to understand our own, as well as others', philosophical orientations. Prior research on teacher beliefs suggests that teaching beliefs strongly influence practices (see for examples, Albion 1999; Albion and Ertmer 2002; Scrimshaw 2004); further literature concludes that teacher beliefs act as filters that guide educational practitioners in both their instruction and curricular decision-making processes (Pajares 1992; Prawat 1992). While acknowledging that much of the past research may only be telling us half the story (e.g., Kane, Sandretto and Heath 2002), more than two decades of research continue to indicate that teaching beliefs have an impact on practice. At a minimum, the past research provides us with insights into the reasons educators act the way they do (Levin and Wadmany 2006).

Irrespective as to whether one views technology as constructive or destructive, as described in the introduction (e.g., *The Chronicle of Higher Education*), the results of this study reveal that it is accepted by Scandinavian academics whose areas of research are teaching with technology that uses of net-based tools in higher education are a non-neutral medium, whereby transformations arise within the teaching and learning experiences. The data from this case study also documents and contributes to the existing understandings of transformations, as well as forms a critical foundation with respect to what Scandinavian academics believe about the technology-teaching-learning relationship.

Bibliography

Albion, P. R. (1999), "Self-efficacy beliefs as an indicator of teachers' preparedness for teaching with technology". In: Price, J. D., Willis, J., Willis D. A., Jost, M. and Boger-Mehall, S., eds., *Technology and teacher education annual 1999*, pp. 1602–08. Association for the Advancement of Computing in Education: Charlottesville, VA.

Albion, P. R. and Ertmer, P. A. (2002), "Beyond foundations: The role of vision and belief in teachers' preparation for integration of technology", *Tech Trends*, vol. 46, no. 25, pp. 34–38.

Dahlberg, L. (2004), "Internet research tracings: Towards non-reductionist methodology", *Journal of Computer Mediated Communication,* vol. 9, no. 3. Available at http://jcmc.indiana.edu/vol9/issue3/dahlberg.html

Draper, J. A. (1993), "Valuing what we do as practitioners". In: Barer-Stein, T. and Draper, J. A., eds., *The craft of teaching adults,* pp. 55–67. Culture Concepts: Toronto, ON.

Elias, J. L. and Merriam, S. (1980), *Philosophical foundations of adult education.* Robert E. Krieger: Malabar, FL.

Elias, J. L. and Merriam, S. (1995), *Philosophical foundations of adult education,* 2nd edn. Robert E. Krieger: Malabar, FL.

Elias, J. L. and Merriam, S. (2005), *Philosophical foundations of adult education,* 3rd edn. Robert E. Krieger: Malabar, FL.

Freire, P. (1973), *Education for critical consciousness.* Seabury: New York.

Kane, R., Sandretto, S. and Heath, C. (2002), "Telling half the story: A critical review of research on the teaching beliefs and practices of university academics", *Review of Educational Research,* vol. 72, no. 2, pp. 177–228.

Kanuka, H., Smith, E. and Kelland, J. (2013), "An inquiry into educational technologists' conceptions of their philosophies of teaching and technology", *Canadian Journal of Learning and Technology,* vol. 39, no. 2. Available online at http://www.cjlt.ca/index.php/cjlt/article/view/722/366

Kelly, G. A. (1955), *The psychology of personal constructs, vol. 1: A theory of personality.* W. W. Norton: New York.

Levin, T. and Wadmany, R. 2006, "Teachers' beliefs and practices in technology-based classrooms: A developmental view", *Journal of Research on Technology in Education,* vol. 39, no. 2, 157–81.

Pajares, M. (1992), "Teachers' beliefs and educational research: Cleaning up a messy construct", *Review of Educational Research,* vol. 62, no. 3, pp. 307–32.

Prawat, R. S. (1992), "Teachers' beliefs about teaching and learning: A constructivist perspective", *American Journal of Education,* vol. 100, no. 3, pp. 354–94.

Zinn, L. M. (1990), "Identifying your philosophical orientation". In: Galbraith, M., ed., *Adult learning methods,* pp. 39–77. Robert E. Krieger: Malabar FL.

Appendix A

Part 1: Opening Statements: Philosophical Orientations

(from Elias and Merriam 2001)

Before responding, think of a senior undergraduate course you currently, or in the past, have taught (please write this down).

I believe the aim of a university education is (choose the one that resonates closest with your teaching beliefs) . . .

1   **To bring about change in the political, economic and social order in society**
    People: George Counts, Theodore Brameld, Jonathan Kozol, John Holt, Paul Goodman, Ivan Illich, Paulo Freire and Jack Mezirow. [Radical orientation]

2   **To search for truth and intellectual development**
    People: Greek philosophers (Socrates, Plato, Aristotle), Mortimer Adler, Robert Hutchins, Jacques Maritain, and Mark Van Doren. [Liberal orientation]

3   **To promote personal growth and maintenance, as well as a better society**
    People: John Dewey, William Kilpatrick, Knowles, Rogers, James, Houle, Tyler, Lindeman, Bergevin, and Freire. [Progressive orientation]

4   **To develop rational thinking through the transmission of the truth (which is also morally, socially and politically neutral)**
    People: Israel Scheffler, R. S. Peters, Thomas Green, Lawson, and Patterson. [Analytical orientation]

5   **To foster individual growth or self-actualization**
    People: Heidegger, Sartre, Camus, Marcel, Buber, Maslow, Rogers, May, Allport, Fromm, and Knowles. [Humanist orientation]

6   **To bring about observable changes in behaviour**
    People: Thorndike, Pavlov, Watson, Skinner, and Ralph Tyler. [Behaviourist orientation]

Part 2: Progressive Philosophical Orientation

My most preferred instructional STRATEGY is (are) . . .	–	Experimental/inquiry-based, problem-solving and/or situation approaches to learning – which is organized to relate to experiences of the learners
I believe the FOCUS of the learning is . . .	–	Toward democratic cooperation, personal growth and insights

I believe the CONTENT is . . .	– Is secondary to the method (emphasis is on process, not product) but includes the practical, pragmatic and utilitarian
	– To facilitate cognitive, affective, and skill development – which are stressed equally as they relate to student's social context
	– To enhance social order
I believe the ROLE of TEACHER is . . .	– To organize, stimulate, instigate, and evaluate the highly complex processes of education
	– Helper, consultant, and/or encourager
	– To provide a setting that is conductive to learning; in doing so, the teacher also becomes a learner
	– A relationship with the student, best characterized as a partnership
I believe the role of the university in RELATION-SHIP with SOCIETY is . . .	– Symbiotic – the individual learner and society cannot be separated; the learner's interests, needs, problems, and ambitions are products of society and the environment
I believe LEARNING . . .	– Is something that students do for themselves
	– Involves experience, which is both reflected and acted upon by the learner. The result is knowledge which is inseparable from the ever changing experiences
	– Is not enough; sooner or later one must act as a consequence of their learning
I believe EDUCATION should be . . .	– The enactment of democracy – the highest ideal is education for democracy
	– To maintain the standards of competence, knowledge, wisdom, and skill which society requires
	– For social reform and social reconstruction
	– Aimed at improving the individual's life in society and, as such, improving individuals through education leads to a better society
	– Concerned with personal growth and maintenance
	– Promoting a better society

Part 3. Technology Beliefs (choose the one that resonates closest with your teaching beliefs)

1   **I believe the aim of teaching with technology should be . . .**   _____   **to meet the teaching and learning needs of teachers and students.** Such uses would include the ability of individuals to use/manipulate technological tools to meet needs with respect to motives, interests, and/or attitudes of those who use it for educational purposes.

_____   **to use technologies as a tool for learning.**
Technological tools can produce new contexts in
the learning process and/or within educational
systems, such learning contexts will include using
technology as mind tools for critical thinking.

_____   **to expose how the Internet is socially, culturally,
politically, and/or economically embedded within
educational systems.** Such uses would be to build on
the notion of students already being "digital native"
and/or "Net-geners" and adjust the curriculum to
reflect how students communicate.

_____   **to gain a better understanding of the role and
recursive effects that occur between the users,
the technology and our environment** (e.g., social,
political, economic, cultural).

2   When teaching   _____   creating **neutral artefacts**, with the capacity to satisfy
with technology,   the purposes/needs of educators using it.
technological   _____   creating **technological artefacts** that inscribes
tools should be   meaning, which shape the way teachers and
viewed as   learners think and this impacts the choices they
make.

_____   creating **social (political, economic, cultural)
artefacts**, which shape the form and content of its
use within educational systems.

_____   creating a **mutual shaping process between the
context, the technology, and its users**

Appendix B

Dahlberg's philosophical orientations of technologies

Uses determinism

This position emphasizes technological uses and focuses on the ways in
which we use technologies within learning and teaching transactions. In
this approach, technologies are perceived as neutral tools and are simply
devices that extend our capacities. As users, we determine the effects of
technological artefacts. Scholars commonly associated with this orientation
have included Fiske (1987), Harrison and Stephen (1999), Katz and Rice
(2002), Sudweeks, McLaughlin and Rafaeli (1998), Garramone, Harris and
Anderson (1986), Ebersole (2000), and Welchman (1997).

Social determinism

In this perspective, educators are concerned with the integration of technological artefacts within social systems and cultural contexts. This perspective
emphasizes the way our uses of technology are affected by social structures

and the social construction of technological artefacts. Educators holding this view are concerned about the way social and technological uses shape the form and content of the learning experiences. Scholars commonly associated with this orientation have included Golding and Murdock (1997), Mosco (1996), Garnham (1990), Woolgar (1991a, 1991b, 1996, 2002), Schiller (1995), and Harris and Davidson (1994).

Tools determinism

Within this orientation, technology is viewed as a causal agent, determining our uses and having a pivotal role in social change. Scholars most commonly associated with this orientation have included Dubrovsky, Kiesler and Sethna (1991), Sproull and Kiesler (1986), Argyle (1996), Spears and Lea (1994), Marcuse (1941), Habermas (1970), Bell (1973), Lyotard (1984), Baudrillard (1983), Castells (1999), Gates (1995), Pool (1983), Toffler and Toffler (1994), Ellu (1964), Heidegger (1977), Postman (1993), and Marx (1997).

6 Educating pharmacists

The perfect prescription?

Claire Englund and Maria Wester

Introduction

In this chapter the question of professional identity is interwoven with the question of Academic Bildung and the theme of this book: How can we educate students through net-based education and still facilitate Academic Bildung? Using a net-based bachelor of science in pharmacy programme (BSc Pharm) as an example we will examine if and how the development of Academic Bildung and professional identity can be facilitated by the pedagogical design of the programme.

As we have seen in chapter three, Academic Bildung is a concept describing a developmental process towards enculturation and the formation of identity. Further, the concept of Academic Bildung has two dimensions: one associated with critical thinking, society-oriented reflection and autonomy, and a parallel dimension associated with the ethical dimensions of human development, existential- and being- related reflection and authenticity. Correspondingly, professional identity is not only constituted in the practical skills and knowledge associated with a particular professional practice and its culture but also in the individual's sense and understanding of the "being-dimension": "What do I really think and feel about my profession as a pharmacist?" "What is the deeper meaning of this profession for me, for the community?"

The theoretical framework of situated learning, which we understand as the social engagement that provides an environment for learning in specific forms of social co-participation (Lave and Wenger 1991) is used in this case study to examine the main theme of the book, where the environment or situation is a net-based educational programme for pharmacy education. Neither Academic Bildung nor professional identity are concepts that can be assessed and identified in an easy and obvious way, being constituted in the interplay between the individual and the world. However, we would suggest that it is possible to examine the conditions of their formation by exploring how the pedagogical design of the learning environment can provide the prerequisites necessary to facilitate the development of both aspects of Academic Bildung and professional identity.

The use of a three-dimensional virtual learning environment to support communicative and experiential learning activities is therefore described in addition to the overall design of the BSc Pharm programme.

Professional identity and Academic Bildung

In traditional pharmacy education, the acquisition of professional identity is mainly concerned with the ability of the students to think and reflect on the practices, knowledge and skills of being a pharmacist (Taylor and Harding 2007; Taylor et al 2004). This dimension can be interpreted as the autonomous dimension of Academic Bildung, involving critical and analytical thinking, society-oriented reflection and that in higher education also includes the graduate attributes or generic skills expected of a university student. In the sense of Academic Bildung, a well-educated, vocationally trained academic can also be linked to Hanna Arendt's notion of authenticity, albeit in a more prosaic sense; it might not perhaps be described as "being one's true self" but is concretised such that the education provides a professional identity (Arendt 1958). This can be interpreted as the sense of *being* a pharmacist, compared to just *working* as a pharmacist. For Arendt, being is concerned with the "who" of the individual, as opposed simply to the "what". In *The Human Condition* Arendt explores the notion of the *vita active* and the various components, such as labour, work and action, which comprise "being-in-the world". Authentic learning is a process of deepening our understanding of ourselves and occurs in and through action. It is through action in word, deed and thought that we establish and re-establish our connection to the world and others and form our identity. The space of learning is always essentially communal, for we are dependent on others for crucial insight into our being. "It is more than likely that the 'who,' which appears so clearly and unmistakeably to others, remains hidden from the person himself'" (ibid., p. 179).

With reference to Barnett's (2004) thoughts on personal knowledge, we can thus conclude that it is not sufficient to know chemistry, biology, pharmacology etc., the student needs to *be* a pharmacist (Barnett 2004; Siemens 2004). In his book *A will to learn: Being a student in an age of uncertainty* (2007) Barnett points out that this also means a shift in pedagogy; the teacher must also change: "Learning for an unknown future calls, in short, for an ontological turn. . . . A pedagogy of this kind will be a pedagogy that engages students as persons, not merely as knowers." (p. 247) and further, " . . . instead of knowing the world, being-in-the-world has to take primary place in the conceptualization that informs university teaching" (p. 795).

Accordingly, the teacher also has an important role to play in the students' process of identity formation. According to Barnett (2007) one of the most important tasks of the teacher is to create, and themselves be an example of, a learning space and way of being that inspires the student to "stand in the open" and thrive in the encounter with the familiar and the unknown. The teacher must not only design the learning environment, making the facilitation of Academic Bildung and professional development possible, but also participate in the learning process together with the students. Also for Arendt, educators are never only *teachers*, but are also first and foremost *learners*.

Situated learning

For Lave and Wenger (1991) learning is also concerned with identity and becoming a part of a community: "learning as increasing participation in communities of practice concerns the whole person acting in the world." (p. 49). The model of situated learning suggested by Lave and Wenger proposes that learning involves a process of engagement in a "community of practice". Learning is not seen as the acquisition of knowledge by individuals so much as a process of social participation where the nature of the situation impacts significantly on the process and where the professional person is invited into and grows into the professional culture, including aspects such as language, actions and attitudes. Also for Arendt, education prepares students for the transition from the private realm to the public; they move from legitimate peripheral participation to "full participation in a community of practice" (Lave and Wenger 1991, p. 37).

Experiential learning: Virtual worlds in education

Learning environments for professional education must support the achievement of both generic skills, such as communication, IT-literacy, collaboration, critical thinking and problem solving, and also more discipline-specific skills. Increasingly, generic and discipline specific skills are being developed using experiential learning approaches. These can be digital simulations of challenging workplace situations or actual workplace learning placements in the field. Experiential learning can be seen as an integrative strategy drawing on attributes of student-centred approaches, emphasising the dynamic interaction between experience, theory and practice (Kolb 1984; Lave and Wenger 1991).

To create the opportunity for practical, hands-on professional experience, a three-dimensional (3D) virtual immersive environment was developed on the Bsc Pharm to provide a platform for authentic (used here in the sense of true-to-life), communicative learning activities on the programme. The unique immersive 3D features of virtual worlds such as Second Life (SL) or OpenSim (OS) provide online learning opportunities that are both immersive and collaborative at a time and place convenient to the learner. A virtual world such as OpenSim has the potential to create engaging and realistic learning experiences that support many aspects of situated learning. It is possible to act in a real context with authentic tasks (Dickey 2005; Lombardi 2007) and take advantage of phenomena from different perspectives through role playing and simulations (Antonacci and Modaress 2005; Warburton 2009). Virtual worlds can thus offer a wide variety of opportunities for learning but also require new approaches to teaching in terms of the creation of learning activities, involving the adoption of new roles for teachers grounded in a sociocultural pedagogical philosophy of teaching and learning.

There has been some disagreement as to whether computer-based simulations are able to facilitate experiential learning (Tripp 1993) and it has been contended that "true expertise is learned by being exposed to experts" (Hummel 1993, p. 75). Nonetheless, current research findings suggest that in the immersive nature of virtual worlds, crossing physical, social and cultural dimensions can provide a compelling educational experience and a powerful and acceptable vehicle for the critical characteristics of traditional apprenticeships. As McLellan (1994) emphasised, while knowledge must be learned in context according to the situated learning model, the context can be the actual work setting or a highly realistic or "virtual" surrogate of the work setting.

Communication

Academic Bildung is a reflective, creative form of self-realisation or self-cultivation that is achieved with and through relations and communication with others. Communication between students and students, and students and teachers, within the BSc Pharm programme needs to facilitate both the cultivation of a community of practice and the development of the students' own voices if their Academic Bildung and professional identity are to be developed. Opportunities to discuss and reflect on questions concerning being a pharmacist and to develop a deeper understanding of their role should be provided for students. We use language and speaking here in a broad sense: as an action *in* the world, not just talking *about* it (Lave and Wenger 1991). This means that all uses of language – talking, writing, chatting, mailing and so on, provide active possibilities to improve, or at least facilitate, learning and can thus be seen as stepping stones towards being educated as a pharmacist and thus *becoming* a pharmacist.

Pharmacists frequently need to provide detailed information for patients, health care workers and customers with regard to the administration of medication and possible side-effects. Increasingly, they are also required to provide consultation and advice concerning non-prescription medication for pharmacy customers. Thus for pharmacy students the development of good communication skills with customers and colleagues is an important part of their future profession and high-quality training for students is a necessary constituent of the programme. Hands-on training experiences are necessary to move learners to deeper levels of learning by affording them practice in the application of the basic skills and knowledge necessary for the provision of patient/customer care. This deeper kind of learning includes the generic skills of critical thinking, analysis and reflection, competences that provide the ability to act as a professional (Lave and Wenger 1991). As Lave and Wenger emphasize, there is a relational interdependence of agent, world, activity, meaning, learning and knowing. Hands-on experience is based on that interdependence, and these processes of learning can thus be of benefit in the process of becoming professional.

Net-based education

An increasing number of students in Sweden study vocational programmes by means of net-based courses and programmes. Despite the many advantages offered by net-based education there are certain aspects, such as the development of communicative skills, the ability to work collaboratively with peers, team training and relational skills that are challenging for distance learners. Finding ways to solve these difficulties requires alternative ways of thinking with regard to course design and the pedagogical use of digital technology. In addition, campus-based courses also increasingly employ digital technologies to enhance their delivery, and the distinction between campus, blended and net-based courses is becoming more and more indistinct (Hunt, Huijser and Sankey 2012). Consequently, there is a need to reflect on the inclusion of an Academic Bildung aspect in all courses, not simply net-based education.

With regard to pharmaceutical education, Chung (2003) has argued that while net-based education has a lot to offer students in the form of increased flexibility, some educational and social experiences may be lost: "Daily interaction with pharmacy faculty and peers may assist in developing values and skills for socializing students into the profession" (p. 944). However Cain argues that "Web 2.0 applications create a participatory architecture for supporting communities of learners" (Cain et al. 2009, p. 10). Net-based students will always miss some aspects of the process of socialisation into the academic community such as discussions over coffee and informal conversations with fellow students and lecturers that give information central to an understanding of the academic community. There are, however, also indications that this is somewhat offset by the fact that communication between student and teacher can be more personal in an online context and that the power structures that exist on campus are less strict in a net-based environment (Bordia 1997; Jaldemark 2005; C. Taylor and Robinson 2009). For net-based programmes the social aspects of learning are harder to achieve, but as we will demonstrate, absolutely not impossible.

Although there are studies taking into consideration more practical aspects of net-based professional learning (Segrave and Holt 2003), the facilitation of existential aspects is not commonly considered in course design studies, with the exception of educational programmes within the field of theology. Diane Hockridge (2013) describes the challenges of designing net-based courses to prepare students for relational professions requiring communicative "people skills" and a certain maturity of character. She describes research into the concerns of educators in theology with regard to the ability of net-based education to facilitate "formation" or character development, which is comparable to Academic Bildung in the present context. Hockridge suggests that

> . . . it is overly simplistic to conclude that formational learning cannot occur in distance and online modes. Formational learning is complex and not easy to achieve regardless of the mode of study. . . . [A] more productive way forward . . . is to be more intentional about the ways in which formation is addressed whether on campus, distance or online.
>
> (p. 158)

Case study: The bachelor of science in pharmacy programme

In 2003 the University of Umeå, Sweden, started a net-based bachelor of science in pharmacy programme (BSc Pharm). The programme was developed in response to the need for qualified pharmacists in rural, sparsely populated areas and to increase equity of access to higher education; the use of net-based education makes it possible for citizens living in remote areas to gain access to higher education without having to disrupt their lives by moving to a university campus, thus losing contact with their future professional environment. When taking part in net-based education, students also develop competency in areas such as computer literacy, information retrieval and the critical analysis of resources. Skills such as proficiency in accessing information online, the use of electronic prescriptions and ability to communicate via internet with customers living far from the nearest pharmacy are also becoming increasingly important in the working life of the pharmacist.

The BSc Pharm programme is almost entirely net-based; however students meet a few times per semester on campus for laboratory work and assignment presentations etc. Students choose to participate in local study groups based at learning centres or enrol as individual distance students not linked to any particular locality. Digital course materials including assignments and lectures are delivered using a learning management system (LMS),[1] and tutorials and seminars are distributed via internet. All study groups, including students studying independently, are assigned an experienced pharmacist as tutor who is able to provide a pharmaceutical, work-related thread throughout the programme and to link the theoretical content of the individual courses to their practical application in the field of pharmacy. Unlike faculty responsible for individual courses, the local tutors follow the students throughout the whole programme and are able to provide continuity and a degree of social support for the students.

Teacher-student communication and student-student communication is facilitated by means of digital technologies (the LMS, Adobe

Connect,[2] discussion forums, e-mail and a virtual immersive 3D environment: OpenSim[3]) combined with personal or net-based meetings with local tutors and lecturers at the university. Students participating in study groups gather on average once per week together with their tutor for group discussions or question sessions either at a local study centre or online. These meetings provide an opportunity for the enculturation and informal discourse necessary for the students to develop their professional identity and personal autonomy. Students also have the opportunity to contact teaching faculty by e-mail or via the LMS, and the majority of teachers arrange regular online meetings with students to discuss any questions or problems arising in the course.

It is of prime importance for students on the BSc Pharm to develop knowledge and experience of their future profession as pharmacists. Therefore, with the purpose of facilitating this process the programme organises an introductory week at the beginning of the programme for students, where visits to a variety of pharmacies, pharmaceutical companies and other stakeholders in the field of pharmacy are included. The programme also includes ten weeks practical experience at a pharmacy, with the assistance of an experienced pharmacist or dispensing chemist as supervisor, which further facilitates the development of professional identity.

Creating an authentic, virtual learning activity

As previously discussed, virtual worlds can offer a wide variety of opportunities for experiential learning in authentic environments that can enculturate students into authentic practices. Consequently, teaching staff from the BSc Pharm programme, pedagogical developers and educational technologists worked collaboratively to design a virtual environment and educational activities that would enable learners to achieve the learning objectives of the course (Biggs and Tang 2009). After having determined the properties of the virtual environment necessary to implement the learning activities, the educational technologist created a virtual pharmacy in OpenSim, which as far as possible replicated the working environment of a real-world pharmacy. The building process began by taking photographs and documenting the real-life environment and appearance of a local pharmacy. The challenge for the team was not to create an exact replica in OpenSim, but to create a sense of realism sufficient to induce a feeling of "presence" for the students when acting in the virtual world. This was achieved by identifying the elements of the environment necessary for realism without the need to include exact details.

The role-play activity developed to test and evaluate the use of virtual environments in the programme took place during the course *Pharmacotherapy in the Elderly, 7.5 ECTS*. This is an elective course undertaken during the third and final year of the BSc Pharm. The activity focuses on several of the learning objectives of the course concerned with the pharmacist's ability to communicate with both specialists and nonspecialists in the field of pharmacotherapy and the elderly.

The student, adopting the role of pharmacist, was instructed to provide advice and information to a concerned relative of an Alzheimer patient. This activity had previously been carried out as a written assignment and the use of the virtual world was intended to improve the learning task and provide a more challenging and authentic learning activity. The in-world activity was recorded and direct feedback provided to the learner individually by the teacher. A debriefing session was also held online with the student group to discuss the implementation of the activity and content of the assignment.

Data collection

Both qualitative and quantitative data were collected during the development and implementation of the virtual pharmacy activity. This consisted of the following:

- Semi-structured interviews with teaching staff involved in the course both during the development process and after implementation of the activity. These interviews were recorded, transcribed verbatim and the content analysed thematically.
- Informal observation of students and teachers was carried out during the face-to-face introduction.
- The virtual learning activity carried out by the students was recorded and assessed by the course tutor to determine if the students had achieved the required learning objectives of the activity.
- Online questionnaires were delivered to students immediately after completion of the activity.

In addition, semi-structured focus group interviews on the programme were carried out with first-, second- and third-year students over a period of three years. Students were chosen at random and at least two groups of around eight students were invited to participate from each cohort. The students were asked to respond to questions concerning the delivery of the programme. The questions varied to cover topics that were of particular interest for the programme management and also topics that were of repeated interest such as quality, continuity, communication and the development of the students' professional identity. The interviews were transcribed and analysed thematically.

Results

In total fifty students have now carried out activities in the virtual pharmacy, over a period of three years (the course runs once per year). Answers provided in the online questionnaire indicate that students are very satisfied with the experience of carrying out the activity in a virtual world and had no difficulty adopting the role of a pharmacist. There were some difference in the students' attitude to the authenticity of the virtual pharmacy: although the majority perceived the environment to be sufficiently realistic, those students who had previously worked in a real-life pharmacy commented that certain details in the virtual environment needed to be improved in order to increase authenticity.

Other comments by students were that the role play felt more meaningful when the identity of the other party was unknown (which is not the case in face-to-face role play) and that they felt less nervous and found it easier to adopt the role of the pharmacist as an avatar in OpenSim (OS) than in a classroom role-play situation. Learners felt that they had the opportunity to practice and make mistakes without real-world repercussions.

Contrary to expectations based on earlier research (Warburton 2009; JISC 2009), the students reported few technical difficulties. This may be explained in part by the fact that the learners involved were distance students in the third year of a net-based programme and as such had both good computer skills and equipment. Another contributing factor was the face-to-face introduction and online technical support provided by the Centre for Teaching and Learning throughout the project. Observation during the introduction provided evidence that social interaction between students served to allay the apprehension of those students who were more negative towards carrying out activities in a 3-D environment.

In the online questionnaire the majority of students commented that they experienced the activity as engaging, motivational and that they could see the potential for its use in other courses in the programme. Subsequently, although concrete evidence that the use of the virtual pharmacy had made a significant contribution to improved learning outcomes is lacking, it can be proposed that the activity had a positive effect on the students' learning and provided the opportunity for experiential learning in an authentic environment. The use of virtual environments for communication training created a novel approach to learning and it could be argued that there may be some bias in this project, with students enjoying the experience because of its uniqueness as opposed to a shift in pedagogical practice.

The teaching staff engaged in the development and implementation of the virtual activities were also positive to the experience and commented that it had inspired them to develop their ideas and explore the pedagogical possibilities offered by virtual worlds further. Although it was considered time-consuming initially to gain the skill and expertise necessary to navigate and teach in OpenSim, the implementation and assessment of the student activity in the virtual pharmacy did not require more time than the previous feedback on the written assignment. The importance of a good introduction to the virtual environment and availability of technical support was stressed by the teachers involved as a contributing factor to the success of the project. One very positive aspect of the role play in OS for the teacher was the possibility to provide direct feedback to the student by watching the recording of the activity together with the student and reflecting on the activity together. This provided the student with the possibility to explain the choices he/she had made throughout the role play and for the teacher to provide constructive feedback on both the communication skills of the student and content of the conversation.

"Becoming" a pharmacist: Development of the students' "voice"

> I just feel like I'm studying chemistry, biology and so on. . . . I don't feel like I'm studying to become a pharmacist.

This statement was made by a first-year student in the net-based BSc Pharm during a focus-group interview, a sentiment echoed by many of her fellow students. Overall, first-year students did not experience that they were studying to become pharmacists, however they did comment that the introductory week provided a good overview of what it means to work as a pharmacist. During the first year students study core science subjects: chemistry, physiology etc. with little opportunity to experience or discuss their professional identity. Moreover, the majority of science teaching staff on the first year courses are subject experts rather than pharmacy professionals. Current research has also shown that pharmacy students frequently do not formulate their professional identity until they feel that they have established competency in core science subjects (Taylor and Harding 2007). At this stage the local tutors, who are themselves pharmacists, and the study groups provide a connection to the future profession of the students and facilitate the creation of a community of practice

For year-two students their professional identity is becoming clearer. Many students commented that they were able to see the practical application of their knowledge more clearly and although they did not yet feel themselves to be pharmacists, they recognised that the courses studied contained the skills and competencies that were essential for their future profession. Year-two courses are increasingly held by pharmacologists and pharmacists, and contain practical laboratory work that further increases the enculturation of the students into the profession together with increased participation in the community of practice formed by the study groups and programme activities.

Year-three students seem to have a well-defined picture of their profession; by this stage of their education they have completed a work placement and several advanced courses in customer communication, ethics etc. The majority of year-three students interviewed felt that they had had great benefit of their theoretical and practical knowledge, especially computer skills, during the work placement and felt confident of their ability to carry out their duties as pharmacists. They felt that their identity as pharmacists, which had slowly been developing throughout the programme through participation in authentic learning activities and opportunities to discuss and reflect on their future role, was well founded. Although perhaps not complete, their professional identity would continue to develop as they entered their professional lives as pharmacists.

So how did it go for our first-year student: did she become a pharmacist? At the end of her third year the answer to this question was:

> Yes! Now I feel like a pharmacist. I feel ready to begin work, to take care of customers and help them with their medication. It's a bit scary to think that I'll have so much responsibility for others, but I feel confident that I can do it and that I will continue to learn and develop as I work.

Discussion

As previously mentioned, some educational and social experiences such as opportunities to meet with teaching staff informally, enculturation and socialisation into the role of the pharmacist are lacking in net-based education. Counteracting this loss is most probably not entirely possible, however the provision of multiple channels for communication and use of a virtual learning environment can compensate to some degree. Students are provided with opportunities to exercise their voice, give advice to customers, and build confidence in their competence as pharmacists in group work and together with the local tutors. However there is insufficient evidence at present to determine if the students in the BSc Pharm do develop a true sense of *being* a pharmacist and more importantly, what the contributing factors are in this process.

The virtual environment, as discussed earlier, can provide increased opportunities for the students for professional development and communication in an authentic learning environment. There are of course limitations in the use of a virtual environment for experiential learning and communication; a virtual environment can never provide the same authenticity as a face-to-face environment. Nevertheless, in the pedagogical design of the BSc Pharm as a whole and the virtual pharmacy in particular, the focus has been on the achievement of learning outcomes and skills, and the facilitation of students' profession identity. Facilitation of more existential aspects of the students' education, such as Academic Bildung, were not expressed by faculty as being important features of the course design of the BSc Pharm. In contrast, the question of professional identity has always been an important consideration in the programme and the role of the local tutors has from the very beginning of the programme been to provide students with a strong connection to their future profession.

The immersive and social affordances of virtual worlds offer many new opportunities for educators, however these must be weighed against barriers to managing a new technological environment and the impact the use of virtual worlds may have on the role of the teacher. In virtual worlds the teachers' position becomes that of a facilitator and co-constructor of knowledge, indicating a shift away from the traditional role of teacher as lecturer and purveyor of knowledge. The teachers involved in the current project were enthusiastic innovators, student-focused and well-prepared to adopt the role of mentor and member of a common community of practice. However, the complexity and shift in roles necessitated by virtual environments and situated learning may prove more of a challenge for some teachers, and support in the development of new strategies for teaching and the creation of innovative learning experiences in virtual worlds is needed. After the completion of the trial in the *Pharmacotherapy in the Elderly* course, several other teachers have included the virtual pharmacy environment in their courses on the programme. However, there are also examples of teaching faculty who, although not explicitly negative, resist using the virtual pharmacy despite its suitability in their particular subject.

In total, 50% of the students taking the *Pharmacotherapy in the Elderly* course over the three years studied chose not to carry out the virtual pharmacy activity. This decision was in the majority of cases due to technical problems such as insufficient broadband capacity or hardware problems, and also perceived lack of time required to learn how to navigate and use their avatar. A further 5% were directly negative to the idea of entering a virtual world. It is also important to take into consideration these students when planning learning activities in virtual worlds. Is it reasonable to make this type of activity obligatory for all students on a programme? It could be considered provocative for students to be "forced" into a virtual world. Students who, out of principle or for other reasons, do not wish to take part in activities in an open virtual world should be offered alternative methods of carrying out the activity. However, ensuring that these alternatives are of equal value can be difficult; they must provide the same opportunity for students to achieve learning outcomes but use a different mode of delivery.

Research has indicated that unless learners perceive the virtual world as authentic (true to life) they may be resistant to the idea of learning in it (Childs and Peachey 2010). Further, if the view is taken that cognition is situated and that learning is inseparable from the activity in which it is meant to be used, the authenticity of the virtual world is vital (Brown, Collins and Duguid 1989). As we have seen, although some students did not perceive the virtual environment to be entirely authentic it was sufficiently authentic for them to be able to adopt the role of the pharmacist. Similarly, although the students were able to carry out the communication activities successfully, the average time spent in-world by the students (six to seven short visits prior to taking part in the activity) was most probably too short for them to be able to identify with their avatars and achieve a sense of presence or embodiment in the virtual environment. Childs (2010) found a strong correlation between satisfaction with the learning activities in a virtual environment and an experience of presence, and vice versa. He also suggests that until learners have acquired a sense of "embodiment" or presence in a virtual world their ability to learn may be impaired:

> [A]s learners in the physical world we take embodied cognition for granted and so can be unprepared for the difficulties that occur when moving into a virtual world; learners have the need to learn to become learners again but within a new environment.
>
> (p. 15)

The time required for students to equip themselves with the necessary skills and gain a sense of presence in the environment precludes the use of virtual worlds on shorter courses and seems to indicate that the use of immersive virtual worlds would be more effective if used throughout the programme.

Although the students perhaps did not gain the sense of presence necessary for total immersion in the environment it would appear that their experience was sufficient for them to enter the role of the pharmacist, to communicate, and carry out their assignment of providing information and counselling for the customer at a correct level, thus contributing to their professional identity. Unfortunately the questionnaires and focus group interviews with students do not provide evidence that the experience also contributed to the development of more existential, being-related aspects of Academic Bildung.

Net-based education does however have advantages to offer as well as drawbacks. For example, studying in a net-based programme fosters increased autonomy and independence in students, as shown in alumni questionnaires and feedback from employers. The structure of the material on the net facilitates independence in the students; they become increasingly self-disciplined, independent, and take more personal responsibility for their learning as they progress through the programme. The design of the programme provides a form of scaffolding for the students: first-year students receive a relatively generous amount of support, their assignments are well-structured, there are weekly meetings with the local tutor, and detailed study guides are provided. In interviews with teaching staff, it is evident that as the students progress through the programme they work more independently with project work, case studies etc. and the degree of support necessary decreases (Diaz and Cartnall 2010; Andersson 2013).

Net-based education definitely has the potential to support students in the process of learning but are both dimensions of Academic Bildung and professional identity equally supported? Is the student able to develop critical thinking, society-oriented reflection, autonomy and also existential- and being-related reflection and authenticity?

To answer these questions, further research is needed into the structure and process of the study groups and relationships between the local tutors and the students/groups. Are the students truly participating in a community of practice? Is this a forum where students can discuss questions of *being* a pharmacist, ethics and their role as pharmacists? Do the learning activities in the virtual pharmacy contribute significantly to their professional identity and sense of *being* a pharmacist? Are autonomy and authenticity developed in balance?

Conclusions

From the responses provided by students in the Bsc Pharm programme, and a review of current research, it is apparent that the pedagogical design of the learning environment plays an essential role in facilitating the development of Academic Bildung and professional identity. The provision of multiple channels for communication, designing for authentic experiential learning activities and creation of a community of practice to enable development of the students' voice and professional identity are all essential aspects that need to be considered when designing net-based vocational programmes that also facilitate Academic Bildung and professional identity.

Academic Bildung is becoming not less relevant to higher education but more, possibly as a reaction to the current emphasis on evidence-based teaching (Biesta 2007) and a striving for life-long learning as set forth in ET 2020 (Council of the European Union 2009). Essentially, there is a need to achieve a balance between the instrumental dimension of professional competence and the existential dimension of Academic Bildung, between autonomy and authenticity (Arendt 1978).

If this is to be achieved, it is our conclusion that it is necessary to design a learning environment that can provide the student with multiple opportunities to develop their own voice in communication with others, to formulate and practice their understanding and to interact with others as part of a community of learning.

From our examination of the BSc Pharm programme, situated experiential learning, community and inter-personal interaction and communication are key factors in the facilitation of Academic Bildung and professional learning. The ability of technology-enhanced forms of education to provide these prerequisites is dependent on pedagogically sound design and is essential for the facilitation of professionalization and Academic Bildung in net-based courses.

Notes

1 A commercial LMS, Ping Pong, developed in Sweden by Partitur, is used. http://pingpong.se/index.en.html
2 The communications software Adobe Connect is used for net meetings.
3 A virtual 3D immersive environment including a pharmacy and hospital created in Open Simulator.

References

Andersson, W. (2013), "Independent learning: Autonomy, control and meta-cognition". In: Moore, M. ed., *Handbook of distance education*. Routledge: New York.

Antonacci, D. and Modaress, N. (2005), "Second Life: The educational possibilities of a massively multiplayer virtual world", conference presentation. Available online at http://www2.kumc.edu/netlearning/SLEDUCAUSESW2005/SLPresentation Outline.htm (accessed 15 Oct. 2009).

Arendt, H. (1958), *The human condition*. University of Chicago Press: Chicago.

Arendt, H. (1978), *The life of the mind*, McCarthy, M., ed. Harcourt Brace Jovanovich: New York.

Barnett, R. and Coate, K. (2004), *Engaging the curriculum in higher education*. McGraw-Hill International: Berkshire, UK.

Barnett, R. (2007), *A will to learn: being a student in an age of uncertainty*. Society for Research into Higher Education and Open University Press: Maidenhead, UK.

Barnett, R. (2012), "Learning for an unknown future", *Higher Education Research & Development*, vol. 31, no.1, pp. 65–77.

Biesta, G. (2007), "Why what works won't work: Evidence-based practice and the democratic deficit in educational research", *Educational Theory*, vol. 57, no. 1, pp. 1–22.

Biggs, J. and Tang, C. (2009), *Teaching for quality learning at university*. Open University Press: Berkshire, UK.

Biocca, F. (1997), "The cyborg's dilemma: Progressive embodiment in virtual environments", *Journal of Computer Mediated Communication*, vol. 3, no. 2.

Bordia, P. (1997), "Face-to-face versus computer-mediated communication: A synthesis of the experimental literature", *The Journal of Business Communication*, vol. 34, no. 1, pp. 99–120.

Cain, J. (2008), "Online social networking issues within academia and pharmacy education", *American Journal of Pharmaceutical Education*, vol. 72, no. 1.

Cain, J. and Fox, B. (2009), "Web 2.0 and pharmacy education", *American Journal of Pharmaceutical Education*, vol. 73, no. 7.

Childs, M. (2010a), "A conceptual framework for mediated environments", *Educational Research*, vol. 52, no. 2, pp. 197–213.

Childs, M. (2010b), "Learners' experience of presence in virtual worlds". PhD thesis, University of Warwick, UK. Available online at http://archive.alt.ac.uk/news letter.alt.ac.uk/files.warwick.ac.uk/mchilds1/files/childs%2bthesis%2bfinal. pdf (accessed 15 Dec. 2010).

Childs, M. and Peachey, A. (2010), "Fur and loathing in Second Life: Students' concerns and resistance to learning in virtual worlds". Conference presentation at Plymouth eLearning: Learning without Limits, 8–9 April, 2010, UK.

Chung, U. (2003), "Maintaining quality pharmaceutical education in the digital age", *American Journal of Health – System Pharmacy*, vol. 60, no. 9.

Council of the European Union. (2009), "Strategic framework for European cooperation in education and training (ET 2020)". Available online at http://eur-lex. europa.eu/LexUriServ/LexUriServ.do?uri=CELEX:52009XG0528(01):EN:NOT

Diaz, D. and Cartnal, R. (2010), "Students' learning styles in two classes: Online distance learning and equivalent on-campus", *College Teaching*, vol. 47, no. 4.

Dickey, M. (2005), "Two case studies of Active Worlds as a medium for distance education", *British Journal of Educational Technology*, vol. 36, no. 3, pp. 439–51.

Engestrom, Y. (2001), "Expansive learning at work: Toward an activity theoretical reconceptualization", *Journal of Education and Work*, vol. 14, no. 1, pp. 133–56.

Goldberg, K. (2000), "The Unique Phenomenon of a Distance". In: Goldberg, K., ed., *The robot in the garden: Telerobotics and telepistemology in the age of the internet*, pp. 2–20. MIT Press: Cambridge, MA.

Hansen, F. T. (2007), "Phronesis and authenticity as keywords for philosophical praxis in teacher training", *Paideusis*, vol. 16, no. 3, pp. 15–32.

Hew, K. F. and Cheung, W. S. (2010), "The use of three-dimensional (3D) immersive virtual worlds in K-12 and higher education settings: A review of the research", *British Journal of Educational Technology*, vol. 41, no. 1, pp. 33–55.

Hockridge, D. (2013), "Challenges for educators using distance and online education to prepare students for relational professions", *Distance Education*, vol. 34, no. 2, pp. 142–60.

Hummel, H. G. K. (1993), "Distance education and situated learning: Paradox or partnership", *Educational Technology*, vol. 33, no. 12, pp. 11–22.

Hunt, L., Huijser, H. and Sankey, M. (2012), "Learning spaces for the digital age: Blending space with pedagogy". In: Keppel, M., Souter, K. and Riddle, M, eds., *Physical and virtual learning spaces in higher education: Concepts for the modern learning environment*, pp. 182–97. IGI Global: Hershey, PA.

Jaldemark, J. (2005), "Ett deltagande för alla? En kritisk diskussion". In: Jobring, O., Carlén, U. and Bergenholtz, J., eds., *Att förstå lärgemenskaper och mötesplatser på nätet* (pp. 149–72). Studentlitteratur: Lund, SE.

Jisc. (2008), "Serious Virtual Worlds: A scoping study" [report], Jisc: Bristol, UK. Available online at http://www.jisc.ac.uk/media/documents/publications/seriousvirtualworldsv1.pdf (accessed 15 Oct. 2009).

Kirremuir, J. (2008), "A spring 2008 'snapshot' of UK higher and further education developments in Second Life", *Eduserv Virtual Watch*. Eduserve Foundation: Bath, UK. Available online at http://www.scribed.com/doc/7063700/ A-spring-2008-snapshot-of-UK-Higher-and-Further-Education-developments-in-Second-Life (accessed 2009).

Kolb, D. A. (1984), *Experiential learning: Experience as the source of learning and development*. Prentice-Hall: New Jersey.

Lave, J. and Wenger, E. (1991), *Situated learning: Legitimate peripheral participation*. Cambridge University Press: Cambridge.

Lombardi, M. (2007), "Authentic learning for the 21st Century: An overview", [report], Educause Learning Initiative: Louisville, CO. Available online at http://www.educause.edu/ir/library/pdf/ELI3009.pdf (accessed 15 Oct. 2009).

McLellan, H. (1994), "Situated learning: Continuing the conversation", *Educational Technology*, vol. 34, no. 10, pp. 7–8.

MOOSE (MOdelling of Second Life Environments), available online at http://www.le.ac.uk/beyonddistance/moose/ (accessed 20 Oct. 2009).

Norwegian Association of Higher Education Institutions, Education Committee. (2011),"Aspects of Formation/Bildung" [report]

Open Simulator, available online at http://opensimulator.org/wiki/ (accessed 10 Jan. 2012).

Savin-Baden, M. (2008), "From cognitive capability to social reform? Shifting perceptions of learning in immersive virtual worlds", *ALT-J*, vol. *16*, no 3: pp. 151–61.

Second Life, available online at http://secondlife.com (accessed 10 Jan. 2012).

Segrave, S. and Holt, D. (2003), "Contemporary learningeEnvironments: Designing e-learning for education in the professions", *Distance Education*, vol. 24, no. 1.

Siemens, G. (2004), "Connectivism: A learning theory for the digital age", available online at http://www.elearnspace.org/Articles/connectivism.htm

Taylor, C. and Robinson, C. (2009), "Student voice: Theorising power and participation", *Pedagogy, Culture & Society*, vol. 17, no.2, pp. 161–75. doi: 10.1080/14681360902934392

Taylor, K. and Harding, G. (2007), "The pharmacy degree: The student experience of professional training", *Pharmacy Education*, vol. 7, no. 1, pp. 83–88.

Taylor, K. M., Harding, G., Bissenden, B., Shepherd, O. and Shooter, B. (2004), "'It made me feel like a pharmacist, not just a science student': Pharmacy undergraduates' attitudes towards extemporaneous dispensing practical classes", *Pharmacy Education*, vol. 4 no. 3–4, pp. 137–42.

Tripp, S. D. (1993), "Theories, traditions and situated learning", *Educational Technology*, vol. 33, no.3, pp. 71–77.

Warburton, S. (2009), "Second Life in higher education: Assessing the potential for and the barriers to deploying virtual worlds in learning and teaching", *British Journal of Educational Technology*, vol. 40, no. 3, pp. 414–26.

Wenger, E. (1998), *Communities of practice: Learning, meaning and identity*. Cambridge University Press: Cambridge.

7 Net-based guerrilla didactics

Søren S. E. Bengtsen, Helle Mathiasen and Christian Dalsgaard

Introduction

This chapter is based on an empirical study of teachers' experiences with a range of educational technologies. The study looks at net-based communication between students and between students and teachers in the master education programme course "IT educational design". We study how the course experiments with different technologies with the intention both of attracting students from all over the country and of supporting students' and students/teachers' collaborative activities, sharings and discussions. We ask: How can technologies facilitate communication and learning in different teaching environments? The sub-questions are: (1) what categories of communication appear in different communication forums; (2) what do the findings indicate when the focus is on pedagogic and didactic perspectives; and (3) what initiatives follow in net-based communication in higher education? Thus we are aiming at reflecting the meaning of a digitally influenced form of Academic Bildung, in which the net-based tools used, and not their human counterparts, are of special interest to us.

In this chapter we undertake an analysis and critical reflection of the IT educational strategy and practice applied in the graduate course "IT educational design" which took place in the fall of 2012 at Aarhus University in Denmark. We discuss the pedagogical and didactical conditions for realizing graduate education across digital and physical teaching formats. The term "didactics" refers to the use of the term in the Scandinavian-German tradition, in which it designates the relation between Bildung and planning, understanding and evaluation of the subject content (see Hopmann 2007; Gundem and Hopmann 2002).

The teachers' didactical intention for the course element was to make use of different designed IT educational platforms, where each would prefer particular communication forums and conditions. As such, the course was designed with a variety of different digital platforms intended for (1) communication about the specific subject matter, (2) communication of social character, and (3) study techniques.

Early on in the research we discovered that the students did not use the different platforms in the way didactically intended by the teachers.

Discussions on social matters and study planning were absent in forums where they were expected, and discussions on the subject matter arose in digital forums where they were not intended or wanted. This meant that the balance between forums for communication about the specific subject matter, communication of social character, and study techniques was displaced, and the teachers partly lost control over which discussions were present in what forums and with what content.

This has led us to rethink traditional didactical and pedagogical categories such as subject matter/social content and intended/actualised course content. We conclude this chapter with the position that IT educational phenomenon presented in our case study can be understood as a "guerrilla didactics"; a didactical pulse which continually dislocates itself from within the specific platforms used for communication. Revolving around the constructs put forward by American philosopher Graham Harman (2002, 2005) we argue that each digital platform assumes a life of its own, and thus becomes a pedagogical world in itself with its own subcultural norms, habits and values. This, we argue, makes room for a more potent and inclusive understanding of educational IT within the higher education sector.

Background

The object of the case study is the master's degree programme in IT educational design, at the Faculty of Arts, Aarhus University, Denmark. The primary target group for the programme is teachers in primary school and kindergarten. In 2012, the programme was redesigned with the aim of attracting students to Aarhus University from across Denmark, as well as students with time and place barriers (e.g., part-time employment which prevents travel to Aarhus University for on-campus classes). In order to attract this wider group of students, the programme was redesigned with the objective of developing a course programme that is flexible in relation to time and location. Thus the programme should be suitable for students unable to travel to the university every week, and for students who need to study at certain times of the day/week.

Prior to the redesign, the courses within the programme followed a structure traditionally employed in Danish higher education with two or three lessons each week. Lessons would typically last three hours and consist of lectures and student presentations. In contrast to this, the redesigned course programme has a minimum of face-to-face meetings and other forms of synchronous communication. Instead, net-based communication forums and other digital tools are employed.

In September 2012, around 40 students enrolled in the programme. The students were from different regions in Denmark, and a few students lived abroad. Many of the students (around 40%) worked more than 25 hours a week. Also, many of the students stated that the partly web-based nature of the courses was very important to their enrolment.

Thus a flexible and partly web-based course programme was necessary for a majority of the students. However, there were also a number of students who did not enrol in the programme because of time, place and situational barriers. The diversity of students' background, expectations, education and practical conditions is a fundamental challenge when the educational settings are designed by means of different communication platforms. In any case the basic condition for the redesigned programme is that it should be flexible. Further, there is the intention of developing new teaching methods and new ways of organizing and planning courses, which utilize digital media. Hence the students as well as teachers at this master degree programme called IT educational design were, so to speak, tasting their own medicine during their activities.

The first semester of the master's degree programme forms the case study for this chapter. The case study focuses on the different conditions for learning and teaching provided by the combination of communication tools and diverse teaching methods in the redesigned programme.

Behind the described design of digital media were a number of pedagogical considerations. The idea was to use the different forums for different kinds of communication and purposes. Thus, it was expected that certain forms of communication would occur in the different forums. These objectives behind the digital media usage are presented in the case below.

Presentation of case study

The first semester of the master's degree programme in IT educational design will make up the case study of this chapter. During the first semester, there were only two face-to-face seminars; a two-day kick-off seminar at the beginning of the semester, and a one-day seminar in the middle of the semester.

Tools and communication forums

A range of net-based tools and digital materials were employed during the first semester to support communication and collaboration in the periods between the seminars. The most central tools and materials were a forum for each course (Buddypress), a blog for the class (Wordpress), tools for collaborative writing (Google Docs/Drive), screencasts for short video lectures (YouTube), and videos for student presentations (YouTube). Further, students and teachers used email, the students created a Facebook group for the class, and finally for group work, some groups created group forums using primarily Facebook groups or Google+. None of the teachers were members of the Facebook group or the group forums.

Each week, students were given an assignment to be handed in the following week. The assignments were primarily in the form of a screencast supplemented with written text. In the screencasts, the teacher made brief presentations of the theme, literature and assignment for the week. Most often students worked on the assignments in groups using Google Docs/ Drive. They created a document, which they shared within the group and with the teacher, who was then able to follow the work in the process. During the week, students were offered supervision and feedback from the teacher within the Google documents. After the assignment was handed in, the teacher would provide feedback to the groups also using the Google document. Whereas some assignments were handed in via Google Docs/Drive, other assignments were required to be posted on the joint public blog, thus giving students the opportunity to view the work of the other groups.

A blogging platform called Pages with social networking features was used as the primary communication platform for the courses. The platform was set up using Wordpress with a Buddypress plugin. A group forum for communication was created for each of the two courses the first semester. The objective of the Pages group forum was to create an open space for student communication with the presence of the teacher. The groups were presented to the students as forums for all kinds of posts related to the course, and students were encouraged to share relevant thoughts and resources. A joint blog was created in Pages for the class. The blog is open to the world, and everyone outside the class could access the blog. The blog is to be used throughout the two years of studies across the different courses.

Similar to the group forums, the objective of the blog was to provide an open space for both students and teachers to write posts related to the course. The blog was intended to contain more comprehensive and academic posts related to the subject matter of the courses. The blog was also used by teachers to post video lectures and assignments, and students were required to post some of their assignments on the blog.

The teachers used a YouTube channel to upload screencasts with video lectures. The videos were relatively short presentations of themes, concepts and theories of the courses.

Finally, the courses used Google Docs/Drive for student group work. Google Docs/Drive enables synchronous editing of documents, comments with discussions, and a chat within the documents. Students used Google Docs/Drive to create shared documents for collaborative writing. The students shared the documents with the teachers, enabling them to follow the writing process and provide feedback. The objective of Google Docs/Drive was to support close collaboration between students, who were oftentimes not able to get together.

Students' use of forums

It soon became obvious for the teacher that the students did not use the different communication forums the way they were intended in the course design. For instance, posts and comments of a social nature were absent from the intended course forums, while discussions related to subject content appeared in forums, where they were not intended. Discussions on course-bound subject matter were dislocated from the Pages communities to the participants' Facebook group. And stories about more private matters appeared in Google Docs, a programme meant for discussions on course-bound matter only. As a result, the teachers experienced a loss of control with respect to communication tasks related to the courses. These initial discoveries of the students' (or the teachers') unintended use of the communication forums form the motivation for the case study below.

Theoretical framework and empirical method

We have chosen the following theoretical perspectives to underpin the case study, based on the thought that they describe in a particular illustrating manner how systems (Luhmann), objects (Harman) and digital platforms (Suler; Friesen) "strike back" or "play back" at the teacher and students using those platforms during online courses. By applying these theoretical perspectives we try to elucidate how potent and forceful a digital platform can become when interacting with other communicative systems (Luhmann) or objects (Harman); that is, students and teachers. By combining Luhmann and Harman we aim at presenting a new understanding of Bildung and autonomy, which focuses on the tools used and not (in the first place) the people using them. By this we mean that the software applied (social systems in Luhmann's sense, and objects in Harman's sense) should also be acknowledged as real and poignant forces to be reckoned with on their own terms and not (only) in relation to the human counterparts in the communication.

The empirical point of departure in this case study is about observing the communication in the presented digital platforms. The theoretical key concept is communication – hence we begin with a definition.

Definition of communication

Inspired by the German sociologist Luhmann's systems theory (Luhmann 1995) one communication unit is described as a three-phased selection process in which three selections are synthesized:

Selected by utterer, for example, the teacher:

1   the selection of information,
2   the selection of utterance,

and then selected by the addressee, for example, the student:

1   the selection of understanding (Luhmann, 1992).

The two first selections are visible while the third selection is invisible. One cannot observe what the addressee (or listener) chooses to understand by the uttered information.

The definition of communication indicates that one needs a minimum of two people to make a communication unit. And a communication unit is, so to speak, unpredictable in the sense that one cannot be sure that one's uttered information is understood by the addressee as one might intend. Similarly in the educational system a communication unit can involve two people; however it is often the situation that there is one teacher and many students. The students then process an understanding based on the teacher's utterance and/or possible utterances from fellow students. This increases the complexity, as each student processes understandings arising from his or her ability and potential as an observing system.

Systems are characterized by being *operationally* closed, self-referential, and autonomous (Luhmann, 1995). These system characteristics have consequences for the way we define learning and teaching. Furthermore as a consequence of these characteristics, we can infer that systems are observed to be non-trivial systems (Foerster and Pörksen, 2006; Luhmann, 2002), and can describe systems as also analytically indeterminable, unpredictable, and dependent on the previous operations *and* the concrete context. The consequences of such an approach to systems is that we can reject the idea of causality. This means that we cannot predict the outcome of a defined input. We do not know what happens when the specific system operates in its self-referential mode. For example, when a student has listened to a lecture one cannot tell what the outcome will be in terms of the student's understandings. While teachers' intentions about students' knowledge construction is one thing, the student's own construction of knowledge is another. This approach to systems has consequences for the way we consider the possibility of the fulfilment of the required purposes of the educational system.

When the learning environment is situated in net-based forums, or in a combination of face-to-face and net-based forums, the complexity increases due to the conditions for the single communication unit. The term *selection* describes that each choice is made between a range of possibilities. In this way both information and utterance are selected from a range of possibilities in the sense that the utterer selects which information to utter, and the selections are context dependent. Thus selection of utterance includes paralinguistic cueing (e.g. facial expressions, pauses, gestures and intonation) when the communication is face-to-face. In a net-mediated communication, for instance a written-based discussion forum, the utterer of the information has other premises, hence the utterer has to use other effects, such as space between letters, capital letters, emoticons (e.g., smiley etc.) to "compensate" for the lack of paralinguistic cues.

The third selection, the selection of understanding, concerns the way that the addressee selects how the information uttered will be understood. Thus we can only talk about communication when all three selections are synthesized.

When we relate this concept of a communication unit to the concept of teaching, we can define teaching as a specific and distinguished form of

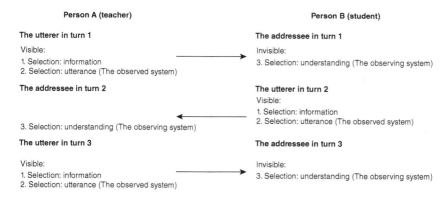

Figure 7.1 Teaching as dialogue; discussion as communication

communication that is intended to bring about changes by participants, concerning educational aims and requirements, thus allowing the possibility of facilitating knowledge construction. Hence, the underpinning assumption of this chapter is that teaching is understood as communication involving participants in the roles of students and teachers, while learning is understood as knowledge construction in its broadest sense.

With that point of departure we can conclude that "teacher talk" is one part of a communication unit – specifically when the teacher selects information as an utterance (e.g. a podcasted lecture). Before we can talk about communication, and accordingly teaching, the student has to focus on the uttered information and select an understanding. In a systems theoretical lens a student is seen as an observing system, while the teacher is the observed system. If the communication expands in the sense that one communication unit follows the next in a thread (often on the same theme) we talk about teaching as, for example, discussions. Thus the observing systems and the observed system will take turns in an iterative process. Hence the concept of teaching takes a variety of forms, from the one-way communication of the lecture, to discussion and mentoring where both teachers and students participate, a mode that includes net-based as well as face-to-face communication (Mathiasen, 2012).

A pivotal point is that communication can be successful if a horizon of expectations is established, which can happen over time. These expectations might concern teacher and student roles and functions, and how to behave in class and participate in net-based forums. It deals with culture in its broadest sense. Persons are not becoming transparent to each other, due to the foundation that sees systems as non-transparent, non-linear and autonomous. Systems will always observe each other as black boxes but can over time build up a horizon of expectations as a construction, and thus it does not follow that systems become transparent to each other.

According to the definition of a communication unit, we can only observe the first two selections in a communication unit. The third selection is based upon thoughts, and these do not "leave" a system (person) as thoughts, but if something is uttered, it is then "linguistic reconstructions of thoughts" – which is not the same as thoughts themselves. The pedagogic decisions concerning choice of the concrete communication forums have implications for the proceeding of the communication (e.g. teaching). The conditions are different depending on the possibilities to couple to the uttered/written information and hence the possibility to continue, for example, a dialogue or just try to understand the uttered information by questioning the content. Each forum has its advantages and disadvantages and the pedagogical choice must depend on the aim of the course, content, purpose and students' abilities (Mathiasen and Schrum, 2009).

Methodological reflections

The methodological reflections of the case study draw on research into the relation between communication and pedagogical actions in net-based forums (Friesen 2005, 2011; Manen and Adams 2009; Suler 2004; Evans 2009; Stokes and Jones 2009). The method used for analysis is a patchwork ensemble consisting of communication theory, phenomenology, and literature on net-based counselling. Research into supervision and text feedback at the university has a long tradition focusing on the relation between the didactical act and the contextual communication framework between organisation, supervisor and student (Bengtsen 2011, 2012). However, despite the obvious practical and theoretical implications when introducing net-based communication in supervisory settings at the university, literature on this aspect is scarce, wherefore we look to the tradition in net-based counselling where net-based communication and its implications for psychological/pedagogical actions long has been the focus of research. How students perceive the teacher's or facilitator's pedagogical intention with his or her net-based communication is deeply connected to the writing style used. How invitations to different forms of contact are understood relates to how the teacher and students use their writing as a prolongation of the invitation they wish to convey. In some part of the research tradition this is described as "online presence", as for example pointed out by Jane Evans (2009). Whether the content of the dialogue is experienced in a formal or informal way depends on the language used in the communication between supervisor and supervisee. As pointed out by John Suler, the net-based relation can to a high degree be said to present itself as a quality of the writing used in communication:

> Writing affects the relationship and the relationship affects the quality of the writing. The same reciprocal influence exists between the text relationship and *writing style*. Concrete, emotional, and abstract expression;

complexity of vocabulary and sentence structure; the organisation and flow of thought – all reflect one's cognitive/personality style and influence how the other reacts.

(2004, p. 21)

Taking this point into phenomenological-inspired research on net-based education Norm Friesen stresses the importance of paying attention to writing style as the designator and framing device for the purpose and possibilities of the specific net-based forum used in IT educational courses (2011). Where the research into net-based counselling described above focuses on the importance of the style of writing as a tool to form and facilitate the pedagogy emerging in the flow of contact between supervisor and supervisee, the phenomenological research undertaken by especially Max van Manen (2005, 2009) and Norm Friesen (2005, 2011) furthermore focuses not only on the persons using net-based platforms, but the potentials and limitations of the digital platforms themselves used for communication. As Friesen points out:

[I]t is important to recall how Web technologies foreground their own "function": In contexts of online education, different configurations of Web technologies are referred to explicitly as specific tools suited to quite different educational and communicative ends. For example, one tool will be for chatting, a second specifically for collaborative document development, and a third for more specialized "knowledge building" activities.

(2011, p. 156)

An important notion Friesen stresses in this quotation is the difficulty of obtaining knowledge of relational pedagogy in net-based communication in general. The conditions for communication are never uniform and homogenous across the different platforms used in net-based courses. Typically, several digital platforms are used during the same course, and often with different purposes and didactical intentions. Even if only one net-based platform is used, the different students and teachers connect to that platform in different ways which makes it impossible to foresee the specific communicative outcome, compared to the introduced concept of communication. As is reflected in our previous work we have, in line with Friesen and Suler above, made visible the ways that conditions for pedagogical action change as the conditions for communication change (Bengtsen 2012; Mathiasen 2004). A common point is that educational IT invites a variety of pedagogical relations between teachers and students, but at the same time the mixing of different media for communication increases the complexity, and thereby challenges the strategies for planning and evaluation sought for in didactical designs.

Analysis

The points above regarding the link between communication and pedagogical action have been made operational for closer analysis of the data material used. The empirical materials of the case study consist of the following: two course forums, students' Facebook group, posts and comments from a blog, excerpts from the Google documents, and videos on a YouTube channel.

The focal point of the analysis is communication in the different forums, also called platforms, with an emphasis on analysing how the different forums are used, and how they are used differently. The empirical study is primarily based on communication within the two course forums and the Facebook group in the period from late August 2012 to February 2013.

The main question that the case study sought to explore is: What were the different communication forums used for? First of all, the analysis will study the forms of communication within the different forums. How do the participants address the forum? Do they ask questions, post updates, links, etc.? What kinds of communication forums do the students use, and what kinds of communication categories are observed? The following categories will be used in the analysis.

We make a distinction between two categories of contributions:

- Asking questions – responses expected, which requires two communication units
- Providing information – responses not expected, in principle requiring only the uttered information (selection 1 and selection 2 of the communication unit)

The objective is to make an initial distinction between posts (which are text-based contributions by the course participants) that call for responses, and posts that provide information and do not require a response. The analysis based on these categories also entails an analysis of whom the participants address in their posts.

Related to this distinction, we also examine whether teachers and students use the forums to initiate discussions and dialogue, or whether they use them to send out information. This elucidates the dialogical potential of the particular design applied. Thus, it is also important to study whether there are responses to the questions and also to the information provided with no call for response. Do the contributions initiate dialogue, or is it one-way communication?

- Dialogue (more than two communication units in a thread)
- One-way communication (one communication unit)

Following this initial analysis, we make an analysis of the content of the contributions within the forums. What do the participants write about? Since the group forums in Pages were intended to be open spaces for students' interaction – both of a subject-specific and a social nature – it is relevant to make an analysis based on the following two categories:

- Contributions of a social nature (how style of writing invites this type of communication)
- Contributions related to the course and subject content (as above)

Because our study has a focus on communication related to subject content, we also further investigated the nature of the second category. To this end, we also analysed the forums based on a distinction between the following kinds of contributions related to the course and subject content:

- Concepts and theories relating to the course
- Study technique
- Administrative issues

These categories are coupled with those on contributions of a social nature and contributions related to the course in order to analyse who initiates discussions, and what the discussions concern.

Findings

The different communication forums of the case have been analysed on basis of the categories presented above.

Pages groups

The analysis shows that the two Pages groups are very similar, and are presented together below. The groups contain examples of the two first categories: asking questions and providing information. However, there is a clear distribution of roles between students and teachers. Whereas the students primarily use the forum to ask questions, the teachers primarily provide information to the students and answer their questions. In the majority of the student posts, the students address the teachers directly by beginning their posts with "Hi [teacher]." However, there are also many examples of students themselves answering questions from other students.

The analysis from the second set of categories shows that there is dialogue and discussion between students and teachers and also between students. There are also many examples of one-way communication, where information from the teachers has no response from the students. The forums contain many "providing information" posts with no answers, and the forums are generally dominated by the teachers' information to the students – often information that does not require a response.

The analysis of social vs. course-related content of the forum shows that communication related to the course and the subject content dominates the forum. There are *no* examples of communication of a social nature in the Pages groups. No "small talk". Instead, all the posts of the Pages groups relate directly to the course and the subject content.

Going into the content of the communication, the contributions primarily concern administrative issues. Most of the contributions are from the teachers, and the majority of the posts are concerned with information about administrative issues related to assignments, literature, exams, deadlines, seminars, etc. In other words, the Pages groups are primarily used by the teachers to provide administrative and practical information to the students. The teachers also use the forum to share links of relevance to their course. There are only a few of these examples from the students. This is in contrast to the expectations and intentions made beforehand about using the Pages groups as forums for discussions of subject matter and theoretical reflections.

Whereas the administrative and practical issues dominate the communication of the forums, there are also a few examples of questions from the students in relation to study technique, and fewer examples of contributions on concepts and theories related to the course.

The Facebook group

An analysis of the number of questions versus information shows that questions dominate the student-initiated Facebook group. Also, in comparison to the Pages group, there are many more examples of students providing information to each other – without the expectation of a response.

Whereas the Pages groups showed many examples of one-way communication from the teachers, the Facebook group is dominated by dialogue, where students answer and comment on each other's posts. The nature of communication within the Facebook group is primarily dialogic in the sense that the students answer each other's posts and comment extensively. There are very few posts that are not commented on by other students.

Similar to the Pages groups, an analysis of the content of the contributions shows that communication related to the course and the subject matter dominate the Facebook group. However, as opposed to the Pages group, there are several examples of contributions of a social nature that do not relate to the course. Students coordinate their activities and arrange meetings and dinners.

Within the course-related communication, students primarily ask questions concerning administrative and practical issues related to their studies, including questions on how to interpret the assignments, where to locate literature, when and where to hand in assignments, etc. Students also discuss subjects relating to study technique. Finally, there are only very few discussions related directly to the content of the course, for instance discussions on texts or concepts. Interestingly, this is very similar to the use of the Pages groups. In many cases these are questions that might as well have been asked directly to the teacher. In many cases the teacher would most definitely know the right answer. Instead, the students ask and provide answers to each other.

Apart from asking questions, students also use the Facebook group to provide information related to the course. Students use the Facebook group to exchange ideas, tips and links of relevance to their studies. For instance they link to events, articles, videos, etc. that deal with the subject matter of their courses. These are the kinds of contributions that were intended for the Pages group, but they are more numerous within the Facebook group. Thus, the Facebook group was used far more often and for several other means than any other forum. This is interesting as the Facebook group was the only forum that the teachers did not intend to use in the course design. In this way the students took action themselves and "moved" the communication to their own preferred platform for communication, hereby, on their own, aligning their social and institutional realities.

The Facebook group represents a forum where the students can share and discuss their questions and doubts related to their studies. An important question is why they chose to have the discussions without the teacher. This finding suggests a need for further research into similar matters seen from the students' perspective.

Google Docs/Drive

Google Docs serve a double agenda. It is used for communication with the teacher who is able to comment on the paper in the writing process, and as a tool for communication between the students about subject content and discussions about how to structure the paper, planning of group work and socialising. Google Docs makes visible the writing and working process of the group in the form of linguistic "trails"; minor and major changes in the text and the communication about these changes. A closer analysis of the students' working/writing processes on this platform makes it possible to understand a closer relation between product and process dimensions of student assignments and student work, which becomes visible as a form of communication that is dynamic, intertextual, collaborative, collective and spontaneous due to the possibility for synchronous communication. Google Docs as a medium is a hybrid form that merges synchronous and asynchronous communication, product and process, individual and group-oriented work options to a degree where it is difficult to separate these different dimensions of communication.

The analysis shows that Google Docs was used by the students to a variety of purposes as a communication tool for the students to discuss both social and course-bound subjects. The comment-feature of the platform was used at times for synchronous and chat-like purposes while the students were engaged in working on the document simultaneously. In these situations the chat-like feature was used both in order to make practical arrangements for the particular group's next meeting, and furthermore was used to comment on each other's formulations while working synchronously on the document. Google Docs was at other times used in a more traditional way for asynchronous text feedback between teacher and students. The teacher took a "peek" at the particular group's document in progress, from time to time, to write a comment and give suggestions for improvement of the text. The students used this feedback mode as well, writing comments on each other's contributions at different times whenever they seemed to have an opportunity.

Overall Google Docs was the platform used most explicitly for discussions on course-bound subject content. It was at the same time the "workshop" in which the documents the students had to submit as weekly assignments were produced. It can be argued that Google Docs was the IT educational tool which was used most as planned beforehand by the teacher. It was intended primarily as a net-based "workshop" for assignment production, and was used for this purpose accordingly. However, regular social talk and private communication were also present on this platform, although to a lesser degree.

The two key findings are that (1) in order to understand students' working processes as a group using a partly synchronous tool such as Google Docs, the working processes were on one hand *more* visible as the study of minor and major changes showed the choices and "negotiations" made as a group. On the other hand the process became *less* visible as the many changes often blurred the actual substance of change, which may be better seen from a distance. When many of the changes in a document or a writing/thinking process, which formerly were tacit, suddenly become visible, information overload may occur and create a "blurred" view. And (2) that the peek into the "black box" of collective writing processes partly produced several more black boxes, as the teachers became attentive to the many different corrections and comments embedded in each group-document. Furthermore the teachers came to understand that they did not necessarily get closer to peeking into the black box, as it was clear that the group had often also communicated by other means or through other platforms before they made use of Google Docs. However these findings support the notion of an IT educational potential which could be further reflected in a didactically suitable manner that would facilitate, in a more tailored way, the actual needs of the students. This finding suggests the need of further research into the ways the renewed access into details of change in the students' working documents can be structured and managed didactically.

Weblog

A study of the weblog shows that it is used for two kinds of posts. First of all it is used by the teacher to present video lectures and by students to present their answers to assignments. There are no examples of posts on the initiative of the students. All posts are either by the teacher or directly encouraged by the teacher. The same pattern is repeated when analysing the comments on the blog posts. There are only very few comments. Again, they are primarily by the teacher, who provides feedback to the students' posts. Or students comment because it has been required by the teachers. There are very few examples of dialogue within the comments.

The weblog does not serve as an open space for students' contributions outside of the assignments. Apart from the assignments, there are not examples of students writing subject-related posts of relevance to the courses

YouTube channel

The YouTube channel contains video lectures from the teachers. The channel is used only by the teachers, and the videos are not commented on by the students. It is obvious that the students primarily see the course groups in Pages as a forum for communicating with the teacher. This is evident in the many posts, in which students address the teacher directly by writing "Dear [teacher]" at the beginning of the post. The same is the case with the joint weblog and the YouTube channel. These forums are viewed as domains of the teacher. The Facebook group on the other hand is given the role of an open space for communication, both of a social nature and related to course content. The use of the Facebook group was an especially unexpected event.

Discussion: Net-based guerrilla didactics

The analyses disclose the following challenges concerning the IT educational point of departure. Firstly it seemed a disadvantage trying to think across different IT educational tools within the same didactical "worldview" or "panorama". It becomes evident that the teachers thought it possible to use the same general didactical framework to encapsulate all the different tools used for the course – and thus tried to align the working processes with the learning goals across the platforms. This proved to be a difficulty as shown above; the distinction between contributions of a social nature and contributions related to the course and to subject content did not hold a demarcation line between different platforms, but actually existed within each platform – in several ways at the same time, changing as the course progressed. Talk of a social and personal nature sifted in through the platforms marked out for text feedback and supervision, as was the case with Google Docs. Thus a clear distinction between formal/informal communication used regarding classroom/out-of-classroom communication did not hold when dealing with net-based communication across different forums. The very conditions for formal/informal communication seemed to change during the course even though the same platform used for communication did not change. However, the different platforms used offered "hidden" possibilities for new modes of making social/course-bound communication manifest, which were not initially obvious for the course planners. In particular, the use of Google Docs as a mix of chat and peer/teacher feedback, and the use of Facebook as a platform for discussions of course-bound material, were unexpected. Thus the potential occurred for using Google Docs for other forms of communication than those strictly course-bound, and the use of Facebook as other than a social media.

Secondly the analyses show that course planners face a challenge of what can be called a "blurred perspective". When communication unexpectedly moves from one platform to another, thereby assuming a new format and maybe even a new topic or communicative framework, it is difficult for the teacher to locate the thread or topic he or she initiated. The teacher-initiated or intended discussion might be believed to have never taken place, when it may be very much alive and intense – merely in a different forum and/or under different discursive framing. This was evident with the use of Pages as an almost exclusively one-way communication between teachers and students, even though intended as a much more dialogical forum. And it was equally evident with the use of Facebook for course-bound discussions and peer commentaries, though primary intended for social chatter. This second major challenge is one of "communicative plummeting"; the experience of sending a topic or a question onto the platform design for exactly this form of communication, just to see it crash and never fly, or to see it suddenly disappear merely to reappear on another platform – but transformed, maybe even "mutated" or transfigured into something completely different. And what then – has it become didactical "trash" or "waste", or does the new form contain new and unforeseen potential? Great potentials lie in this didactical wasteland. By this we mean that these communicative "errors" and mishaps experienced by the teachers in the case study show themselves as holding rich and powerful potentials for rethinking IT educational designs. Communication "gone bad" or "led astray" is actually communication assuming an autonomous form not thought of before, and thereby enriching our preconceptions concerning the use of net-based education. Here autonomy is not attached to the students and teachers using digital tools applied in net-based forums. On the contrary we argue that the platforms themselves obtain a particular kind of autonomy as "tool-beings" (Harman 2002,); they communicate in terms of shared or cross-linked meaning connected by the entangled relations that the different platforms have with each other – also when no human being is actively using them. This calls for an attempt to reconceptualise didactical challenges in net-based education. Tentatively we term these "mishaps" anti-didactical knots of communication, and unintentional dimensions of didactical strategies (Luhmann, 2002) – which, like kryptonite, dissolves the strategies made by the teachers, and forces them to reconfigure their didactical framework *during* the course.

The challenges described here also brought forth new possibilities for rethinking educational IT. By framing the didactical conditions differently, new modes for IT educational pedagogy present themselves. In this rethinking we present the concept of "guerrilla didactics" to point out that IT-educational didactics can never be viewed from above or beyond the different digital platforms used, but must be planned, re-planned, broken up and displaced in order to remerge as a dynamic and plastic pulse through different contexts as they change during the course. The term "guerrilla" is borrowed from the American philosopher and phenomenologist Graham Harman (2002, 2005) who uses the term in a more abstract philosophical manner. Harman claims to be able to present a guerrilla metaphysics and argues that any endeavour that tries to formulate one overall metaphysical doctrine (either an essentialist or anti-essentialist one) is in vain. There are multiple metaphysical dimensions at work around us all the time, and each thing is its own metaphysical galaxy holding powers and a capacity for being that is never entirely grasped or disclosed by the other things it engages with, and it even escapes the grasp of the human being as well. Harman describes this in the following way:

> An object is a box of surprises, never fully catalogued by the other objects of the world. As soon as one accepts that there are multiple relations to the same things, and that neither animate nor inanimate actors are able to sound the depths of their neighbours, the standpoint of object-oriented philosophy has been established. What lies behind all events are inscrutable tool-beings or substances lying in some sort of still-undetermined vacuum. And somehow, the vacuums must manage to communicate with one another. This is guerrilla metaphysics.
>
> (2005, pp. 78–79).

Drawing on Harman's understanding of this guerrilla warfare between different ontological planes of the world we argue that the same holds for digital platforms used in net-based education. Each platform has it own logic and "laws of nature" which must be taken into account when outlining the didactical structure for a net-based course. However this is, we argue, the very essence of an IT educational didactics: That because of each individual platform's own didactical or logical set up, the course didactics are never entirely stable and predictable. As every experienced teacher knows, this holds true for any course taught whether net-based or not. However, the cardinal point here is that traditional pedagogical and didactical bipolar categories like course bound/social communication do not hold in net-based education, as the specific net-based tools and platforms used do not contain one-sided possibilities for communication. Any net-based didactical intention must view itself as embedded in the particular worldviews or paradigms which each platform projects. So, compared to classroom teaching, or campus-based education, the didactical challenge differs as the teacher does not only have to reflect and manage the differences of students, but also the differences between the digital platforms used. This is not an argument which is trying to turn software programs into pseudo-human beings, but an argument which foregrounds the status of communicative agents of the tools in play. They play their own game, only partially aligning with their human operators.

On one hand this demands a certain amount of effort and resources on behalf of the IT educational course planners, as the didactical set up may be evaluated and revised several times during a single semester course. On the other hand it creates unique didactical potential, as the net-based platforms themselves become pedagogical actors on the same footing as teachers and students. From a conservative point of view this seemingly loss of control may not be desirable because of the entropy or escalating complexity it might generate. From a progressive point of view this inventive disorder opens doors to new dimensions in university teaching, because the digital platforms, like a mirror reflects light, reflect the didactical intention in new and possibly unforeseen directions – making the learning activity space wider and more creative. However, to paraphrase what Bruno Latour (in Harman 2005) writes about Harman, this notion of guerrilla warfare within the course does not invite brandishing any pedagogical Kalashnikov or aggressive hegemony of didactical will to power or control. On the other hand it opens a buzzing and enchanting optics on net-based pedagogy as a space for creativity, risk and adventure.

This parallels the point in the introductory chapters of this volume that IT educational strategies must be multi-voiced and pluralistic in their origin. This is exactly the sort of Bildung IT educational designs can promote: The necessity for the students to alter their communicative actions across different platforms, reflective of many different worlds of communications, each trying to be what it is – a specific digital forum – and not trying to be everything at the same time. Thus net-based education holds, maybe, the most powerful opportunity to give students the critical and hermeneutic attitude of understanding so valuable in discourses on Bildung in higher education. By inviting students and teachers alike to be mindful of the different norms of communication, and thus the different criteria for social interaction across different platforms of communication, net-based education teaches students not to assume that their own presuppositions about the world are universal and valid for everyone else.

This leads us to suggest a more "weird" form of Bildung that primarily concerns the net-based platforms in use and only secondary the people who use it. Out of Harman's understanding of guerrilla metaphysics, and as suggested elsewhere in our own work (Bengtsen 2013), we link Bildung-phenomena such as autonomy and authenticity to the net-based platforms and tools themselves used in educational settings. We argue that the particular digital platform itself, partly independent of the people using it, assumes different voices in accordance with the four voices described earlier in this book. Thus, the individual digital tool acquires what Harman (2002) describes as "tool-being", a form of being not necessarily linked to human consciousness but to the thing itself instead. We suggest this unorthodox understanding of Bildung as a way of generating a more subtle and complex understanding of not only the relation between a digital platform and its human counterpart, but also the relations between platforms and between systems independent of the people using them. The different platforms used in educational settings play against each other and strike back at us with voices of their own.

Conclusion

The case study has circled round a central didactical challenge regarding the transformation of communicative practice in net-based education. The primary focus has been on the relation between course content and social discourse across different digital forums. The intended communication was shown to be displaced into new forms on unintended platforms, and not return as a boomerang, but instead act more as a runaway fugitive seeking exile in more fertile communicative environments. As the analysis showed, the teachers did not manage to facilitate the wished-for dialogical communication between teachers and students, and between students, on the main communication platform of the course, the Pages group. Instead the students on their own initiative formed a Facebook group to which they moved the course dialogue, hereby black-boxing it for teachers. Not being able to locate the dialogical communication, as it was closed off for them to review, the teachers thought the course had major communicative problems, until they realized by chance that the dialogue had merely gone "undercover" and wandered off to another, perhaps more inviting, platform of discourse. This was, for the teachers, partly experienced as a pedagogical paralysis where it became hard to structure a didactical design because of the ongoing changing conditions for communicative actions during the course. From the lenses of both systems theory (Luhmann) and phenomenological philosophy (Harman), we can say that communication lives its own life, unpredictable and autonomous. This has been shown to have important didactical implications that need to be studied further in future research.

At the same time we point to new possibilities for understanding the premises for didactical action in net-based education, even if we see the conditions as hyper-complex. This holds its own pedagogical-ontological condition called guerrilla didactics; a form of didactics where the different net-based platforms and forums used influence the communication in each other's systems, though never directly overlapping or touching. By this we mean that each communication forum abide by its own internal logic, not taking into account how the teachers manage to bridge the different forums used. This is maybe the most central task for IT educational didactics – bridging worlds of communication and aligning several horizons of meaning, each proclaiming at the same time to be the most important one.

The new unlocked potential for net-based education is therefore to view the didactical action as a manifold operating on many levels during the course, some of them unforeseen and unpredictable. This calls for new ways of thinking about didactical strategies in net-based education, and moving away from the thought that learning goals and course structure can be aligned on an abstract and meta-reflective level. On the contrary. Net-based didactics seem to hold a great potential for creating dynamic, creative and unexpected learning spaces and experiences. Thus we propose a new agenda for teaching and learning activities at the university in the twenty-first century: to be a teacher is to be a guerrilla leader, to guide the student groups of "freedom fighters" one small step at a time, never knowing exactly where they will end up, but the entire time sure of the potentials of the particular course and the students' will to communicate and engage in dialogue-driven studies.

The case study reveals the following crucial issues for further empirical research into the nature of net-based education and communication: First and most importantly, more knowledge is needed on the way net-based platforms for learning and communication activities become pedagogical worlds and things in themselves, in some respects disconnected from the teacher's pedagogical view in a given course. Second, such pedagogical worlds, in the shape of net-based platforms and tools, hold their own potential for contributions of a social nature and contributions related to the course and subject content, not necessarily grasped in their entirety by the teachers and students. And third, we see the need to continually evaluate and rethink the course structure as the teaching and learning processes take place – which calls for a radical theory of process-pedagogy and process-didactics when dealing with net-based courses in higher education.

References

Bengtsen, S. (2011), "Getting personal: what does it mean? A critical discussion of the personal dimension of thesis supervision in higher education", *London Review of Education*, vol. 9, no. 1.

Bengtsen, S. (2012), "Didactics and idiosyncrasy. A study of the relation between personal and professional dimensions of the supervisory dialogue at the university", PhD thesis, Aarhus University, Denmark.

Bengtsen, S. (2013), "Into the heart of things: Defrosting educational theory". In: Gibbs, P. and Barnett, R. eds., *Thinking about higher education*. Springer: London.

Evans, J. (2009), *Online counselling and guidance skills. A practical resource for trainees and practitioners*. Sage Publications: London.

Foerster, H. and Pörksen, B. (2006), *Wahrheit ist die erfindung eines lügners. Gespräche für skeptiker*. Carl-Auer Verlag: Heidelberg.

Friesen, N. (2005), "Technological experiences: Is there a body in this class?" In: van Manen, M., ed., *Writing in the dark: Phenomenological studies in interpretive inquiry*. Althouse Press: Ontario.

Friesen, N. (2011), *The place of the classroom and the space of the screen: Relational pedagogy and internet technology.* Peter Lang: New York.

Gundem, B. and Hopmann, S. (2002), *Didaktik and/or curriculum: An international dialogue.* Peter Lang: New York.

Harman, G. (2002), *Tool-Being: Heidegger and the metaphysics of objects.* Open Court Publishing: Chicago.

Harman, G. (2005), *Guerrilla metaphysics: Phenomenology and the carpentry of things.* Open Court Publishing: Chicago.

Hopmann, S. (2007), "Restrained teaching: The common core of didaktik", *European Educational Research Journal,* vol. 6, no. 2, pp.109–24.

Jones, G. and Stokes, A. (2009), *Online counselling: A handbook for practitioners.* Palgrave Macmillan: New York.

Luhmann, N. (1992), "What is communication?" *Communication Theory,* vol. 2, no. 3, pp. 251–58.

Luhmann, N. (1995), *Social systems.* Stanford University Press: Stanford, CA.

Luhmann, N. (2002), *Das erziehungssystem der gesellschaft.* Suhrkamp: Frankfurt.

Mathiasen, H. (2004), "Expectations of technology: When the intensive application of IT in teaching becomes a possibility", *Journal of Technology in Education,* vol. 36, no. 3, pp. 273–95.

Mathiasen, H. and Schrum, L. (2010), "New technologies, learning systems and communication: Reducing complexity in the educational system". In: Khine, M. and Saleh, I., eds., *New science of learning: Cognition, computers and collaboration in education.* Springer Publishing: New York.

Mathiasen, H. (2012), "Time to rethink the concepts of knowledge dissemination and transfer in the educational system?" *European Review,* vol. 20, no. 2, pp.153–63.

Suler, J. (2004), "The psychology of text relationships". In: Zack J. and Stricker, G., eds., *Online counselling: A handbook for mental health professionals.* Elsevier Academic Press: London.

van Manen, M. (2005), *Writing in the dark: Phenomenological studies in interpretive inquiry.* Althouse Press: Ontario.

van Manen, M. and Adams, C. (2009), "The phenomenology of spaces in writing online". In: Dall'Alba, G., ed., *Exploring education through phenomenology: Diverse approaches.* Wiley-Blackwell: Oxford.

8   Learning, meaning and Bildung?

Reflections with reference to a net-based MBA programme

Gunnar Grepperud and Frank Holen

> If the purpose for learning is to score well on a test, we've lost sight of the real reason for learning.
>
> Jeannie Fulbright

Introduction

The main question in this book relates to how and if net-based higher education strengthens or weakens the possibility for Academic Bildung, as it is described and discussed in Chapter 3 (Solberg and Hansen). Based on our work with a flexible MBA programme, we want to highlight and discuss some of the preconditions for realising this ideal. More specifically, we investigate how mature flexible students approach their learning process and what determines their approach.

Our issue is as follows: To what extent do the MBA students display learning at higher taxonomic level, and what explains their learning behaviour?

We start by presenting the MBA case and students' approaches to learning. We continue by reflecting on the relationship between deep learning and Bildung. In the last part of this chapter we present and discuss the results in relation to our understanding of Bildung and what might explain the divide between ideals and reality in the MBA case.

The MBA case

The MBA is an experience-based master's degree where the applicants must hold an equivalent to a bachelor's degree and two years of work experience. Hence, students come from various professional and academic backgrounds ranging from nursing and economics to a PhD in physics, to mention some. The programme lasts for two and a half years and has five mandatory courses and a master's thesis, giving a total of 90 study points. The first three semesters are dedicated to the courses and the last two to completing the thesis.

Structure of the MBA

All of the courses are divided into so-called learning paths, smaller parts or steps that all students follow. Each step represents different topics or subjects that are grouped together. Normally, all the steps contain mandatory reading material, recorded lectures, group work and assignments – i.e., all the learning material regarding the topic. Hence the content of each course is made readily available for the students, which makes it quite easy for them to organise their study work. A Gantt chart showing tasks and timeline for the progression in a course is also distributed to the students. The following illustration is taken from the first semester. Students and staff start off with a two-day seminar introducing the main pedagogical ideas and instructional/didactic design, the courses, and the ICT tools and digital media of the programme. The intention is to create both a social and academic foundation for collaboration and learning throughout the rest of the program. In the middle of the semester they meet for two days (one day dedicated to each course). In addition there is an "open hour" on Adobe Connect (online meeting) each week, which is facilitated by the programme's academic coordinator. The students can ask questions and comment, and the lecturers can attend to, answer, or discuss different subjects. Normally, there is a variety of activities such as assignments, lectures, and discussions – both teacher and student driven. The intention with this weekly open hour is to have a social arena for the students to meet up and keep track of their progress.

Within each semester the students have a mandatory assignment that they have to pass in order to take the final exam in the subject. The intention is twofold. First, the assignment's goal is to engage the students in learning activities; second, it gives the lecturers feedback on each student's progress.

Infrastructure and learning media

In order to increase flexibility, parts of the learning material, i.e. lectures and articles, are digitalised. Additional material such as YouTube presentations

Task Progression MBA fall 2010	Duration	Start	Finish	
	39 days?	8/26/10	10/19/10	
Step 1: Introduction to marketing management	39 days?	8/26/10	10/19/10	
Step 2: The marketing plan: Content and	2 days?	8/26/10	8/27/10	
structure	5 days?	8/30/10	9/3/10	
Step 3: Competition: Who we complete with?	5 days?	9/6/10	9/10/10	
Step 4: Competition analysis	5 days?	9/13/10	9/17/10	
Step 5: Customer analysis – consumer behaviour	5 days?	9/20/10	9/24/10	
Step 6: Customer analysis – industrial buying	5 days?	9/27/10	10/1/10	
behaviour	5 days?	10/4/10	10/8/10	
Step 7: Customer analysis – segmentation	1 day?	10/19/10	10/19/10	
Submission of analysis steps 1–7				

Figure 8.1 Progression in the MBA courses

is added to support self-produced material. Adobe Connect is also used to give live lectures on-line when requested or needed. Both these lectures and the weekly "open hour" are recorded and could be used afterwards. In this way, the students who are unable to attend have the opportunity to watch the recordings afterwards.

Flexibility and the student role

The flexibility of the programme has made the time and place of studying less important. At the same time, the students have to take the main responsibility for most of the work, i.e. they must watch and interact with the net-based lectures in order to progress. They cannot simply raise their hand in the classroom; they must actively contact the lecturer. Consequently, the students have to be more self-regulative in this net-based model.

Student learning approaches

As part of the students' course assessment, we asked them to answer a questionnaire specifying their engagement in learning activities. The basis for this is the so-called SAL (Student Approaches to Learning) tradition, rooted in constructivism and phenomenology. This tradition distinguishes between a few main categories of learning approaches. Originally, two such categories were identified: depth and surface learning.

In short, depth learning means that students go "behind" the text to understand ideas and search for meaning. This is done by searching for patterns and principles within and between subjects and topics, by relating their reading to their own experiences, designing and testing their hypotheses, and by creating coherence and continuity. Students with this orientation are also conscious of themselves as learners and their learning situation.

A surface orientation is characterised by the students focusing more on details than the whole, more on facts than meaning. They are more concerned with remembering than understanding, and they are less able to create connections between academic knowledge and everyday life. The students using this as their primary approach are, compared to those with a deep approach, less conscious about themselves as learners and about the learning situation (Prosser et al. 1999; Pettersen 2004; Richardson 1997; Richardson 2000).

Over time, a third category has been included, termed the strategic approach. This approach is characterised by strategic behaviour, i.e. students being more interested in studying than learning and more concerned with cue-seeking, assessments and exams than the learning itself. Strategic students constantly change between a surface and a deep approach (Volet and Chalmers 1992), but like deep surface students their studying is characterized by self-regulation and metacognition (Entwistle and Peterson 2004; Entwistle 2005).

Table 8.1 Defining features of approaches to learning

Deep Approach

Intention: to understand ideas for yourself	Transforming by
Relating ideas to previous knowledge and experience	
Looking for patterns and underlying principles	
Checking evidence and relating it to conclusions	
Examining logic and argument cautiously and critically	
Becoming actively interested in the course content	

Surface Approach

Intention: to cope with course requirements	Reproducing by
Studying without reflecting on either purpose or strategy	
Treating the course as unrelated bits of knowledge	
Memorising facts and procedures routinely	
Finding difficulty in making sense of new ideas presented	
Feeling undue pressure and worry about work	

Strategic Approach

Intention: to achieve the highest possible grades	Organising by
Putting consistent effort into studying	
Finding the right conditions and materials for studying	
Managing time and effort effectively	
Being alert to assessment requirements and criteria	
Gearing work to the perceived preferences of lecturers	

(from Entwistle 2005)

There is some disagreement as to whether these three approaches should be assessed as equal or if one of them should be preferred in higher education; several still assume that pursuing higher education must primarily be characterised by the deep approach (Gibbs 1992; Prosser et al. 1999; Pettersen 2004). It is, however, well documented that both the deep approach and the strategic approach contribute to good learning outcomes in higher education (Diseth and Martinsen 2003).

Academic Bildung and students' approaches to learning

How students approach the task of learning is in our view a highly relevant question when discussing and reflecting on what Academic Bildung is or should be. Although we have registered some resistance to the idea of juxtaposing Academic Bildung and academic skills, there are evident connections between the autonomy part of Solberg and Hansen's "double tracked" Bildung ideal (Chapter 3) and the overall ideals for learning and development in higher education.

Understanding Bildung as learning and development seems to be one of the cornerstones in the liberal arts tradition in American higher education. It is also close to the thinking of the philosopher and educator John Dewey.

Human beings are perceived as acting organisms in continuous interaction with their environment, and the main goal of the Bildung process is to assist individuals in their quest for a problem-solving capability that enables them to meet life's many challenges. The ultimate goal is the formation of democracy, and the role of any higher education institution is to prepare students for their role as citizens in a democracy.

Yale University highlights the following eight talents as their ideal for Academic Bildung:

1   The ability to be probing and curious about the outside world and to ask interesting questions about this world.
2   The ability to put facts into wider frames, gather information from a variety of sources and assess this information in accurate and fruitful ways.
3   The ability to submit a theme to a sustained and disciplined analysis, and where necessary, with more than one method or one understanding.
4   The ability to connect and integrate different frameworks of under-standing, thus creating knowledge or perceptions that were not available when using only one lens.
5   The ability to express one's thoughts precisely and convincingly.
6   The ability to take initiative and mobilize intellectual capacity without waiting for instructions from others. Being able to stretch intellectually.
7   The ability to work with others in ways that produce a result that could not have been created on one's own.
8   The ability to see themselves as members of a larger community, locally, nationally, globally and recognition that one's own abilities and talents are in the service of a greater common good.

(Bostad, 2009, p. 13)

The common denominators in these talents are learning and development, and the idea of in-depth learning fits well within these. If not all learning at all times is to be characterised by such talents and qualities, it must certainly be the overall goal that students move towards them during their studies. To be a master's student should also imply the ability to practice such high level talents that are also found, either directly or indirectly, in the highest levels in Bloom's taxonomy of cognitive learning (Anderson and Krathwohl 2001; Biggs and Collis 1982). Some talents also, in whole or in part, parallel the levels of the taxonomy of attitudes and skills.

In other words, higher education is to be exactly that, high level learning gained in a way that promotes academic insight and democratic citizenship. The overall aim of Academic Bildung is to foster individuals who take responsibility for their own Bildung process and are capable of using their insights and talents to the best of their environment. It is an ideal that rests heavily on the individual's ability to learn, to make informed choices, and to act consciously (Hagtvedt 2009). Bostad puts it this way:[1]

Bildung is in an intimate relationship with concepts such as maturation and reflection; intellectual, moral, and aesthetic maturity and critical reflection that make the individual capable of independent choices and informed decisions. This is the character of the individual, what the individual is, which requires a certain attitude to what it means to learn, and how knowledge and understanding develops.

(2009, p. 119)

This bears resemblance to the notion of exploration and exploitation as discussed in several disciplines (e.g. March 1991; Cohen et al. 2007). As Cohen and colleagues write, there are several kinds of decisions we make in our daily lives that require an exploration of alternatives before committing to and exploiting the benefits from a particular choice. Many of these require further exploration of alternatives in the face of changing needs or circumstances. Cohen and associates state: "often our decisions depend on a higher level choice: whether to exploit well known but possibly suboptimal alternatives or to explore risky, but potentially more profitable ones" (p. 933).

Furthermore, Academic Bildung has more to it that just intellectual development of the critical mind. Academic Bildung has to embrace the whole person, and thus include different types of knowledge and cognition. Bildung must be as much related to the skilled professional practitioner's tacit and intuitive knowledge (cf. Englund and Westers' Chapter 6) as to intellectual analysis and critical thinking. Solberg and Hansen's introduction of "the second track" (Chapter 3) further reminds us that Academic Bildung is also about touching, affecting, and developing the individual in such a way that it contributes to his or her independent voice in the world (Solberg and Fossland 2013). This is in line with how Barnett (2007) applies the concept of authenticity. Through this, he promotes qualities such as intellectual courage, integrity, creativity, dedication and commitment.

The MBA students' approaches to learning

To map the MBA students' learning approaches, we used a Norwegian version of ASSIST (Approaches to Study Skills for Students), which measures the three main approaches through six questions for each of them. One hundred and six students responded to the survey. Not all students took the statements as appropriate:

I see these issues as more aimed at students coming straight from high school . . . so please make questions that are attuned to your audience – we are between 30-60 years [old] and have valuable work experience that would have contributed to a more customised programme.

(our translation)

Table 8.2 Compared results from ASSIST

Approaches to learning	Courses		
	Statics, NTNU	*Hydrodynamics, NTNU*	*MBA, UiT*
Strategic learning	11,17	13,08	14,46
Surface learning	13,53	14,26	14,52
Deep learning	9,36	13,93	14,27

Note. The table show the summation of tendencies in the subject where increased score indicates tendency.

This student promotes some of the criticisms that have been levelled against both the whole SAL tradition and the survey instruments (Haggis 2003; Webb 1997; Sjølie, in press).

The same survey has also been used by Gynnild (2001), asking 470 full-time students in two technical subjects, statistics and hydrodynamics. Table 2 shows a comparison of MBA scores (variation in and between approaches) and results from Gynnild's survey.

All three approaches are found in both the NTNU (Norwegian University of Science and Technology) courses, however, there was a significant difference between the surface approach and the two others, particularly for the hydrodynamics course. The results are partly explained by the study structure and the study habits. For example, it emerged that apart from the last two weeks before the exam, students spent significantly fewer hours studying than stipulated (Gynnild 2001).

Similar differences in approach were not revealed for the MBA students. There were no significant differences between the different categories and neither variance nor standard deviation showed differences among the groups and variables. Instead, we found that many of the students combined all three strategies. The three statements that received the highest score (i.e. closer to 90 per cent of the respondents), represented, for example, each learning approach:

- When I read, I try to remember important data for future use (reproduction): 92.9 per cent.
- It is important for me to do really well in the courses (strategic): 89.9 per cent.
- The main reason why I study here is that I can learn more about subjects that really interest me (in-depth): 87.9 per cent.

The use of these approaches simultaneously is labelled as a disorganised learning approach and this is often linked to so-called "at-risk students". This means students with low performance and with difficulties completing the courses (Pettersen, 2010). Although the dropout rate was not particularly high for this group; the exam results indicate that many of the students were closer to mere survival than to Bildung.

What determines the students' approaches to learning?

Why is it that this group of students, many of them in interesting and responsible jobs and with a background that matches the MBA curriculum, appear as disorganised survivors?

There is, of course, no simple explanation to this, and the causes will vary with each person. Nevertheless, in this chapter we will elaborate on two main explanations, which also determine Academic Bildung in general: constant time pressure and the importance of perceived meaning.[2]

Constant time pressure

Deep learning is not only a question of reading more; an equally important prerequisite for addressing the most advanced taxonomic level is that students are given sufficient time to develop their advanced talents. Working with adults who are also flexible students for several years we have experienced that sufficient time for reading, processing, reflecting, and wondering is a kind of infrequent luxury most of them can't afford. In other words, their everyday studies seem to be far from the kind of Academic Bildung that Kant, Gadamer, Grundtvig, or even Barnett advocate.

In the research on what determines students' learning approaches, emphasis is placed on their interpretation of the learning task and learning situation. More specifically, it has been found that perceived workload is one of the factors that most strongly promotes surface learning (Pettersen 2008). This is also something Gynnild (2001) elaborates in his study.

When dealing with mature flexible students, the perceived workload must, however, not be restricted to the reading and writing; it must include their total life situation. The studies are closely embedded in their everyday life, a point of view emphasized by the MBA students themselves:

> I'm following the lectures this semester. But with three young children with homework from school and leisure activities in addition to a demanding job with long hours, there is little time left. I spent the night studying and cut out exercise. So life is too hectic to study right now. I'm following the lectures and find them very interesting. When the kids get older I will again have the opportunity to study. The study is great, so therefore I will attend until Christmas. But since my employer didn't give me leave for exams and lectures on campus . . . I can't use my 5 weeks of holiday. Sadly. Excellent teachers and very exciting. But at the present time there is not enough time. Since I do not get leave from work it is impossible. The programme is well organised and you motivate your students well ☺!

In their comments about the study, it is not the joy of deep learning, creativity, and existential experiences that dominate, but rather critical views, particularly related to three factors: administration/organisation of the programme, the programme structure, and their lack of time to study. Some students go as far as to say that their study and learning processes have made them more embarrassed than existentially touched. Moreover, their ideal study model was far from promoting the ideals of Academic Bildung as outlined in this book. In an already disciplined and structured study programme, the students wanted even more structure, at the expense of the autonomous and authentic learning experience. They wanted everything clearly defined in advance, to be told what to do, what to learn, and especially which part of the syllabus they should bother to read. Their comments thus provide the impression that many of the students, because of their "overloaded" life situation, wanted to get through "as cheaply as possible". This seems to be of more importance than their learning-related outcomes.

The above quoted student highlights one of the main dilemmas faced by flexible or net-based students: is it possible to combine the need for academic reflection and contemplation with the obligations of everyday life? These students are also employees or executive directors, parents, politicians, bridge players or eager squash players in their spare time. Too often the result is given in advance; in the competition between academic work and the obligations related to job and family, the latter usually wins. In a larger survey of mature flexible students in Norwegian higher education, 55 per cent reported that they had to spend so much time on family and friends that it had negative effects on the studies, 37 per cent were not up-to-date with their progression, and 42 per cent described their behaviour as "on and off". At the same time, only 8.5 per cent were given opportunities to study while at work. In addition, their conditions for studying at home were far from satisfactory. Two-thirds said that they too often were disturbed while working, and almost one-third said that their study habits had developed for the worse over time (Grepperud et al. 2006).

Several international studies have identified the pressures of family and work combined with constant time pressure as the main reasons for dropping out of net-based studies. In an Australian study, 756 former students were asked why they had dropped out: 45 per cent said it was because of their job situation and 56 per cent said it was due to family or personal reasons (Kirkby 2000). In Ashby's (2004) survey the drop-out students said that it was primarily because they were behind with their studies or because of the situation at home or at work. In a similar Swedish study (Westerberg and Mårald 2005) 76 per cent of the drop-out students answered that lack of time and too much to do at work were the main reasons.

So where do these somewhat gloomy perspectives leave us?

First of all it tells us that changing study conditions by no means imply an easier route towards Academic Bildung. There is obviously a price to be paid when giving the students the possibility to attend more flexible study programmes. In particular, it presupposes an even more conscious self-regulation and a stronger self-discipline than in the ordinary on-campus full-time studies. For these flexible students there is much truth in the saying that "*I will* is just as important as IQ".

The question is then, are the mature flexible students willing to pay this price? Some are, others are not. Our dilemma so far is that too many are looking for the easy way out. Our evaluation of the MBA programme has revealed one of the paradoxes associated with flexibility. Expanded access to higher education combined with a flexible study situation makes more students enrol. At the same time an increasing number of students are challenged by factors that make it very difficult to safeguard their own learning process. Possibly the result of more net-based education will be that Academic Bildung is reserved for the few, the truly dedicated who like to have or consciously create the time and space that is required for the study. Maybe it is primarily those who already have acquired Academic Bildung who are the most successful, with the result that Academic Bildung maintains its status as an elite phenomenon.

The importance of perceived meaning

To understand the MBA students we also have to take into account their interpretations and experiences with the programme content and tasks. A crucial factor determining the students' motivation and learning outcomes is perceived meaning, i.e. how the curriculum in one way or other "grabs hold of" and affects students' experience, identity, and life world. This is expressed through the individuals' experience of relevance, detection, utility, application, understanding and motivation. Perceived meaning is, as Bengtsson (1993) puts it, how students rediscover themselves in theory. The phrase "in one way or the other" is consciously chosen because it does not always seem obvious, or given, how and why good matches between subjects and person occur or evolve. There are several factors that determines how students experience and perform a task, whether they have applied their strengths/interests (personal value), the joy of solving the task (intrinsic value), and benefits and costs associated with solving the task (Skaalvik and Skaalvik 2005).

The Norwegian philosopher Anders Lindseth is an eager spokesman for the necessary link between the students' life experiences and Academic Bildung. In his opinion today's Scandinavian higher education is characterised by a fundamental breach between the students' life worlds, the content, and the way the academic curriculum is defined and disseminated. This promotes, in his opinion, an inverted Bildung ideal which belittles the individual's experiences at the expense of authoritative forms of understanding. For Lindseth this is just "academic snobbery". For him, the preconditions for Academic Bildung are the reflections that articulate "lived world conditions". It is what Lindseth calls integrated knowledge

(2009), and the parallel to Barnett's "educational voice" is obvious. Both relate to the student's own personal experiences of "being-in-the-world" and of the construction of meaning.

Not surprisingly, we find that a deep learning approach is best spurred by a subject matter that interests and engages. For this reason, it is also suggested that there is a close and mutual relationship between intrinsic motivation and deep approach (Harper and Kember 1986; Richardson 1994; Grepperud 2007; Pettersen 2008). Within the SAL (Student Approaches to Learning) tradition it is relatively well-documented that mature students appear more deep- or meaning-oriented than younger students (Richardson 1994, 1997, 2000; Grepperud 2007). This is explained by referring to mature students' previous school experiences, their motivation/choice of studies, and their life experiences (Grepperud 2007).

Both Lindseth's line of arguments and the results from the SAL tradition support the basic tenet of any form of training: the importance of linking individual experience with content. Academic Bildung is only possible when the content is acknowledged as meaningful and relevant. If not, knowledge and learning become nothing more than an "outer cognitive shell" with minimum influence on personal behaviour and development. In such cases students may be knowledgeable, but hardly wise. They can probably define or explain excellent leadership; they might even be able to critique concepts and theories of leadership. But if they are unable to exercise it, have they really understood what it is about?

A study investigated the study strategies of adult miners following a vocational training programme alongside their work. Students were asked to complete the Learning and Study Strategies Inventory (LASSI) survey. Based on the results from this survey the students were interviewed about their study strategies and study habits. The survey showed that overall, students scored somewhat below average, but the interviews revealed major differences between subjects. In a subject like mathematics, most students had major problems, primarily because almost all of them lacked some of the basic knowledge. As a consequence the students' work on the subject was characterised by inadequate approaches and strategies. The motivation and effort they put into their work decreased as they failed, not only for mathematics but for the whole programme. As one of them said, it was more inspirational doing the washing up than doing mathematics. Over time, the majority of the students were considering dropping out.

However, it turned out that when the same students were reading geology, they approached the subject matter in a very different way. They encountered content that they understood, were interested in, and had, to some degree, experienced in their job. In meeting this subject content their descriptions of their learning approaches were consistent with the deep approach. They tried to identify the main points, reflected on interesting topics, connected the content to their own jobs, and worked in a focused manner (Grepperud 2009).

To sum up, an important premise in this chapter is that Bildung must relate to the individual's perceived meaning. The very foundation of Academic Bildung is located in the relationship between the individual's personal experiences (in the widest sense) and the reservoir of academic knowledge. Without meaning there is no education, merely replication. Perceived meaning is a relational phenomenon that occurs as a result of the encounter between subject and person. Hence, Academic Bildung is neither concerned unilaterally with content (material Bildung) nor form (formal Bildung), but resides in the relationship between form, content and person. And it is our task as educators in higher education to strengthen these relationships and connections.

From curriculum to wisdom

This book addresses how universities and colleges can meet the challenge of Academic Bildung in their net-based education. The answer is partly dependent on which group of students we are talking about. The MBA student group, i.e. mature, flexible and part-time students combining work and studies, will become an increasingly important target for higher education in Scandinavia. Furthermore, the trend is that the students who up until now have been characterised as young and full-time, will to a greater extent combine work and study, as documented in Chapter 4. Consequently, the number of part-time students is growing.

The longing for a revival of the full-time student in Scandinavian higher education seems like a lost case. We have to search elsewhere if we want to improve learning and Bildung. In accordance with our line of argument in this chapter, we find a possible solution in challenging the rather "neurotic" focus on curriculum and replacing it with a much stronger emphasis on deep/higher learning qualities rooted in the participants' experiences and lives. Our metaphorical claim is "a transformation from reading to studying".

All too often learning at a higher level is confused with an extended curriculum, i.e. more advanced learning presupposes reading more books, writing more papers, or doing numerous exams. The idea of Academic Bildung forces us to re-examine this long-held assumption. Maybe it is time take an opposite view, that it's necessary to reduce the curriculum in order to give students the opportunity to get deeper into the subject, to reflect and wonder. In other words, is it possible that "less is more"?

The challenge is for teachers and students to fill this new "space of learning" with meaningful and challenging activities. It presupposes a relationship between teacher and students, and between students and peers, characterised by equality and mutual recognition. In the adult educational context, this was pointed out by Illeris (2007) in particular. He believes that teachers in adult education should not enter into a clearly defined teacher role, but instead be themselves in relation to their adult participants. At the same time, the teachers must fulfil their duty to support and facilitate the participants' learning, not least as a dialogue partner. In addition, the teacher has to contribute to a constructive existential unrest by always challenging the participants' insights. This constructive instability will also contribute to an attitude to learning and development characterised by openness, curiosity and the quest as Solberg and Hansen underline in Chapter 3.

Although it might sound alluring, such intentions are not easily realised. Many flexible students might find it tempting to reduce their own activity instead of doing the opposite. It would possibly contribute to a better conscience, but probably not to Academic Bildung, seeing as this for many is perceived as a zero-sum game where less on the curriculum implies more time for other "duties".

So what about ICT and the many net-based and digital solutions – will these come to our aid as promised by the powerful ICT rhetoric? In our case, there is no evidence to support this. The MBA case study does not have much to say about the net, or its potential, partly because the students did not make substantial use of these resources. Digital learning resources must be used if they are to matter!

Moreover, through this case study we want to highlight that net-based solutions are by no means a short cut to better learning or Academic Bildung. The answer to how Academic Bildung is to be realised is so far not to be found in the technology as such. This is also the conclusion in a larger meta-study conducted for the federal Department of Education in the United States. In this report a comparison was made of students' learning outcomes in online versus regular (face-to-face) teaching. The findings suggest, first of all, that students in online/web-supported programmes did better than those who followed the same teaching face-to-face. Further the report concluded that students who followed the so-called hybrid models, i.e. combined online and conventional education, did better than those who only followed net-based programme. Upon further analysis it was found, however, that the crucial point was neither the models per se, nor the media, but rather how the teaching and learning processes were designed. The variations were partly explained by the teaching aids, learning methods, students' work, and not least the time spent studying (Means et al. 2010).

To sum up, the MBA case has shown us that the road to Academic Bildung is simple but challenging. It all comes down to what we have always known; it depends on hard work, both from the students and their teachers. Our duty as teachers is to make this a meaningful journey, net-based or not.

Notes

1 Our translation.
2 The results may also be due to weaknesses in the survey instrument. Within the SAL tradition it has been found that these instruments do not always give unambiguous results. Not only have they produced results that could be interpreted

as contradictory (Busato et al. 1998; Vermetten et al. 1999), it has also proved difficult to reproduce exactly the main dimensions (Richardson 2000). Surveys have also revealed other learning approaches than the three used here. This is explained by contextual factors.

References

Anderson, L. W. and Krathwohl, D. R. (2001). *A taxonomy for learning, teaching, and assessing: a revision of Bloom's taxonomy of educational objectives.* Longman: New York.

Ashby, A. (2004). "Monitoring student retention in the Open University: Definition, measurement, interpretation and action", *Open Learning: The Journal of Open, Distance and e-Learning,* vol. 19, pp. 65–77.

Barnett, R. (2007). *A will to learn: Being a student in an age of uncertainty.* Open University Press: Maidenhead, UK.

Bengtsson, J. (1993). "Theory and practice: Two fundamental categories in the philosophy of teacher education", *Educational Review,* vol. 45, no. 3, pp. 205–11.

Biggs, J. B. and Collis, K. F. (1982). *Evaluating the quality of learning: The SOLO taxonomy.* Academic Press: New York.

Bostad, I. (2009). "Kunnskap og dannelse foran et nytt århundre - innstilling fra Dannelsesutvalget for høyere utdanning", Universitetet i Oslo: Oslo.

Busato, V. V., Prins, F. J., Elshout, J. J. and Hamaker, C. (1998). "Learning styles: A cross-sectional and longitudinal study in higher education", *British Journal of Educational Psychology,* vol. 68, pp. 427–41.

Cohen, J. D., Mcclure, S. M. and Yu, A. J. (2007). "Should I stay or should I go? How the human brain manages the trade-off between exploitation and exploration", *Philosophical Transactions of the Royal Society B: Biological Sciences,* vol. 362, no. 1481, pp. 933–42.

Diseth, Å. and Martinsen, Ø. (2003). "Approaches to learning, cognitive style, and motives as predictors of academic achievement", *Educational Psychology,* vol. 23, pp. 195–207.

Entwistle, N. J. (2005). "Contrasting perspectives on learning". In: Marton, F., Hounsell, D. and Entwistle, N., eds., *The experience of learning: Implications for teaching and studying in higher education.* University of Edinburgh, Centre for Teaching, Learning and Assessment: Edinburgh.

Entwistle, N. J. and Peterson, E. R. (2004). "Conceptions of learning and knowledge in higher education: Relationships with study behaviour and influences of learning environments", *International Journal of Educational Research,* vol. 41, pp. 407–28.

Gibbs, G. (1992). *Improving the quality of student learning.* Technical and Education Services: Bristol, UK.

Grepperud, G. (2007). "Til skjells år og alder? En drøfting av studie- og læringsorienteringer hos voksne studenter", *Nordic Studies in Education,* vol. 27.

Grepperud, G. (2009). *Fra gruvegang til skolegang.* U-vett. Universitetet i Tromsø: Tromsø, NO.

Grepperud, G., Rønning, W. M., Støkken, A. M. (2006), *Studier og hverdagsliv: Voksne studenter i fleksibel læring.* Tapir Akademisk Forlag: Trondheim, NO.

Gynnild, V. (2001). "Læringsorientert eller eksamensfokusert? Nærstudier av pedagogisk utviklingsarbeid i sivilingeniørstudiet" [report]. Fakultet for samfunnsvitenskap og teknologiledelse, Pedagogisk institutt, Norges teknisk-naturvitenskapelige universitet, Trondheim, NO.

Haggis, T. (2003). "Constructing images of ourselves? A critical investigation into 'approaches to learning' research in higher education", *British Educational Research Journal*, vol. 29, pp. 89–104.

Hagtvedt, B. (2009). "Kunnskap og dannelse foran et nytt århundre. Høyere utdanning og forskning i Norge møter den globaliserte verden". In: Bostad, I., ed., *Kunnskap og dannelse foran et nytt århundre*. Dannelsesutvalget, Universitetet i Oslo: Oslo.

Harper, G. and Kember, D. (1986). "Approaches to study of distance education students". *British Journal of Educational Technology*, vol. 17, pp. 212–22.

Illeris, K. (2007). *How we learn learning and non-learning in school and beyond*. Routledge: London.

Kirkby, K. (2000). "'I am still studying, I just have not finished': Research into the reasons for student non-completion at OTEN-DE". In: Australian Vocational Education and Training Research Association. *Future research, research futures:* proceedings of the third national conference of the Australian Vocational Education and Training Research Association (AVETRA), Alexandria, NSW.

Lindseth, A. (2009). "Dannelsens plass i profesjonsutdanninger". In: Bostad, I., ed., *Kunnskap og dannelse foran et nytt århundre*. Dannelsesutvalget, Universitetet i Oslo: Oslo.

March, J. G. (1991). "Exploration and exploitation in organizational learning", *Organization Science*, vol. 2, pp. 71–87.

Means, B., Toyama, Y., Murphy, R., Bakia, M. and Jones, K. (2009). "Evaluation of evidence-based practices in online learning: A meta-analysis and review of online learning" [report]. Center for Technology in Learning, U.S. Department of Education. Available online at http:// http://eric.ed.gov/?id=ED505824 (accessed 18 Sept. 2014).

Pettersen, R. (2004). "Studenters lærings- og studiestrategier: Kvalitetsindikatorer i høgre utdanning?" *Uniped*, vol. 27, pp. 44–65.

Pettersen, R. C. (2008). *Studenters læring*. Universitetsforlaget: Oslo.

Pettersen, R. C. (2010). *Lärandets hur*. Studentlitteratur: Lund, SE.

Prosser, M., Trigwell, K. (1999). *Understanding learning and teaching: The experience in higher education*. Society for Research into Higher Education; Open University Press: Buckingham, UK.

Richardson, J. T. E. (1994). "Mature students in higher education: I. A literature survey on approaches to studying". *Studies in Higher Education*, vol. 19, no. 3, pp. 309–25.

Richardson, J. T. E. (1997). "Dispelling some myths about mature students in higher education: Study skills, approaches to studying, and intellectual ability". In: Sutherland, P., ed., *Adult learning: A reader*. Kogan Page: London.

Richardson, J. T. E. (2000). *Researching student learning: Approaches to studying in campus-based and distance education*. Society for Research into Higher Education; Open University Press: Buckingham, UK.

Sjølie, E. (2014), "Pedagogy is just common sense: A case study of student teachers' academic learning practices" [PhD thesis]. Norwegian University of Science and Technology, Trondheim, NO.

Skaalvik, E. M. and Skaalvik, S. (2005). *Skolen som læringsarena: Selvoppfatning, motivasjon og læring*. Universitetsforlaget: Oslo.

Solberg, M. and Fossland, T. (2013). "Akademisk danning – et mulig prosjekt for voksne studenter I fleksible studier?" In: Arbo, P., ed., *Utdanningssamfunnet og livslang læring: Festskrift til Gunnar Grepperud.* Gyldendal Akademisk: Oslo.

Vermetten, Y. J., Vermunt, J. D. and Lodewijks, H. G. (1999). "A longitudinal perspective on learning strategies in higher education - Different viewpoints towards development", *British Journal of Educational Psychology,* vol. 69, pp. 221–42.

Volet, S. E. and Chalmers, D. (1992). "Investigation of qualitative differences in university students' learning goals. Based on an unfolding model of stage development", *British Journal of Educational Psychology,* vol. 62, pp. 17–34.

Webb, G. (1997). "Deconstructing deep and surface: Towards a critique of phenomenography", *Higher Education,* vol. 33, pp. 195–212.

Westerberg, P. and Mårald, G. (2005). "Avbrott på nätuniversitetsutbildningar. Höstterminen 2003 – vårterminen 2004 – när och varför gör studenter avbrott?" Umeå Universitet: Umeå, SE.

9 Interprofessional net-based health education

A possibility to move beyond learning?

Trine Fossland

Introduction

Learning across disciplines has become more significant in the education of healthcare workers as evidence emerges that effective teamwork enhances the quality of patient care and cost-effective service provision (WHO 2012). This can be seen in relation to challenges associated with large student groups and the current discourse addressing the need for more interprofessional knowledge, skills and general competences[1]. Interprofessional education (IPE) can be defined as curricular activities in which students from different professional programs learn from, with and about each other (CAIPE 1997; Thistlethwaite 2012; Barr et al. 2005; Hjerpaasen et al. 2012; Wilhelmsson 2011). Interprofessional net-based courses have emerged as a solution to the facilitation of this interprofessionality within healthcare educations. In this chapter Academic Bildung is addressed in relation to an interprofessional introductory course (HEL-FEL) for 650 students at the Faculty of Health Sciences at UiT The Arctic University of Norway. This interprofessional course included ten different disciplines of first semester healthcare students who studied together in a net-based course as a joint introductory part of their more discipline-oriented programmes. In order to determine whether it is possible to facilitate the development of Academic Bildung in a net-based course with students from ten different healthcare professions, the aim of the study is to identify dimensions of Academic Bildung expressed in the plans, curricula and surveys/interviews done with people involved in this particular endeavour. My research question is therefore: Is it possible to move beyond learning in an interprofessional net-based health education?

In this chapter I address the four voices – "the voice of knowing" "the voice of doing", "the voice of being" and "the voice of the phenomenon"[2] – as they are described in Chapter 3 as four fundamentally different but inter-relating orientations within higher education. According to Barnett (2007) the voice of doing and knowing is connected to standards, norms and the pedagogical side of education (the pedagogical voices) that is realized through autonomy. The educational side of education (the pedagogical voice) is realized through authencity, and has do with the students' own personal experience, engagement and the process of "self-becoming". This can be understood as an approach to life, thinking, and criticality that a university-educated person should aspire to: to become critically able to engage with the world, and themselves as well as, through knowledge. According to Barnett this must be accompanied by a movement into authenticity. These four orientations that we have earlier called the "four-voiced" Bildung pedagogy is a way to clear a space for the more existential and ontological dimensions in university education and the understanding of Academic Bildung. In Chapter 3 Solberg and Hansen defined Academic Bildung as critical, emancipatory, and society-oriented reflection as well as a dimension of ethical-existential and being-oriented reflection (p. 28). They argued that there are both content and attitudinal sides of Bildung. The content side deals with the cultural content, in a wide sense, which students meet in their education. The attitudinal side of Academic Bildung concerns the formation of identity, both the ethical and the existential sides of education (op. cit). Can this double-tracked view on Academic Bildung, the four voices and the more existential and ontological dimension of higher education, be identified within this particular interprofessional course design that is presented in this case study? Before I present the findings related to this particular case, I will discuss the methods used.

The case study, the data and methods used

As a response to demands for new competence, skills and general knowledge among future healthcare students, the Faculty of Health Sciences at the Arctic University of Norway initiated a 10-credit interprofessional course for all the faculty's first-year students. The Faculty of Health Sciences has pointed out that in order to be successful in educating health professionals with the skills required in the future, all health sciences students must experience interdisciplinary collaboration related to specific patient situations and different topics. The interprofessional course was first implemented as a pilot in autumn 2011[3] and was fully implemented in the autumn of 2012 for about 650 students. It includes ten different health programmes, based on the concept of interprofessional collaborative learning.

To determine whether it is possible to facilitate Academic Bildung in this net-based course with students from ten different healthcare professions, some of the main parts of the course design with expressed intentions of facilitating Bildung-dimensions are investigated. The dimensions of Academic Bildung are expressed in the plans, curricula, and notes from meetings. In order to address the possibility of facilitating Academic Bildung, data from process documents, qualitative interviews, observation, and different questionnaires are analysed. I have operationalised my investigation into four sections: 1) the facilitation of content in the course design, 2) how the development of an interprofessional identity is organised, 3) how the relational part of the course is facilitated, and 4) the facilitation of dialogues and discussions as a learning activity.

In many studies, the learning environment or course design are investigated through the perceptions of the students. For instance, in Trigwell and Ashwin (2006), the learning environment was studied with a focus on the variables concerning students' perceptions of good teaching, clear goals, appropriate assessment, and appropriate workload. In the present study, the students' perceptions are captured in my search for Academic Bildung dimensions through questionnaires, including some with open answers, and official documents, evaluations, and observation. These empirical data are seen in relation to the expressed intentions of facilitating Academic Bildung in the official documents (such as the curricula, official documents, minutes from meetings etc.). The study is therefore conducted through a multi-methodology approach to the data from different sources. This method of data collection makes it possible to obtain answers to the questions from a number of perspectives. When one source of data does not provide all the information required, others may cover a broader part of the picture. This means that the quantitative and qualitative data collection and analyses in this single study are integrated (Creswell 2003). The value of this approach is that I get different data connected to the same course design. The weakness is that not all of the questionnaires have a good response rate, and that some of them have a broader viewpoint than this particular study. The following empirical data are used:

Online questionnaire 1

This was distributed to the 200 students who attended the pilot phase; 88 out of 200 answered. Nearly all of these answers came from students in psychology, since the majority of the students attending the pilot programme were from this subject. Only a few cross-disciplinary groups were represented (40 students).

Online questionnaire 2

This was distributed to the 650 students who attended the first inter-professional course: Only 196 out of 650 responded to the survey (from 26 November to 7 December in 2012). Nearly two-thirds of the responses (121 of 194) were students in the three programmes with the most students: psychology, medicine and nursing.

Interviews and observation

Both formal and informal qualitative interviews were conducted with people representing faculty management, participants in the steering group (every discipline was represented in both of these groups), supervisors, and seminar leaders. Both the board meetings and work group meetings (with all disciplines represented) were observed.

Documents

The following documents were analysed: 1) process documents from both the steering committee and working group meetings; 2) minutes from meetings and all possible and available descriptions relevant for the study; 3) internal evaluations (both done by myself and the faculty, similar to the questionnaire mentioned above, and one done by faculty staff among supervisors), etc.; 4) an independent external research report from a research institute focusing on the implementation and the process both from an instrumental and an institutional perspective (Gaski 2013). Different members of the steering group and personnel were also interviewed in this rapport, so there are several interesting parts in the report (particularly related to the leader's role) that were only covered by observation in my own research.

The data in the first questionnaire is from the pilot phase of the course. This is still interesting as it demonstrates challenges and viewpoints that were forming the process from the very start. The interval of 26 November 2012 to 15 June 2013 is the main period for the data collection. Firstly, student perceptions of their course experience within a net-based course design are considered using questionnaires 1 and 2. I examine how these topics relate to the research question and the different data. To investigate how the development of Academic Bildung was facilitated and interwoven in the course design, there was a need to use all of the different types of data.

Results and discussion

The research question is related to the conditions for the facilitation of Academic Bildung dimensions in a particular course. Since one of the main aims of the study was to identify dimensions of Academic Bildung as expressed in the plans and curricula of this particular course design, this is where I start this investigation. Another aim was to investigate the surveys/interviews to find out whether the development of Academic Bildung was facilitated in this net-based course, and to explore this I chose to look closer at some of the main aspects of the course design: the facilitation of the development of a cross-professional identity, the socialisation into the academic culture, and the approach to critical thinking, as these can be understood as aspects related to a concept of Academic Bildung. In this empirical part, the understanding of Academic Bildung is presented and operationalised into these four different sections:

1   Academic Bildung dimensions in the description of the course design,
2   Academic Bildung dimensions related to the development of an interprofessional identity,
3   Academic Bildung as socialisation into the academic culture, and
4   Academic Bildung related to the facilitation of critical thinking in net-based discussions.

Within these four empirical designations I am interested in the common academic values the students meet as they are closely related to generic skills and the development of an identity as a healthcare worker. I investigate whether, in interrelational settings, the students' formation address the four voices of higher education, "the voice of knowing", "the voice of doing", "the voice of being" and "the voice of the phenomenon". Or is the students' approach to higher education more aligned to their own disciplines within this particular course design? Are the students moving beyond learning in accordance with the double-tracked concept of Academic Bildung presented in Chapter 3? In the two last parts, I am interested in the more relational sides of the course design, as the students' socialisation into a specific academic environment and culture can be of great importance to their development of Academic Bildung. As interprofessional discussions were seen as important for the students' Academic Bildung process, and this was expressed in the formal description of this particular course design, the last section focuses more specifically on the facilitation of the dialogues and discussions as learning activities to investigate whether the development of critical thinking skills were supported.

Academic Bildung dimensions in the description of the course design

In the descriptions of the course design several of the goals for the students' development addressed both critical, ethical-existential, society-oriented and being-oriented reflections. The content side of Academic Bildung can be said to deal with the cultural content that students meet in their education. In this particular interprofessional health course the importance of using an outcome based approach to the content and course design was highlighted from the very start of the planning process, however, their ambitions toward several Academic Bildung dimensions were also clearly expressed in the course design. Several generic academic skills associated with becoming an academically oriented person were expressed as goals in this study. The learning objectives were related to becoming critical beings (Barnett 1997), expressed as learning academic values in an academic context, approaching a critical use of literature and net-based resources, producing written and oral presentations of academic material, and being responsible for reflecting on their own learning. The cross-disciplinary learning goals included generic competences and knowledge about the healthcare system, developing the students' ability to discuss ethical issues, understanding different knowledge forms in health science, and learning different communication and constructive problem-solving skills. To achieve the relevant knowledge, skills and general competences involved in this interprofessional health course, students were required to follow the content organised in four different "knowledge pathways":

1) Information literacy (learning in an academic context)

In this part, the students had to do a self-test and answer some questions about plagiarism. The supervisor's task was to approve the assignment online (answers existed, and this was accomplished with the teachers having minimal direct contact with the students).

2) Writing course

This part required two posts related to reading a scholarly text to be submitted in a net-based forum. Students also had to submit a text and get feedback from a peer. The supervisor's tasks were to oversee and give comments on the net-based discussions the day they were supposed to be delivered (if necessary), approve them, and make sure the students fulfilled the requirements.

3) Ethics and communication

In this part, the students were required to post four contributions to net-based discussions. This was, however, only required from the students from biomedicine, pharmacy and psychology. The other students were to participate in three group meetings and seminars. The supervisor's tasks were to give supervision in two meetings, participate in seminar discussions, and to give approval based on students' presence and activity.

4) Knowledge about the healthcare system and structure

In this part, the students listened to a net-based lecture and answered questions related to this lecture.

All four parts of the course design included Academic Bildung dimensions, with the intention of strengthening the students' formation process and their generic knowledge, skills and competences as students and healthcare workers. The learning outcomes were closely related to the development of generic skills and core values associated both with the university community as a whole (information literacy, writing course) and their identity as healthcare workers (ethics, communication, and knowledge about the healthcare system and structure). At the same time, the tasks were also discipline specific (they had to find and work with literature in collaboration with peers from their own discipline). Students had to read, write and discuss content intended to support their understanding of their position as future healthcare workers. This can be related to both the content and the attitudinal sides of Academic Bildung.

As the intention was that the students had to work in a net-based learning environment, they also trained their familiarity with general net-based competences. The students submitted their assessment texts online. The exam content was directly connected to the different learning paths and described learning outcomes, formulated in two parts:

1   Text on knowledge in the health sciences. Work began immediately in the learning path for writing academic texts (see the first learning path above), where students gave each other feedback on the draft text based on certain guidelines. The final text was available online prior to the deadline for submission for the exam.

2   One case related to patient care and the learning path "knowledge about healthcare system" was given (see the fourth learning pathway). Students received a written case report that described a patient's medical history and family situation. On the basis of literature and online lectures students were expected to describe the patient's complex problems and probable journey through the healthcare system. This paper was also delivered online.

The assessments were also meant to strengthen the students' critical thinking, their society-oriented reflection and autonomy. The written case that described a patient's medical history and family situation involved the complexity of a patient's life and health situation, and was also meant to stimulate the ethical dimensions of human formation and self-formation, as these elements are involved in all meetings between patients and health care workers. The assessment was aimed at developing the students' existential and being-oriented reflections, as these are closely related to authenticity.

To summarise, all four thematic parts in the course design were facilitated to strengthen the students' development of Academic Bildung. The learning goals of the generic academic skills were related to learning academic values in an academic context. The cross-disciplinary learning goals included knowledge about the healthcare system, being able to discuss ethical issues, understanding different knowledge forms in health sciences, and learning different communication and constructive problem-solving skills. The development of the students both as critical beings, as Barnett describes it, and the autonomy, authenticity and general knowledge involved in becoming a healthcare worker were clearly expressed in the description of the course design. In the next section I will discuss the interprofessional dimensions of the course design in more detail.

Academic Bildung and the development of an interprofessional identity

Tomorrow's healthcare professionals are expected to have developed common generic knowledge and system understanding, insight into their roles in patient care, and respect for and expertise in interdisciplinary collaboration. This requires a broad and common interprofessional educational knowledge platform involving cooperation between disciplines in their healthcare education (Det Kongelige Helse og Omsorgsdepartementet 2008–09), i.e. students need to get to know other disciplines than their own. In the theoretical section, interprofessional collaborative learning was defined as students from various disciplines who learn from, with, and about each other (Barr et al. 2005; Hjerpaasen et al. 2012; Wilhelmsson 2011). Interprofessionality was one of the main ideas aimed at ensuring students developed what was called a "double identity", related both to the disciplinary part of their future occupation (as nurses, doctors, psychologists and so on) and the more interdisciplinary parts. The purpose of this section is to investigate whether these intentions of interprofessionality addressed dimensions of Academic Bildung, as this can challenge the traditional profession-specific approach to health education.

One main point in the facilitation of interprofessional learning in the course was to support collaboration between disciplines. The reports from students (both questionnaires) demonstrated that their collaboration was very limited. The implementation process described step by step in documents, interviews and surveys revealed several challenges related to the development of a double identity/interprofessionality and other Academic Bildung-oriented dimensions. It has been a top-down process; the time aspect has been problematic because of a tight planning schedule; the training of supervisors has not been well organised; the use of internal evaluations has not been exploited well enough to adjust to the different study approaches; and challenges related to organisation and coordination have not been implemented well enough between the different disciplines. Other challenges were also mentioned in Gaski's (2013) report:

- Lack of common understanding of the different tasks involved in the course design.
- Different professional standpoints and practices made it difficult to establish a common basis for interaction and solving tasks.
- Lack of willingness to collaborate and interact among specific disciplines, because they defined their needs differently.
- Lack of foundation for the development of an interprofessional identity (they had not developed their own disciplinary identity yet).
- Lack of resources, expertise or legitimacy.
- Too large ambitions and expectations about what was possible to achieve with the project's limited time resources.
- Challenges related to different experiences with the use of technology.
- Large variations in exam results between programmes which have contributed to a challenging marking process.

The conclusion from analysing documents and internal evaluations is that this collaboration clearly needed a more thoughtful organisation. Even though the idea was that the collaboration between different disciplines would strengthen the development of a professional identity from the very start of the students' education, the faculty leadership did not allow enough time in the process to ensure that the administrative and academic personnel within the different disciplines were sufficiently involved in the decision making (op.cit). Interviews revealed that many felt that decisions were made before the meetings. To some extent the result was that the different disciplines "lived their own lives" because of the tight deadlines, outside the formal structure that was decided upon. The lack of foundation and development of the interdisciplinary parts of the course design was also related to the fact that some felt that the content had too weak a connection to their own subject (for instance some felt that the video content was not suitable for all disciplines). Instead, different values and traditions shaped local solutions that merged into the local facilitation in their own discipline, different forms of teaching and ways of relating to the content. This may have hindered the possibilities for collaboration and the formation of the students' identity as healthcare workers, insight into other disciplines, and their development of Academic Bildung.

Dissimilar professional standpoints and practices within the different disciplines made it difficult to establish common ground for interaction, especially with regard to the question related to meetings with patients. When different students were supposed to, for example, discuss filmed cases online, some personnel from the disciplines felt that these kinds of questions and meeting with patients could only be discussed in a live setting. Gaski (2013) points out that another problematic issue has been the variation in exam results for autumn 2012, which demonstrated that there were relatively large differences between the programmes in terms of failure rates. The proportion of failures for the pharmacy and nursing programmes was over 40 per cent, for the physiotherapists and radiographers 21 and 20 respectively, and for psychology 12 per cent that year. The programmes for bioengineering, occupational therapy and dental hygiene had zero failures. The large differences in results between programmes were linked to the fact that the instructions for the teachers who carried out the marking were perceived as unclear and the guidance was problematic (op.cit). The lack of willingness to make the students collaborate in the shared online course design seemed to hinder collaboration between the disciplines. This limited the students' opportunities to discuss and strengthen their development of Academic Bildung related to their interprofessional (double) identity and to relate to other disciplines.

To summarise, the development of generic cross-disciplinary knowledge, skills and competences related to being a healthcare worker were seen as an important part of the course design as well as the development of the students' "double identity". The findings have demonstrated that both timing and collaboration between the organisers, teachers, supervisors and peers are essential. However the surveys, interviews and documents revealed several challenges. To succeed with the interprofessional dimensions in this large course design, it seems essential that the implementation of the main ideas needs to be organised and facilitated in a way that the different disciplines can agree upon. To facilitate the students' movement beyond learning, central dimensions concerning the course design, such as better scheduling, real use of internal evaluations, and the framing of cooperation that all disciplines could relate to seem to be obvious and possible improvements. It is impossible to know whether this interprofessional health course would have been successful if these organisational challenges were solved, but one point is definitely obvious: several dimensions related to time and organisation can interrupt cooperation across disciplines and the formation of a double identity as a future healthcare worker.

Academic Bildung as socialisation into the academic culture

As discussed in the theoretical part, being socialised into an academic community –meeting with one's teacher, peers, and other personal connections related to one's study – is a fundamental part of the Academic Bildung process (Solberg and Fossland 2013). In line with the definition of Academic Bildung in Chapter 3, these relations can be seen as important sources to challenge and develop both critical thinking skills and society-oriented reflections as well as ethical formation and existential being-oriented reflections. The content and attitudinal-oriented sides of Academic Bildung can also be developed through supervision and other forms of social relations. In this interprofessional health course Academic Bildung can also be related to social networks between the participants in the course. This was not the case in this particular course design.

The findings demonstrate that many students did not, despite ample opportunity, take time to relate and discuss matters with teachers, supervisors and peers. Older students were leading many of the seminars, and some of them clearly did not spend much time discussing with the younger students the content and attitudinal parts of the tasks. One seminar leader said it like this:

> The different student groups got very dissimilar help. Some of the participants did not get help at all, and in my group the seminars only lasted for five minutes. It was difficult to learn anything from these meetings and to see the point of it.

The opportunities to develop stimulating social networks and connections with others are found to have a positive impact on students' learning outcomes and the development of the students' formation process as future employees (Sawir et al. 2008; Trowler 2010). But it was not only the students who were dissatisfied with the situation. The documents and interviews also refer to criticism related to the role of the supervisors. Some supervisors expressed that they felt frustration associated with their role. They observed students who did not learn what they were supposed to learn; one of them put it like this:

> Students say they want more feedback on what they do. Apart from verifying one work requirement, feedback is not our role as supervisors.

Only fellow students were giving feedback, and this was limited. As a pedagogical issue this was frustrating, because they do not put the same effort into the task. Later, when they were writing a paper . . . in my opinion, they needed extra lessons.

The empirical findings revealed that the supervision and contact with older students did not seem to contribute to challenging the students' knowledge and ideas or contribute to the students' development of Academic Bildung. Moreover, it seems as though the potential of working and communicating with peers or senior students, as discussed in Chapter 2, was not exploited as well as it could have been, mainly because of the lack of clear instructions and regulations for how the senior students were supposed to support and address a stimulating and challenging communication with the younger students. In this health course, the lack of opportunities to build social networks created a situation where several students felt alienated and socially isolated, feelings that have been found to be a common reason for some students dropping out from their studies or experiencing a decline in their learning outcomes (Ramburuth and McCormick 2001; Kim 2011). Despite these findings from other studies, the drop-out rate for this interprofessional health course was low. This may be due to the fact that they were heading for a longer journey as healthcare students, and that this particular introductory course was their ticket to continue this journey.

This dissatisfaction was considered in the internal evaluations. To support more collaboration in the net-based part of the programme a physical meeting between students from different disciplines was organised as a "kick-off party" at the beginning of the semester for student groups that were enrolled in 2013. It was arranged as "stations" where members of the different disciplines were given the opportunity to meet and talk about their work in an inspiring, informative, and creative way with students enrolled in the other study programmes. The purpose was to strengthen the social relationships across professions, and the idea was that if they got some face-to-face contact, the collaboration in the net-based course design would be easier. The present data do not enable me to confirm whether the collaboration was getting better or closer between the different groups of students in this net-based course subsequent to these changes, but I have data suggesting that many students participated in and appreciated this event at the beginning of the semester. Many of them said that this gave them an idea about other disciplines and that they became more aware of them after having been given a chance to interact with them.

In line with Ehlers (2004), the findings demonstrate that supervisor support, two-way communication, and interaction and collaboration between teacher and student are important conditions for the students' learning and their Academic Bildung processes. It is difficult to know whether a closer socialisation into the academic culture would have been a central source for the Academic Bildung dimensions related to these students, but it seems obvious that the environment does not facilitate close relations and socialisation into an academic culture in this net-based study. This finding can be understood in relation to studies that focus particularly on the situation of new students (Hovdhaugen and Aamodt 2009) and studies about international students (Ramburuth and McCormick 2001; Kim 2011), which conclude that the lack of opportunities to build social networks creates a situation where students often feel alienated and socially isolated.

To summarise, the findings demonstrate that the students were not sufficiently socialised into the academic community, which can be understood as a fundamental part of the Academic Bildung process. They were not sufficiently challenged nor critically involved in reasoning and reflections together with their teachers, peers and supervisors, to become what Barnett (1997) calls "critical beings". The facilitation of the collaboration did not develop their society-oriented reflections nor human formation, or self-formation or existential- and being-oriented reflections. As such, it can be argued that Academic Bildung, as defined in Chapter 3, did not appear to take place. In the next section I will go deeper into one of the most important learning activities to investigate in more detail.

Academic Bildung and the facilitation of critical thinking in net-based discussions

In this last section, I look more specifically into the facilitation of dialogues and discussions as a learning activity in order to investigate whether it supports Academic Bildung dimensions in the course design. As outlined in Chapter 3, these dimensions include the development of critical thinking skills, society-oriented reflections, and ethical dimensions of an existential and being-oriented nature. The facilitation of synchronous and asynchronous net-based discussions, which were motivated by filmed role-plays as a starting point, had the potential to move the students beyond subject learning. The idea was that the students could relate to "authentic" situations demonstrating patients and different healthcare workers "in action". This aimed at stimulating the students' formation process, and being an important source to existential and being-oriented reflections involving the students as persons.

In the survey, many students reported that discussions in the online groups were not adequate, and that the guidelines outlined were not good enough to ensure fruitful discussions. Several explanations were suggested. One respondent pointed to the tasks that were given, some to the fact that the group size was too big to get good discussions. Others indicated the fact that many students invested just a minimum of time and effort to deliver whatever was necessary to pass the minimum requirements related to their contributions in the discussions. Several students reported that other students just posted their contribution to the discussion in order to fulfil the participation requirements. Some students witnessed what they called "free riders" who virtually "copied" other's answers, making only small adjustments. Others thought some students posted a substantial contribution that they had prepared in advance, and then only gave a short comment to a peer in order to "get the net-based meeting over with", as one student put it. The questionnaires and student evaluations also revealed a clear impression that net-based discussions risked undermining the purpose of the course, since those who were interested in making an effort became demotivated when other students with their very low effort were approved as "good enough". These challenges were captured in the evaluations of the programme and prompted the organisers to add more restrictions framing the discussions, such as requirements for "unique", self-produced and original contributions.

Even though such changes were accomplished, it seemed like the organisers did not fully see the potential of creating more motivating and cross-disciplinary challenges, which could have ensured a deeper involvement of students with the discussions and their peers. Several challenges that affected the quality of the discussions were pointed out, such as the potential of producing challenging and critical questions. The questionnaires demonstrated that although the students were motivated and prepared for some of the questions that were presented, the topics did not invite them to discuss any further than just posting short answers. The development of their Academic Bildung was clearly not stimulated through these discussions, even though at least some of the students were motivated and wanted to be challenged and go further in their investigations, in terms of questions related to their own and others' discipline, and also to open up for their wonderment and curiosity. Another practical challenge that affected the possibilities for further discussions was that the discussions were open for only an hour and a half during which the supervisors were supposed to give feedback or at least be present. The discussions were open for another two hours for potential further discussion. The students were required to contribute to the net-based discussion meetings with two posts each: a main post and a reply to a fellow student. After the first two semesters it was decided that there was a need to extend the time (the room was open from 8:00 until midnight), making more detailed demands of the content of the discussions, and complying with suggestions for improvement from the students.

To summarise, in this section I have discussed whether the net-based discussions promoted critical thinking, society-oriented reflections, or facilitated dimensions of existential- and being-oriented reflections, in line with the way Academic Bildung is defined in Chapter 3. The findings demonstrate that the discussions have potential to do so, but the interviews and the surveys have revealed that the discussions were not sufficiently organised and thought through, when it came to student group size, the organisation and framing of the discussion, and the requirements and questions posed.

Interprofessional net-based health education: A possibility to move beyond learning?

The aim of this study was to investigate whether it is possible to facilitate Academic Bildung and interprofessional learning in a net-based course with students from ten different healthcare professions. The findings outlined Academic Bildung dimensions related to: 1) the description of the course design, 2) the development of an interprofessional identity, 3) the students' socialisation into the academic culture, and 4) the facilitation of critical thinking in net-based discussions. The findings have demonstrated that this health education programme represents both intentions and ambitions to address all the four voices of higher education – "the voice of knowing", "the voice of doing", "the voices of being" and "the voice of the phenomenon" – in interrelational settings. Students were supposed to be challenged in their academic writing, share and develop texts and content across disciplines, and approach questions addressing the society at large, healthcare and the educational system. The students were also supposed to participate in settings that stimulated the development of their own voices and challenged their theoretical, social and academic understanding in learning activities like net discussions and so on. They were also exposed to interrelational concepts such as caring, ethical principles, and involvement. Together the course design addressed the students' "being in the world", authentic discussions and meeting across disciplines, in accordance with how these different voices were introduced in Chapter 3 as a "four-voiced" Bildung pedagogy, which has the potential to make room for more existential and ontological dimensions in university education. To draw the first part of the conclusion: in line with the double-tracked concept of Academic Bildung presented earlier, this health care education programme had possibilities and potential to address critical, emancipatory and society-oriented aspects, as well as dimensions of ethical-existential and being-oriented reflections, and move the students beyond learning.

However, the findings demonstrated the complexity and multilayered challenges related to both the ambition of facilitating Academic Bildung and interprofessionality, and pointed out the many obstacles that must be considered in order to be in a position to facilitate Acedemic Bildung in net-based environments. These obstacles include different professional standpoints, lack of willingness to cooperate, and lack of appropriate foundations with which to develop an interprofessional identity. The common principles of this facilitation also need to be deeply rooted within the academic personnel and other people with key positions within the discipline. A relevant question to ask is whether there is a possibility – at all – to really facilitate and develop an interprofessional identity in a net-based course of this short of a duration with such recently established groups of students? There are many indications that the students need to develop their individual discipline-oriented knowledge, ideas, experiences, and actions first in order to be able to be confronted by and develop an interprofessional identity. Therefore, to draw the last part of the conclusion, if the aim is to develop the students' Academic Bildung within an interprofessional educational environment, the facilitation of such a programme must take into consideration the whole complexity connected to 1) how the course design, the collaboration and content are planned, implemented in the organisation and facilitated; 2) how the development of interprofessionality is connected to developing the students' autonomy and authenticity; and 3) the socialisation into an academic culture, and how Academic Bildung is reflected in the very learning activities presented in the program.

Independent of whether one thinks interprofessionality is possible or not, this study has highlighted the importance of fostering criticality, society-related reflections (autonomy) and ethical dimensions of human formation, and existential- and being-oriented reflections (authenticity) within higher education. When educating first semester healthcare students in a cross-disciplinary course, both others' and my own findings indicate that a social and relational foundation of Academic Bildung is especially important in order to get a safe and stimulating platform where the students are allowed to challenge and follow their own and others' voices on their journey to become academics.

The findings have revealed that not all students are "naturally born critical beings" when they enter this first semester of healthcare education, and this emphasizes the importance of structure and clear demands related to the facilitation of the different elements of the course design. The present research demonstrates that all four elements identified in this case study must be seen as important when facilitating the development of Academic Bildung in a net-based interprofessional first semester course. The facilitation of the students' development of Academic Bildung must be understood as a progression which follows the students throughout their formational journey towards the status of an educated healthcare worker in the future. The facilitation and support of the students' movement beyond learning can never be more than part of the picture. To really move beyond learning, the students need to challenge themselves in order to actively open up and integrate their own wonderment in accordance with both the self-determining and authentic parts of their educational journey.

Notes

1 A large number of reforms and white papers like "Samhandlingsreformen" [report] St. meld. 47: 2008–2009 and "Utdanning for velferd: Samspill i praksis", [report] St.meld. 13, 2011–2012.

2 See Barnett (2007),Hansen (2013) or Chapter 3 for a more detailed discussion on this concept.

3 The pilot was organized for psychology students (about 200 students) and two interprofessional groups of health professional students (16 students).

References

Barnett, R. (1997). *Higher education: A critical business.* Open University Press: Buckingham, UK.

Barr, H., Koppel, I., Reeves, S., Hammick, M., and Freeth, D. (2005). *Effective interprofessional education. Arguments, assumption and evidence.* Blackwell Publishing: London.

CAIPE (Centre for the Advancement of Interprofessional Education). (1997). "Interprofessional education – A definition", *CAIPE Bulletin*, vol. 13, no. 19.

Creswell, J. W. (2003). *Research design: Quantitative, qualitative, and mixed methods approaches*, 2nd edn. Sage: Thousand Oaks, CA.

Det Kongelige Helse og Omsorgsdepartementet. (2008-09). St. meld. nr. 47: "Samhandlingsreformen: Rett behandling – på rett sted – til rett tid" [report]. Helse- og omsorgsdepartementet: Oslo. Available online at http://www.regjeringen.no/nb/dep/hod/dok/regpubl/stmeld/2008-2009/stmeld-nr-47-2008-2009-.html?regj_oss=1&id=567201 (accessed 19 Sept. 2014).

Det Kongelige Kunnskapsdepartementet (2012). St. meld. nr. 13: "Utdanning for velferd: Samspill i praksis" [report]. Kunnskapsdepartementet: Oslo. Available online at http://www.regjeringen.no/nb/dep/kd/dok/regpubl/stmeld/2011-2012/meld-st-13-20112012.html?id=672836 (accessed 19 Sept. 2014).

Ehlers, U. D. (2004). "Quality in e-learning from a learner's perspective", *European Journal of Open, Distance and E-Learning.* Available online at: http://www.eurodl.org/index.php?article=101 (accessed 9 June 2014).

Gaski, M. (2013). "Ikke 'Hel(t)-Fe(i)l'? Evaluering av implementeringen av fellesemne ved det helsevitenskapelige fakultet ved Universitetet i Tromsø" [report], vol. 2013:4. Norut Northern Research Institute: Alta, NO. Available online at http://norut.no/en/node/1933 (accessed 19 Sept. 2014).

Hansen, F. T. (2013). "Undringsfællesskabet som vej til U-læring på højere uddannelser". In: Belling, L., and Gerstrøm, T., eds., *Fortællinger fra U'et. Teori U omsat i liv, læring og lederskab* (p. 207-234). Dansk Psykologisk Forlag: Copenhagen.

Hjerpaasen, K. J. et al. (2012). "Tverrprofesjonell samarbeidslæring innen helse- og sosialfagutdanningene." Prosjekt Læring i arbeidsliv og utdanning [report], University of Tromsø: Tromsø, NO.

Hovdhaugen, E. and Aamodt, P. O. (2009). "Learning environment: Relevant or not to students' decision to leave university?" *Quality in Higher Education*, vol. 15, no. 2, pp. 177–89.

Kim, H. (2011). "International graduate students' difficulties: Graduate classes as a community of practices", *Teaching in Higher Education*, vol. 16, no. 3, pp. 281–92.

Ramburuth, P. and McCormick, J. (2001) "Learning diversity in higher education: A comparative study of Asian international and Australian students". *Higher Education*, vol. 42, no. 3, pp. 333–50.

Sawir, E., Marginson, S., Deumert, A., Nyland, C. and Ramia, G. (2008). "Loneliness and international students: An Australian study", *Journal of Studies in International Education*, vol. 12, no. 2, pp. 148–80.

Solberg, M. and Fossland, T. (2013). "Akademisk danning – et mulig prosjekt for voksne studenter i fleksible studier?" In: Arbo, P., ed., *Utdanningssamfunnet og livslang læring: Festskrift til Gunnar Grepperud.* Gyldendal Akademisk: Oslo.

Thistlethwaite, J. (2012). "Interprofessional education: A review of context, learning and the research agenda", *Medical Education*, vol. 46, no. 1, pp. 58–70.

Trigwell, K. and Ashwin, P. (2006). "An exploratory study of situated conceptions of learning and learning environments", *Higher Education*, vol. 51, no. 2, pp. 243–58.

Trowler, V. and Trowler, P. (2010). "Student engagement evidence summary" [report], Department of Educational Research, University of Lancaster. Higher Education Academy: York, UK. Available online at: https://www.heacademy.ac.uk/http%3A/www.heacademy.ac.uk/resources/detail/evidencenet/Student_engagement_evidence_summary (accessed 19 Sept. 2014).

Wilhelmsson, M. (2011). "Developing interprofessional competence. Theoretical and empirical contributions", *Linköping University medical dissertations*, no. 1189. Linköping University: Linköping, SE.

World Health Organization. (2010). *Framework for action on interprofessional education and collaborative practice.* WHO Press: Geneva.

Part III

Rethinking university education

10 Pedagogical considerations

A new discourse based on Academic Bildung

Mariann Solberg, Gunnar Grepperud and Finn Thorbjørn Hansen

Education: A normative enterprise

Let us start by summing up some of the important assumptions and conclusions from the theoretical chapter on the concept of Academic Bildung. And then let us see how we can – now inspired by the different cases of teaching and learning in net-based higher education – rethink net-based higher education through a new discourse based on a Scandinavian conception of Academic Bildung.

One of the first things that must be mentioned is a basic difference to be found between those fields of human activities that *must* be talked about in normative terms, and those that *can* be talked about in such terms. We would say that education, and thus teaching, is a necessarily normative enterprise. The main reason for this is that education and teaching concerns relations between people, between teacher and student. Teaching in a university cannot be a neutral craft, as the teacher's interpersonal relation to the student is normative. Teaching thus cannot be *reduced to* a skill, the competence of bringing about effective learning in the students. Subsequently, effective student learning is not the only goal for university education. There are *attitudinal* and *normative* sides to education, and these are not covered in the concept of learning, at least not in the concept of learning as cognition. Nor are the concepts of knowledge, skills and competences, the three main learning outcomes defined in the EQF, the European Qualification Framework for lifelong learning, inherently or unquestionably normative. Just as the concept of education is an inherently normative concept, so is the concept of Academic Bildung. It is timely that the normative concepts in education are coming into focus again. Education as well as research also has existential dimensions. We believe that choosing Academic Bildung as the optic through which to look at net-based higher education will enable us to see the *values* in and of education.

As noticed in Chapter 3, Academic Bildung is a concept covering personal development processes in relation to formal and informal learning in higher education. It is connected to critical thinking, society-oriented reflection and autonomy on the one hand, and to ethical dimensions of human formation and self-formation, existential- and being-oriented reflection and authenticity on the other hand. We have elaborated on this through our descriptions of how Kant and Gadamer in different ways connect Academic Bildung to both a critical and an existential form of reflection and attitude. But the concept also draws heavily on Scandinavian conceptions of education, which is to say welfare state conceptions of education, and we have also linked it to adult education, people's enlightenment and enlightenment for life. Bildung is an egalitarian project in Scandinavia.

We also saw that, when it comes to higher education, Wilhelm von Humboldt's thinking about the university is at the historical roots for a concept of Bildung, and also for our concept of Academic Bildung. A Humboldtian idea of particular importance for our understanding of Academic Bildung is the idea of the unity of research and education. Thus the Bildung process to be expected in the research university is first of all the process of a search for new knowledge. This search is not about acquisition of knowledge already available, though that is most definitely a prerequisite for finding new knowledge. Humboldt's idea of the freedom of research is still crucial here.

We do not think there is a particular form of Academic Bildung for net-based education. What we have been asking in this book is whether the principles of Academic Bildung that traditionally have applied to education on campus in Scandinavian higher education, in terms of development of autonomy and authenticity, can apply to net-based higher education as well. The question posed in this chapter is: How can we rethink net-based higher education through a new discourse based on a Scandinavian conception of Academic Bildung? If a new discourse can lead to new analysis and make us see things differently, what practical differences can this bring about when it comes to, first, the quality of net-based courses and programs and, consequently, to the Academic Bildung of the students? And what difference could this make for the empowerment and meaningfulness of the life of the individual, for the quality of the new knowledge produced, and for the overall capability for innovation in societies?

We first sum up the different Bildung dimensions found in the case studies of this book and discuss these dimensions and their corresponding conceptions of Bildung in relation to the concept of Academic Bildung developed in Chapter 3. Based on the case studies we explore what we can say about the relation between Academic Bildung and the conditions of net-based education. Can net-based learning environments mean "value added" when it comes to Academic Bildung dimensions? Do net-based learning environments block processes of Academic Bildung? Is the balance between the critical and existential dimension in Academic Bildung, which Chapter 3 saw as crucial, seen and retained in the cases of contemporary net-based higher education learning? Finally, we discuss whether the practical empirical reality uncovered in the case studies has implications for the theoretical concept of Academic Bildung. We also discuss the extent to which this concept can function as a basis for a new discourse on

net-based higher education. But now let us look at the Bildung conceptions and dimensions of the case studies.

Conceptions of Academic Bildung in the case studies

What kinds of understandings and practices of the phenomenon of
Academic Bildung emerge when we read and reflect upon the case studies?
We focus on the ways in which they do (and do not) touch upon the topic of
Academic Bildung in light of the concept developed in the first part of our
book. We also comment upon commonalities as well as differences between
the unified Bildung approach of the book and the diverse approaches of
the case studies.

The first study in Part II, "Philosophical orientations of teaching and
technology: A Scandinavian case study", is not a case study in the same sense
as the four other case studies. It is in a sense a view of Scandinavian net-
based education approached from the side on rather than from within, as
Scandinavian higher education teachers' beliefs and opinions concerning
teaching and technology have been studied in comparison to teachers in
four other countries. In this respect, the study can function as a test of
a claim of the existence of a specific Scandinavian approach in net-based
higher education. Kanuka has examined opinions and beliefs held by
teachers concerning what they see as the aims of university education and
why they use educational technology. She found that all the Scandinavian
participants selected the same orientation, the Progressive one, as closest to
their own teaching philosophical orientation. This orientation is illustrated
by the statement that "the aim of a university education is to promote personal growth and maintenance, as well as a better society".

When it comes to the Scandinavian-oriented concept of Academic
Bildung developed in our book and the philosophical orientations of
teaching of the Scandinavian scholars found in this study, there are close
connections on some dimensions. The participants' focus on "personal
growth" is perspicuous, and this is at the core of many conceptions of
Bildung. That the personal, individual growth connects to the social systems is expressed to be important by the participants is at the core of the
society-oriented Kantian concept of Bildung, as we have seen in Chapter 3.
It is also a central element in the Scandinavian orientation of the concept
of Bildung, particularly when it comes to the critical emancipatory tradition
of pedagogy and adult learning. Furthermore, the view that knowledge is
constructed as a social process, aimed to support personal growth with a
critical stance, is common among the Scandinavian interviewees. This orientation also aligns well with the autonomy dimension in our concept of
Academic Bildung.

Why is this group of Scandinavian higher education scholars in the area
of educational technology so unanimous? Are these views a feature of a
general Scandinavian university culture in the field? We must of course be

careful to draw peremptory conclusions on the basis of a small cohort, but it certainly is remarkable. Kanuka's study seems to some degree to support our original assumption of there being something common in Scandinavian net-based higher education, and that this "something" is different from the world of English-speaking higher education that we otherwise compare ourselves with. However, we must remember that the study covers the opinions and beliefs of the fifteen specific teachers and not their practice.

It must be noted that Kanuka's study has not explicitly touched upon existential and being-oriented dimensions of Academic Bildung. When Kanuka identifies six teaching philosophical orientations (Radical, Liberal, Progressive, Analytical, Humanist, and Behaviourist) she has not included teaching philosophical orientations such as existential pedagogy (Bollnow 1969; Dupont and Hansen 1998) or phenomenological-oriented pedagogy (van Manen 1991; Friesen 2011) or enlightenment for life and people's enlightenment pedagogy, which indeed are a unique Scandinavian approach. Other results could then of course have come up.

In the second case study, "Educating pharmacists – the perfect prescription", Bildung is professional proficiency. Professionalism is defined as the combination of good reflective practice and a well-developed awareness and understanding of oneself as professional. This is expressed in the idea that it is not sufficient to exercise the pharmacy profession – one must also *be* a pharmacist. Professionalism, as it is here stated in terms of being the aim of vocational education, however does not concern only those attending courses at the higher education level. It applies to all professional training. Thus, Englund and Wester have indicated a general Bildung or professionalism ideal. A question that remains to be answered is whether vocational education at tertiary level should or must include something more, something different or more special than such a universal authenticity ideal of professional proficiency.

The concept of authenticity at play here includes not only ethical awareness and self-formation, it is also about learning through action and in practical life, where the personal lived experience is both the starting point and the goal. They differ from the other case contributions in terms of their emphasis on experience and practical knowledge as part of their Bildung ideal. However, Englund and Wester's conception of Bildung focuses less on the existential- and being-oriented sides of Bildung than the concept of Academic Bildung developed in Chapter 3. Englund and Wester are not directly focusing on the autonomy side of Academic Bildung.

In the third case study, "Net-based guerrilla didactics", Academic Bildung is seen mainly as a form of autonomy, where the independent action of the students takes the form of "disobedient" dislocation of intended contents of communication between the various platforms in use in the course. Bengtsen, Mathiasen and Dalsgaard further argue that each platform takes on a life of its own and "becomes a pedagogical world in itself with its own subcultural norms, habits and values". This means that the autonomy exercised, the freedom from the teachers' didactical design, is not exclusively in the hands of the students. The students share this freedom from the intended design with the platforms in which they operate, and the authors also argue that communication itself is an autonomous being. Together this creates a disturbance in the didactical design made by the teachers.

When the students become aware of the different criteria for interaction and norms of communication across different platforms the authors hold that they will experience a pluralism of perspectives. They see this as the students gaining a critical and hermeneutic attitude. Students and teachers in this form of didactical design are invited to be mindful about different criteria for interaction and norms of communication across different platforms, and thus learn "not to assume that their own presuppositions about the world are universal and valid for everyone else". Development of perspective expansion as a form of Bildung is not directly touched upon in our two-dimensional concept of Academic Bildung, however it is vital in the concept of Bildung as developed by the Norwegian pedagogical philosopher Paul Martin Opdal (2000, 2008), on basis of the British pedagogical philosopher R. S. Peters(1919–2011). Perspective expansion does seem to have favourable conditions in net-based education of the sort described in this case study.

In the fourth case study, "Learning, meaning, Bildung? Reflections with reference to a net-based MBA programme", the possibilities of Bildung are seen through the question of the possibility for deep learning. As opposed to surface learning, deep learning is defined as "going 'behind' the text in order to understand ideas and seek meaning". Deep learning can be achieved through looking for patterns and principles within themes and subjects, by relating to one's own experience, forming and testing one's own hypothesis, and by creating wholeness and coherence. Students who have this approach to learning are also conscious about themselves as learners and their own learning situation. According to the understanding of the authors, the process of Bildung should, in short, be about stretching towards the ideal of "the exploratory human being". Here they adhere to the American liberal arts tradition, which they connect to the philosopher and psychologist John Dewey's (1859–1952) thinking. From this Anglo-American, pragmatic and society-oriented view on Bildung it follows that the ultimate goal of education is to be able to take an active part in a democratic society.

Grepperud and Holen thus see Academic Bildung as inevitably connected to development and learning, and they connect Bildung with the higher levels of taxonomies for cognitive learning, attitudes and skills, which they find that higher education must promote. They also emphasise that Academic Bildung must include all dimensions of the individual ("the whole person"). They find that there is a lack of a deep learning approach in the students of the programme due to lack of time and a possible lack of experienced meaning. In this way they touch upon both the autonomy and some parts of the authenticity side of Academic Bildung. Autonomy, since they find that independent time management could have helped the students in reaching the higher levels of the taxonomies, and "experienced meaning" belong to the authenticity side of Bildung. However, they do not focus on authenticity as existential- and being-oriented. They do not go into how the students could have done better when it comes to dwelling, wondering and listening to and leaning from "experienced meaning", but it seems that the time factor could be of importance also here.

In the fifth case study, "Interprofessional net-based health education – A possibility to move beyond learning", Bildung is about academic values and skills, and Academic Bildung is about developing an academic identity and behaviour, and an academic mode of being. Fossland includes development of the students' professional identity as health workers into her understanding of Academic Bildung. Fossland also uses the term "academic socialisation" about this phenomenon, a socialisation which she holds will have somewhat different expression depending on the professional and academic subculture students are in. She focuses on the conditions for realisation of an ideal of Academic Bildung, and she finds that little has been achieved in terms of development of the students' Academic Bildung. This is the case at the least when judged by the potential of the didactic design of the program, and the impression is no better when judged by the development of academic skills nor by the development of academic identity. Fossland thus relates to factors on both sides of our two-dimensional concept of Academic Bildung in that she sees professional identity as being connected to the personal dimension and authenticity (albeit not to authenticity as existential- and being-oriented), while academic skills, such as critical thinking, as being connected to autonomy.

Conditions for Academic Bildung in the case studies

The many entrances and understandings of Bildung launched in this book notwithstanding, let us agree that Bildung as a superior quality in higher education requires enduring "virtues" in teaching and learning, like peace, commitment, reciprocity, processing, specialisation, wondering and personalising. Our task as educators and educational institutions is to facilitate and provide the best possible conditions for this, but ultimately the responsibility lies with the learner him- or herself. Learning at the level of higher education cannot and should not include consumerist students who effectively are being served easily digestible "dishes" by smart educators and convenient technology. This is just the way it is; Academic Bildung must and should in all respects be a bold and demanding as well as wondrous exercise.

If we apply this view to the case studies presented in Part II of this book, two conclusions stand out. First it is, on the basis of these cases, difficult to say anything definitive about the extent to which the courses have contributed to the individual student's Bildung. However, all the cases are saying quite a lot about the conditions that must be present for Academic Bildung to take place. If we look closely at the parts of the courses that take place in net-based environments, the second and most obvious conclusion is that the net-based/technological solutions that have been employed do not seem to have made the road towards the goal of Bildung considerably better and wider. As such, it is not surprising that when Englund and Wester are looking for Academic Bildung in terms of professional proficiency in pharmacy students, they see it as a result of the whole academic programme (four years), and thus as a result of all and any measures (including the students' own work). They find that this form of Bildung, professional proficiency, is not a consequence of a limited didactic experiment that only covered half the student group. For this reason, it is not straightforward to assume a simple and unambiguous relationship between Bildung and educational technology.

Let us elaborate on these two conclusions. The most prominent in the cases presented is that they both directly and indirectly highlight some key conditions – or in some cases lack thereof – that are necessary to safeguard and fulfil the ideal of Academic Bildung. This is particularly visible in Fossland's chapter, which points out a number of factors that specifically led to students having experiences (and probably also learning outcomes) that were far from the program's goals and aspirations. Evidence indicates that the ambitions were far too extensive in relation to the existing frameworks and the complexity of the course. After exploring Fossland's analysis, there are in particular two questions that arise: is it possible to develop an interdisciplinary professional identity in such a short time (cf. Englund and Wester's analysis in Chapter 6), and is it possible to develop cross-professional identity without the participants having first developed their own professional identity?

One of the matters stated in Fossland's analysis is what we might call the classic blunder of the curriculum. This means that, with the best intentions, a large amount of subject material and many different means are included in a four-month ten-credit program, to the extent that it almost seems to be counterproductive. We find reading, writing and discussions, face-to-face-meetings, use of the net and case-based assignments and supervision. The students were to work both individually and in different groups. In addition there were the examination tasks. Moreover, Fossland points out that the instructional design was insufficiently anchored among the teachers and in the different professional disciplines. The result of this appears to be that qualities such as calmness, specialisation, wondering and reflection have not had particularly fertile ground.

A similar accumulation of good measures gone awry is found in Bengtsen, Mathiasen and Dalsgaard in their chapter on "Net-based guerrilla didactics". The designers of this course have been inspired by the possibilities inherent in various digital media for communication. Interestingly, they have attempted to divide and distribute the student's communication within the different media according to purpose and function: academic, social, and administrative. The authors draw inspiration from Harman (2005) and his concept of "guerrilla" to explain why the strategy fails. It turns out that the students made use of these arenas in their own way, which can be summarised briefly as students more or less talking about everything everywhere and frolicking verbally at venues where the teacher was not present. This might show that it is neither possible nor desirable to divide the academic, social and personal dimensions of the teaching and learning context. Bengtsen, Mathiasen and Dalsgaard recognise that students' "didactic disobedience" suggests that it is impossible to establish watertight bulkheads between the various themes and dimensions of students' digital communications. In face-to-face teaching on campus the students interact and communicate about subject, learning, leisure, and other more personal matters both within and outside the lecture theatre, and during and after lectures. We would suggest that it is this web of ideas, input and relationships that together make up the academic culture. From the perspective of Bildung, it could thus be argued that the goal must be to unify and strengthen these dimensions, not split them up according to digital solutions.

There are a number of conditions for teaching and learning in net-based environments, inside or outside the teacher's control, that influence and override the teacher's wishes and aspirations. In other words, teachers' attitudes to teaching and learning are not easily and directly expressed in their teaching practice. It is interesting that Kanuka, in spite of somewhat limited empirical data, finds that the Scandinavian higher education staff she interviewed appears to be unified in their views on learning and teaching, at least when it comes to the progressive emancipatory pedagogy. In relation to the aspirations of this book, it is encouraging that the values and perspectives expressed to some degree are located close to a general Scandinavian Bildung perspective for higher education. What we lack, however, is the "second track", the existential and being-oriented perspective in our double-tracked concept of Academic Bildung. Although we believe this second dimension to be of equal importance as the first one in the Scandinavian educational culture, it nevertheless seems to live a more quiet or invisible life. Perhaps it lies inherently in the more existential and being-oriented experiences and events of educational life, as for example van Manen has shown through his phenomenological investigations (van Manen 1991, 2002a, 2002b).

Having mentioned both the visible and more invisible sides of Scandinavian educational culture, it is also important to point out that this hardly reflects only the academic culture of the three Scandinavian countries. We would posit that it primarily reflects some of the most fundamental values of the Nordic countries. And, as Solberg and Hansen point out in

Chapter 3, these values have been central to the diverse Nordic people's enlightenment traditions that, with their many stakeholders, have been key carriers and disseminators of this egalitarian as well as life philosophical culture. We consider it a clear strength of higher education in our countries that it reflects fundamental and important aspects of social culture as well as what Grundtvig would call the "school of life": Anything else would have been questionable. At the same time, such a realisation means that it is difficult, if not impossible, to assume that universities are isolated and closed institutions that manage and develop knowledge regardless of social and human interests and values.

The egalitarian perspective is particularly evident in Grepperud and Holen's chapter. The main topic here is the students and their preconditions. Over the past 30–40 years higher education has passed from being an experience for the few to being available to the large majority. This is often described as a transition from elite to mass education, and it challenges our educational institutions in a number of areas. One of them is about teaching a very heterogeneous group of students, not only in terms of skills, abilities and interests, but also in terms of background, age and life situation. With an increasing number of mature flexible students, life situation is a variable that must be considered when optimal learning situations are planned for. This presents challenges. In light of the unambiguously positive rhetoric that flexible education provides opportunities to study when one wants and where one wants, the authors draw a somewhat more pessimistic picture. It appears that one's everyday living conditions have the power to control study behaviour in a direction where Bildung loses out to more strategic and instrumental perspectives. It appears that this force is strong enough to override even the most creative and advanced didactic solutions, as everyday life often strikes where it hurts the most: right in the time squeeze. In such a study and life situation Bildung can seems a luxury that only a few people can indulge in. There is every reason to take into account experiences like this, not least since students' living conditions gradually have become more influenced by work outside their studies.

For all four Scandinavian cases the net-based component constitutes a part of the program, albeit to varying extents. In Fossland's and in Grepperud and Holen's chapters digital media play a relatively peripheral role, both for students and teachers/tutors. The authors also point to issues outside educational technology and digital media as being of importance when explaining processes and outcomes. Despite their finding that students choose their own ways in and between the platforms, Bengtsen, Mathiasen and Dalsgaard do not provide definite answers as to whether digital communication led students closer to qualities we associate with Bildung processes and Bildung outcomes. The closest we come here is to reiterate what we know from other contexts; students can communicate online and this communication thematically revolves around the same issues that can be found in face-to-face communication. But communication itself is notoriously no guarantee of Bildung taking place, as Mathiasen also argues in Chapter 2. There must at the least be a communication, or a discourse, that is characterised by certain qualities. The qualities of the discourse are not a topic in the chapter by Bengtsen et al.

Through their analysis of the relationship between authentic learning situations and use of virtual worlds, Englund and Wester's chapter touches on the basic tenet of this book, the question of how net-based education can help facilitate Academic Bildung. Simulation, with or without technology, is basically a form of working and learning that fits well in professional studies because it is based on the specific profession and not the subject as such. This form of learning is thus well suited to develop and strengthen that which Englund and Wester describe as occupational or professional proficiency, what we could call professional Bildung. For that reason, this has been widely applied in health sciences, and good results are reported. With the development of technologies related to virtual worlds, many opportunities open up to further develop simulation as a teaching method and form of learning. In part, it is about providing students with an expanded repertoire of training practices without involving a number of practical and economic incremental costs. Moreover, it is about expanding the simulation to areas where in practical life it would be impossible for students to test their knowledge and skills. An interesting result presented by Englund and Wester is that students' backgrounds determined the extent to which they considered the virtual case study realistic. It turned out that those who had previous experience with pharmaceutical work or with the pharmacy as a workplace perceived the case to be less realistic than those without such experience. However, the virtual environment was found to be sufficiently realistic for them to adopt the role of the pharmacist (p. 101).

The four case studies from Scandinavian net-based higher education in this book clearly show the complexity teachers face in their net-based teaching practice. We also see that none of the four cases explicitly focus and articulate issues or experiences concerning the more existential and being-oriented dimension of Academic Bildung. We would guess that one of the reasons may be found in the theoretical framework used to describe and analyse those cases. The four cases are mainly using a learning theoretical and pragmatic constructivist or critical-emancipatory approach to learning and Bildung. What would have happened, we wonder, if the authors and researchers had arrived with a phenomenological or Socratic philosophical approach to cases of net-based higher education? Would that have opened up the analysis for experiences and visions that seem to be covered up by the vocabulary used here? Answers must be sought in further investigations.

Can we now say more about the relation between net-based education and Academic Bildung? Do net-based learning environments seem to mean "value added" as concerns Academic Bildung dimensions, or do net-based learning environments block processes of Academic Bildung? Based on the case studies we have found that the didactic design of the courses can seriously hamper the possibilities for development of Academic Bildung. We have not, however, found there to be something inherent in a net-based environment in itself that hampers these possibilities. We have further found that the time-factor is vital, both the time spent within and outside of the net-based environments. Moreover, communication in a variety of digital platforms and media can open new horizons for the students and give good opportunities for perspective expansion. With this exception, the case studies of this book do not suggest that ICT and the digital necessarily means "value added" in terms of development of the student's Academic Bildung.

A new discourse on net-based higher education based on Academic Bildung?

What can we now say about the concept of Academic Bildung as developed in the first part of our book? Have the case studies revealed a need for an expansion, or other forms of revisions of this concept? Does the actual reality of Scandinavian net-based education as shown in the case studies have implications for the status of Academic Bildung as an ideal? Or is the situation rather that the case studies have shown that we need to increase the effort and rethink the didactical designs of net-based higher education in order to facilitate development of Academic Bildung?

We have seen that there are many different conceptions of Academic Bildung at play, and when considering the Scandinavian literature on Bildung, it seems that all that is valuable, good and virtuous in education constitutes Bildung. The concept of Academic Bildung can thus be at risk of losing any distinct meaning and significance. The case studies have found Academic Bildung to be all the following: (i) professional proficiency, (ii) professional identity, (iii) autonomy in terms of being able to free oneself from didactical design, (iv) ability for perspective expansion, (v) exploration so as to achieve deep learning, (vi) ability to take an active part in a democratic society, (vii) being a whole person, (viii) acquisition of academic skills, (ix) acquisition of academic values, (x) acquisition of academic identity and behaviour, (xi) ability to think critically, (xii) ability to foster personal growth and maintenance, and (xiii) concern with the aims of a better society. And indeed we do find all of these aspects to be connected to Academic Bildung. In the first part of the book we have, on a more general level, developed a concept from a Scandinavian educational perspective where Academic Bildung is about becoming an academically oriented person with integrity and creativity, a person with an autonomous and authentic presence in academia and in society. And these different understandings of Academic Bildung are all pointing to the transformation that is expected and desired in students of higher education.

All the case studies of this book deal with different disciplines, and consequently there have been different kinds of contents that the students of these courses have met. On this basis, we should expect there to be differences in the understandings and practices of the phenomenon of Academic Bildung, and therefore we should expect the authors of the case studies to focus on different dimensions of Academic Bildung. There is indeed a close connection between acquisition of disciplinary content knowledge and Bildung. Formation of attitudes and Academic Bildung can hardly come about without a specific content. The Norwegian philosopher Jon Hellesnes said in an interview in 2012:

> My main point is that we must avoid a principled opposition between Bildung and acquisition of knowledge. Professional training is possible without Bildung, but the converse is not possible. A process of Academic Bildung must always also involve acquisition of knowledge. Critical thinking without relevant knowledge is opinionising. Opinionising is exercising prejudices, which makes them stronger.
>
> (Finstad 2012, para. 5, our translation)

We agree with Hellesnes' views on this point – Academic Bildung without knowledge is impossible – and we need to add: different contents do make a difference to the very processes of Bildung.

But equally important, to remind us of what Ronald Barnett (2007) calls the "ontological turn in higher education", we also emphasise that Academic Bildung without "the voice of being" is a spiritless and instrumental approach to Bildung and higher education. Therefore we also acknowledge the fundamental importance in research and academic work that the truth- and knowledge-seeking person engage in another movement toward existential contemplation. And in this "movement" the truth-seeking person is driven not by an epistemological ethos of knowing, but rather by an ontological ethos of wanting to be, and to "be-in-a-relation-with-the-phenomenon" in order to "understand-from-within" (see also Shotter 2010). Thus, in other words, there should also be time and space in net-based higher education for this kind of Socratic "not-knowing" (*docta ignorantia*), and being in a fundamental community of wonder and dialogue about our deeper longings, inspirations and intuitions of what we experience as important values and meaningfulness in our lives. In order to exercise one's practice in the university (research, teaching and learning) in an optimal manner, one needs to be and form oneself in this practice. Maybe this calls for a new wonder-based and phenomenological-oriented pedagogy in net-based higher education?[1]

So where does this leave the normative concept of Academic Bildung? The concept actually has helped us to see values in and of net-based higher education, even if the existential dimensions have been difficult to pinpoint. On this basis we find it hard to deny that all these different conceptions of Academic Bildung are valuable in a further discourse on net-based higher education. Can we live with a concept that demonstrably has an empirical life of such multitude and that seems to have such blurry boundaries? Can we live with a concept that has so many different theoretical interpretations and empirical instantiations? We believe that the need for strict definitions in this case should be weighed against the fruitfulness of rethinking and rephrasing, over and over again, this basic educational concept that has proved its value as an optic in our pedagogical understanding. It might be that such a seeking and open, yet critical, attitude is itself the proof of the pudding.

Note

1 For an interesting attempt to connect a critical-emancipatory pedagogy with a more phenomenological approach to higher education, see also Dupont (2012); and a so-called "four-voiced Bildung pedagogy" in higher education is developed by Hansen (2010, 2014). See also chapter 9 and 11 in this book where the four-voiced pedagogy is addressed and employed.

References

Barnett, R. (2007). *A will to learn: Being a student in an age of uncertainty*. Open University Press; McGraw Hill: Berkshire, UK.

Bollnow, O. F. (1969). *Eksistensfilosofi og pædagogik*. Christian Ejlers' Forlag: Copenhagen.

Dupont, S. (2012). *Pædagogik og fænomenologi mellem demokrati og dannelse*. Roskilde Universitetsforlag: Roskilde, DK.

Dupont, S. and Hansen, F. T. (1998). *Eksistenspædagogik – på vej mod en ny Voksenpædagogik?* FOFU, Roskilde Universitetsforlag: Roskilde, DK.

EQF, the European Qualification Framework for lifelong learning. Available online at http://ec.europa.eu/eqf/home_en.htm

Finstad, B. J. (20 Nov. 2012). "Med danning på timeplanen" [article], Sogn og Fjordane fylkeskommune [Sogn og Fjordane County, NO, website]. Available online at http://sfj.no/cmssff/cmspublish.nsf/$all/D7CB213F14AB7288C1257 ABC0052C2E3?open (accessed 19 Sept. 2014).

Friesen, N. (2011). *The place of the classroom and the space of the screen: Relational pedagogy and internet technology*. Peter Lang: New York.

Hansen, F. T. (2010). "The phenomenology of wonder in higher education". In: Brinkmann, M., ed., *Erziehung. Phänomenologische perspektiven*. Königshausen & Neumann: Würzburg, DE.

Hansen, F. T. (2014). *Kan man undre sig uden ord? Design- og universitetspædagogik på kreative videregående uddannelser*. Aalborg Universitetsforlag: Aalborg, DK.

Harman, G. (2005). *Guerrilla metaphysics: Phenomenology and the carpentry of things*. Open Court: Chicago.

Hellesnes, J. ([1969] 1992). "Ein utdana mann og eit dana menneske: Framlegg til eit utvida daningsomgrep". In: Dale, E. L., ed., *Pedagogisk filosofi*. Ad Notam Gyldedal: Oslo.

Opdal, P. M. (2000). *Danning som initiering, R. S. Peters' pedagogiske filosofi*. Oplandske Bokforlag: Vallset, NO.

Opdal, P. M. (2008). "Hva er danning", in *Pedagogisk-filosofiske analyser*. Fagbokforlaget: Bergen, NO.

Shotter, J. (2010). *Social construction on the edge: "Withness" thinking and embodiment.* Taos Institute Publications: Chagrin Falls, OH.

van Manen, M. (1991). *The tact of teaching: The meaning of pedagogical thoughtfulness.* Althouse Press: Ontario.

van Manen, M. (2002a). *Writing in the dark: Phenomenological studies in interpretive inquiry.* Althouse Press: Ontario.

van Manen, M. (2002b). *The tone of teaching: The language of pedagogy.* Althouse Press: Ontario.

11 Rethinking net-based higher education?

The facilitation of a four-voiced pedagogy

Trine Fossland

Introduction

Over the last decade, net-based teaching and learning environments have become an increasing part of higher education. Findings from the current research literature and our case studies have demonstrated both new challenges and possibilities related to net-based studies. The use of technology can provide teachers better access to stimulate and follow how students develop academically, and teachers can more easily challenge and reach out to a large number of students. Students can work together with peers or stimulating networks around the world, but can also face both academic and social loneliness in net-based education. To facilitate the students' development of Academic Bildung we argue that there is a need to rethink and be aware of both possibilities and challenges in different net-based course designs. In Chapter 3 we argued that Academic Bildung and a four-voiced pedagogy – "the voice of knowing", "the voice of doing", "the voice of being" and "the voice of the phenomenon"[1] – must be interwoven in the facilitation of net-based education. In this chapter, we want to find out what this really means, in relation to the main question in our book: "How can we educate students through net-based education and still facilitate Academic Bildung?"

To find out whether there is a need to rethink net-based education, this chapter outlines the broader pedagogical picture when it comes to facilitating Academic Bildung. Inspired by our findings in the book as well as findings from a study of more than twenty teachers with extended experience of using technology in teaching (Fossland 2015), the more practical and didactical consequences of facilitating Academic Bildung are addressed. We ask whether there is a need to rethink quality issues and pedagogy, learning outcomes, learning environments and activities, the teacher's role, and the role of assessment, in order to facilitate Academic Bildung.

Rethinking quality issues and pedagogy – is it necessary?

Is there a need to rethink pedagogy when planning net-based education? When it comes to the practical and didactical dimensions of facilitation, a number of existing quality assurance frameworks, guidelines, and benchmarks have been outlined to "secure" quality in net-based education. Uvalić-Trumbić and Daniel (2013) have investigated several different defined and tested benchmarks or quality standards that are in use around the world in their search for quality aspects in net-based studies. Although the terminology and emphases differ, they have identified the following common aspects of quality experienced in different net-based learning environments:

- Institutional support (vision, planning and infrastructure)
- Course development
- Teaching and learning (instruction)
- Course structure
- Student support
- Faculty support
- Technology
- Evaluation
- Student assessment
- Examination security

Several quality assurance standards and guidelines have been developed within the European Higher Education Area to secure the quality in net-based education, such as the European Association for Quality Assurance in Higher Education (ENQA)[2] and UNIQUe, which is a "high quality institutional certification for outstanding use of ICT in learning and teaching".[3] The certification is awarded to universities or institutes by the European Foundation for Quality in e-Learning (EFQUEL) after a process of self-assessment and external peer review, for renewable periods of three years. The criteria can be articulated in three areas: resources, processes and context, each with criteria and sub-criteria.

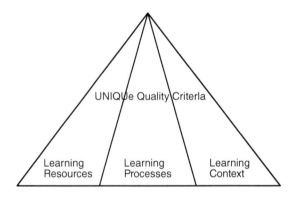

The Quality Matters rubric[4], which provides inter-institutional quality assurance in net-based learning, is another example. Their eight general standards are: course overview and introduction, learning objectives (competencies), assessment and measurement, instructional materials, learner interaction and engagement, course technology, and learner support and accessibility. Even though each and every one of these cross-disciplinary key quality issues, as well as dimensions related to the more complex "quality chains" within higher education (Nordkvelle et al. 2013), can be crucial for any net-based education, it is relevant to ask whether they can be related to the facilitation of Academic Bildung. Asked in another way, if we follow these quality lists as closely as we can, is this sufficient to secure the students' development of Academic Bildung, or is there a need to rethink pedagogy as well?

In their book *Rethinking pedagogy for a digital age* Beetham and Sharpe (2013) ask the following questions: Do we need to rethink pedagogy again? Does technology innovation imply the continual renewal of what we mean by pedagogy? Their answer is that no one has yet shown why we need to change our understanding of how students learn. The research-based fundamentals of what it takes to learn in the twenty-first century have not been seriously challenged and theoretical approaches still call on thinkers such as Dewey, Vygotsky, Bruner, Papert, Lave, and Wenger. To address the importance of developing the students' Academic Bildung, maybe the time has come to challenge these understandings?

The findings in our book and my interviews with innovative teachers (Fossland 2015) have not demonstrated that the use of technology represents a change in our fundamental understanding of the requirements of learning in formal education. We have, however, revealed a need to rethink pedagogy to make sure that both the pedagogical voices (voice of knowing, voice of doing) and the educational voices (voice of being, voice of phenomenon) are addressed in net-based education. The findings in our book and the interviews with the innovative teachers have aslo revealed the importance of students' development of Academic Bildung, as this has been defined earlier. The students need to reflect and become personally and critically involved not only with the course content, but also in the relationships with peers and teachers in order to be socialised into the academic culture. If the goal is to facilitate the students' development of Academic Bildung and become what Barnett defines as "critical beings" (2007), this can be understood as an approach to life, thinking, and criticality that a university-educated person should aspire to and meet within higher education. This includes both the autonomy and the authentic sides of the student's process of becoming an academic. When Barnett stresses that students must be critically engaged with the world and themselves, as well as with knowledge, he says: "Learning for an unknown future calls, in short, for an ontological turn. . . . A pedagogy of this kind will be a pedagogy that engages students as persons, not merely as knowers" (Barnett and Coate 2004, p. 247).

But what does it mean to engage students as persons? As discussed in Chapter 3, a four-voiced pedagogy and the facilitation of Academic Bildung need to address critical thinking and society-oriented reflection (autonomy), as well as the ethical dimensions, the students' developmental process, and existential- and being-oriented reflections. Even though not all the students are fully engaged, they still need to aspire to criticality in order to develop their own voices. Academic Bildung reaches far beyond the traditional concepts of learning when addressing the four voices of higher education, into the development of reflectivity of who we are and how we experience others and ourselves "inwardly" within a complex society. To answer my question: To facilitate Academic Bildung within formal educational settings, it seems necessary to rethink both quality issues and pedagogy. Although pedagogy is still seen as guiding the learner to learn in the net-based environments that have been investigated, it seems extremely important to plan for the students' engagement and involvement, as authenticity needs to be a central part of the learning outcomes, the learning environment, the teachers' approach, and the role of assessment. However, when addressing the double-tracked Academic Bildung concept outlined in this book, some issues seem to be of special importance: the learning outcomes, learning environments and activities, the teacher's role, and the role of assessment. In this chapter, we will therefore discuss these aspects of net-based education in more detail.

Rethinking learning outcomes in net-based higher education?

Do we need to rethink the learning outcomes to facilitate Academic Bildung? A current aspect that higher education institutions need to relate to when rethinking net-based education is the recent implementation of the European Qualifications Frameworks (EQF). In Norway, as all over Europe, this framework was implemented within higher education by the end of January 2013. The question is: Is there a need to rethink these required outcomes in net-based educations to ensure that they enable Academic Bildung? If we follow our definition of Academic Bildung as developing the students' autonomy and authenticity, can this thinking also be built into the learning outcomes of net-based courses and programs, and do we have to rethink how we formulate and relate to our learning goals within net-based higher education in order to secure Academic Bildung? If so, how can they be formulated to bring about student engagement and shape students' learning process to "move beyond learning" in such a way that their approach to education becomes a constructive, motivating and challenging journey?

Friesen (2013) argues that the language used to frame and discuss educational issues, in scholarly publications and in everyday life, both enables and limits ways of defining and addressing pedagogical concerns. According to Andersen (2010), several researchers have been sceptical to a narrow understanding of outcomes. Many researchers have characterised the Qualifications Framework as an expression of how new public management is shaping higher education, as the framework aims to integrate and coordinate national qualifications subsystems (Andersen 2010; European Communities 2008; Fossland 2013a).

Traditionally what Barnett calls the voice of knowing and the voice of doing are expressed in outcomes, but to follow Barnett and the educational voice, it seems important to also address the students' voice of being and voice of the phenomenon in these outcomes. Andersen (2010) argues that detailed learning outcomes are not enough; they need to be rethought in line with the rest of the learning design. She argues that it is important to remember that students do not get their primary motivation from expected learning outcomes, and because there is a clear danger that students have a too narrow view of their expected learning goals, learning outcomes often have to be formulated and operationalised in relation to the actual contexts the students are meant to be engaged in. Andersen argues that there is a need to apply a broader view to both the learning goals and the learning process, as many parts of it cannot be included in specific learning outcomes. The EQF focuses on "what a learner knows, understands and is able to do on completion of a learning process, which are defined in terms of knowledge, skills and competence" (European Communities 2008, p. 11). Academic Bildung only partly concerns the acquisition of a certain amount of knowledge, skills and general competences. More importantly, it concerns the student's personal and independent experience, processing, and evaluation of the content that one acquires. The EQF focuses on definitions and descriptions of specific qualifications to set educational and professional standards, describe curricula, conduct evaluations, or calculate credits. This can to some extent be seen as a contradiction to Academic Bildung, because it limits the students to a process of narrowed goals for learning. Academic Bildung has to do with a very different kind of engagement with the world – and this can only partly be facilitated in formal educational settings. Learning goals need to address critical thinking, society-oriented reflections (autonomy), and ethical dimensions of human formation and self-formation (authenticity).

To answer the question whether there is a need to rethink learning outcomes in net-based higher education, the answer is *yes* – we need to make sure that the learning outcomes are formulated in a way that directly or indirectly fosters the students' development of Academic Bildung, for instance in accordance to the thirteen different Bildung dimensions found in the analysis of the case studies presented in Chapter 10. The issues of students' learning outcomes, use of technology, and pedagogic approaches are so complex that they cannot be understood only in relation to simple causal chains; they need to be rethought in each case, with the students' Academic Bildung in mind. Sometimes the most advanced technology is used in net-based learning environments to implement very traditional approaches to teaching and learning. How Academic Bildung can come into play in net-based learning environments will be discussed in more detail in the next section.

Rethinking net-based learning environments and activities?

If one of the core duties of today's universities is to develop the students' authenticity and autonomy, is there a need to rethink how this engagement can be built into the facilitation of the net-based learning environments? The following design principles, presented as a guide to faculty of Southern Polytechnic State University (Georgia, US)[5], summarise one of many "instructional designs"; this one with the following four main areas:

- Consistent layout and design;
- Clear organisation and presentation of information;
- Consistent and easy-to-use navigation; and
- Aesthetically pleasing design and graphics.[6]

All these dimensions seem important when facilitating Academic Bildung, but findings in this book as well as interviews with innovative teachers have demonstrated that belonging and engagement appear to be among the most important factors for using technology in net-based activities. Bryson (2014) argues that the students' sense of engagement with their experience as a student is enhanced by feeling part of something: belonging, affiliation, and feeling integrated. We know from the case studies in this book that the feeling of being integrated into an academic culture is an important premise for the development of the students' Academic Bildung. So how can net-based learning environments be facilitated to develop the students' academic development in line with a four-voiced pedagogy? Is it possible that dimensions of Academic Bildung can be interwoven in the facilitation of net-based learning environments in a way that also develops the student's own voice? What does it mean to facilitate what Barnett (2007) calls authentic learning, which involves the person's existential reflections, engagements and "self-creational" learning process, rather than only a process of knowledge acquisition, skill learning or competence development, as discussed in Chapter 3? As Academic Bildung addresses both the autonomy and the authentic side of the students' development, can this be addressed within the learning activities themselves?

Several digital resources – from discussions, games, simulations, blogs, wikis, and different forms of social networking – can be seen as sources that have possibilities to support the students' development and Academic Bildung. Uvalić-Trumbić and Daniel (2013) argue in *A guide to quality in online learning* the importance of using different media in net-based learning, through the instructional design, as this can stimulate the variety of learning strategies and multiple learning styles employed. They also argue that using multimedia materials can "bring a course alive" and facilitate a stimulating experience including both visual and auditory senses in the learning process. Different learning platforms or web 2.0 technologies provide new opportunities for the development of the students' Academic Bildung. But as Barnett

(1997 p. 100) concludes in one of his chapters, learning is not enough. The students may have acquired some knowledge and skills and even some understanding, but such learning is insufficient in itself. He poses the following questions: Has she emerged with a voice of her own? Is it a strong voice? Is it sensitive to other voices? Is it authoritative? Is it authentic? These kinds of questions may follow our approach to rethinking net-based education.

To foster both critical and society-oriented reflection (the voice of doing and knowing that can be realised through autonomy), as well as a dimension of ethical-existential and being-oriented reflection (which can be realised through authenticity), the student's own personal experience, engagement and the process of "self-becoming" must be called upon. How can we ensure that this happens? In a study of more than twenty skilled Norwegian university teachers with several years of experience using IT in net-based teaching (Fossland 2014), I found empirical evidence of both autonomy and authenticity that clearly had the potential to move the students beyond learning, in line with how we have defined Academic Bildung in this book. The main dimensions of autonomy and authenticity found in the teachers' story of their use of technology in teaching can be summarised as follows:

- *Pedagogical added value:* Diverse empirical examples of technology that promotes authentic examples, variation, new possibilities for exam revisions, student engagement, preparation, involvement, and motivation that have potential to advance the students' development of Academic Bildung.
- *Collaboration:* Using technology that contributes positively to the way students are integrated into the academic community, through providing new forms of collaboration that stimulate sharing of resources, more supervision, peer feedback and national or international collaboration with networks or academic key personnel or others who have the potential to enhance the students' development of Academic Bildung, and develop and train their own academic voice.
- *Student activity:* Using technology that can promote more active forms of inquiry, problem solving, and authentic styles of learning, using for example social media or filmed cases as a starting point for critical discussions and active approaches to the student's academic journey.
- *Content creation:* Using technology to allow the students to create and edit their own content, which has the potential to encourage their own creative process, authenticity and develop their own academic voice. This makes the content represent more personal and creative commitment and investments, and it has the potential to transform knowledge in a way that influences the students' development of Academic Bildung.
- *Workplace relevance:* Using technology to make it easier to be virtually in contact with workplaces (inviting interesting people to teach, or hosting discussions via digital tools), or easier to connect with processes and digital resources linked to different occupations, both teachers and students

can find and make use of authentic digital material in ways that can stimulate the students' development of Academic Bildung.

- *Digital literacy and twenty-first century skills:* Using technology to enhance the students' thinking, flexible problem solving, collaboration and communication skills (referred to as twenty-first century skills in Chapter 1), which they need to be successful in work and life, so that students can act in innovative ways in the information society and thereby develop their Academic Bildung.
- *Self-directed learning:* Using technology to stimulate authentic tasks and creative approaches that strengthen the students' ownership of their own learning process can develop their Academic Bildung.
- *Accommodation and democracy:* Using technology to give voice to students who face extra challenges such as social, physical, or psychological health problems. For example, introvert or shy students can be given more time and a democratic "space" in net-based environments to find their own voice in collaboration with others. Students who are hindered in other ways can be given creative approaches to find their own voices on their way to becoming an academic.

What these dimensions have in common is that they go beyond the argument of accessibility, freedom and flexibility. If we take a closer look at the various dimensions, we can identify all "the voices of knowing", "the voices of doing", "the voices of being", and "the voices of the phenomenon", as we have discussed these concepts in chapter 3. The voices of doing and knowing are connected to the pedagogical parts of these findings (the pedagogical voices), as realised through autonomy (such as critical thinking and society-oriented reflection), while the educational side (the educational voices) as realised through authenticity, have to do with the student's own personal experience, engagement and process of "self-becoming". All these dimensions can be understood as an approach to life, thinking and criticality that a university-educated person should aspire to; to be able to critically engage with the world and with themselves, as well as with knowledge. So to answer whether there is a need to rethink the learning environment and activities in order to encourage the students' development of Academic Bildung, the answer is that a four-voiced pedagogy can be seen as a way to clear a space for the more existential and ontological dimensions in university education so as to develop the students' Academic Bildung.

Rethinking the role of assessment in net-based studies

Is there a need to rethink the role of assessment to support Academic Bildung? Assessment is one of the core concepts for several reasons when discussing facilitation of net-based education. A variety of assessment techniques can be used in a net-based learning environment. Whitelock (2010) demonstrates different examples of using web 2.0 in assessment, ranging from multiple-choice polls to approaches involving the use of e-portfolios. The Swedish National Agency for Higher Education (2008) has summarised the different ways in which net-based assessments can be organised, with an analysis of their pros and cons. Many different types of assessment can be used as net-based resources to not only follow the students' learning process, but also to challenge them, provide responses, and allow the students an opportunity to follow up on their own progress. Below is a list of a few of these:

- Written assignments
- Participation in net-based discussions
- Essays
- Net-based quizzes
- Multiple choice questions to test understanding (formative) or as a test (summative)
- Collaborative assignment work
- Debates
- Experiential activities such as role play and simulation
- Learning portfolios

When addressing the development of students' Academic Bildung, assessment that stimulates students to see the "broader picture" of higher education, that motivates and encourages them to ask their own questions, seems important. The alignment of the curricula we teach, the teaching methods we use, the learning environment we choose, and our approach to assessment must address the students' development of Academic Bildung. For net-based educators, assessment can be seen as a fundamental element of curriculum design, because it appears as one of the main determinants of students' approach to their studies, and therefore assessment methods can be seen as having prime pedagogical importance (Havnes 2002; Baud and Falchnikov 2007; Fossland 2014). IT has already begun to change traditional educational assessments in accordance with more effective and efficient delivery methods. The use of IT has also expanded and enriched assessment tools so that assessments can more easily include more authentic tasks, for instance filmed cases from real life that students can analyse in relation to relevant theory or actualised cases aimed at preparing students for involvement in their later working life. Another example can be the use of IT to investigate the dynamic interactions between student and assessment material. In my study of digitally competent teachers (Fossland 2014), digital tools were used for assessment in ways that had potential to develop the students' Academic Bildung. Some of the examples were:

- *Formative assessment and access to the students' learning process:* Technology provided access for teachers to follow the students' collaboration and discussions, for instance in a net-based forum. Following student activities described how they progressed in different learning activities. The use of technology also made it easier to give students formative feedback and to create new forms of digital exams that promoted the students' access to higher education in new ways (videos from "real life" for instance that were a starting point for analytical and theoretical approaches in assessment).

o   *Authentic discussions were delivered as a part of their examination requirement.*
o   *Tasks were given before lectures to give the teacher and the students feedback on the students' development in particular topics. This revealed both what the students found difficult and what they did not need that much help with.*

- *The use of authentic cases:* Some of the students got what we can call authentic cases to work with.

    o   *Their summative exam was built up of three different parts.* In the first part the students were given theoretical questions in a multiple choice test, in the next part the students were asked to analyse a filmed case, and in the last part the students were asked to use theoretical perspectives to describe the case.
    o   *An authentic case* was presented at the start of the semester. The students were required to work together in pairs and to follow lectures that challenged their views on their particular case. They developed their authentic case by approaching both theoretical perspectives and information found in any kind of digital resources to analyse and understand important economical dimensions within the particular case that they had chosen. At the end of the semester the same case was used to assess the students, as their final results were delivered.

Interviews with the innovative teachers demonstrated how net-based learning environments offered increased flexibility for assessment, and how this was used to approach the students' creativity, critical thinking skills, and in-depth involvement with their subject –which can be seen as essential for the students' development of Academic Bildung (Fossland 2014). This is particularly the case for formative e-assessment, which involves a process aimed not only at improving students' learning and teachers' teaching, but also at improving the students' learning processes with the purpose of guiding them in a particular direction (Gipps 2002) or opening up new landscapes to support their Academic Bildung. To move beyond learning, assessment also needs to address the unknown, the wonderment, and to open the students' minds to the world, according to the values expressed within the four voices of higher education.

To facilitate Academic Bildung, the assessment has to move from stimulating simple remembering of knowledge to more complex analyses, syntheses and evaluations that really challenge the learners as critical beings (Barnett

1997). Instead of traditional ways of assessment that focus on content recall, and only the student's voice of knowing and doing, the interviews revealed that the more innovative teachers saw a need to adopt assessment methods that encourage and strengthen the students' position as critical beings, and that also involved a closer interaction with the phenomena that was studied, in line with Barnett's voice of being and voice of the phenomenon (Barnett 2007; Fossland 2014). In relation to both formative and summative assessment methods, these teachers wanted to approach both critical and society-oriented reflection as well as a dimension of ethical-existential and being-oriented reflection, in line with the way we have defined Academic Bildung in Chapter 3. The voice of knowing and doing was approached through autonomy, encouraging the students through different ways of inciting their critical thinking and their society-oriented reflections. The more educational voice, as Barnett defines it (the pedagogical voice), can be seen in relation to the voice of being and the voice of the phenomenon, and was realised through authenticity, addressing more the students' own personal experience, engagement and process of "self-becoming" in terms of ethical, existential- and being-oriented reflections. This involves the development of assessment methods that critically involve and engage the students with the content, and challenge them to approach the content in more analytical, complex ways. This, in turn, can become an important part of their development of Academic Bildung.

Rethinking the role of the teacher?

Is there a need to rethink the role of the teacher to facilitate Academic Bildung? The interviews with teachers revealed that in net-based education there is a clear danger of instructional thinking and instruction-oriented designs focusing on what the students' should be doing, and not enough focus on the importance of a present authentic teacher (Fossland 2014). Even though many of the facilitators can be called enthusiasts, there is a clear tendency that net-based courses not often are led by professors or other key academic staff at the universities (op. cit.). We know that authentic teachers and more authenticity in university teaching is important to address the students' personal engagement and their development to become academics (Kreber 2013), but the teachers' skills, knowledge and general competencies related to both net-based teaching and the actual topic are important. If the goal is to facilitate Academic Bildung, there is a need to rethink the facilitators' role in net-based education, a role that needs to address both autonomy and authenticity.

The overall picture from interviews with teachers demonstrated that the teacher needs to be present, follow the students' academic development, and be a trusted, skilled academic and social support (op. cit.). To facilitate Academic Bildung it seems important to safeguard the students and put effort into the social and relational part of the facilitation, to create a learning environment where students feel safe and can express, encourage, and challenge themselves and others, without feeling uncomfortable or insecure (Fossland 2013b). Our findings can be understood in relation to what Beetham and Sharpe (2013) say about learning, teaching, pedagogy and education:

> Learners need teachers. As learners, we cannot know what is possible to know, or how to make that journey to what we want to become. We need guidance. Pedagogy is about guiding learning, rather than leaving you to find your own way. . . . There have always been libraries, friends and experiences to enable us to do that, now supplemented with digital resources and internet friends and virtual experiences. Informal learning continues with even better opportunities.
>
> (p. xvii)

Even though students need guidance and structure, especially in fully net-based environments, we argue that teachers also need to move the students beyond this. It appears that a decent teacher in net-based education doesn't see a contradiction between the students' need for guidance in relation to knowledge and what they are supposed to do, and the importance of developing their more being-oriented voices and reflections, both in relation to their self-formation and the voice of the phenomenon involved. According to Barnett (2007), students need to be involved in a more authentic learning process, where both the teacher and the students constantly try to put themselves into play and at risk, by approaching wonderment and placing themselves in the open and uncertain. The teacher who contributes actively and professionally in different learning settings, as an inspirational, knowledgeable lecturer who manages to be passionate and authentic in her approach to teaching, seems to be the one with a good overview of the students' development of Academic Bildung. The teacher also needs to coordinate and facilitate complex interaction that stimulates the students' critical engagement with the world. This authentic engagement needs to be seen both in relation to the students' approaches to the presented content, and also in relation to the social and relational contexts where the students are supposed to develop their own academic voice.

As earlier argued, several guidelines and information resources are available to support the net-based teacher's role. But if a net-based teacher's mission is to facilitate Academic Bildung and develop students as critical beings, this must be interwoven in the facilitation and also in the teacher's specific feedback to the students. Based on the students' contributions to different learning activities, collaborative tasks and discussions, providing timely and qualified feedback to the students seems significant. According to Hattie (2008), feedback combined with effective instruction can be very powerful in enhancing learning. Hattie conducted a meta-study of more than 800 research articles on approaches to learning published over a ten-year period, concluding that teachers are among the most powerful influences in learning. He says:

> They need to be directive, influential and caring and actively engage in the passion of teaching and learning. . . . Teachers need to be aware of what each and every student is thinking and knowing to construct meaning and meaningful experiences in light of this knowledge, and have confident knowledge and understanding of their content to provide meaningful and appropriate feedback such that student moves progressively through the curriculum levels.
>
> (p. 238)

In line with Hattie the findings in this book and the findings from interviews with teachers have demonstrated the importance of a present and authentic teacher. The facilitation of students' engagement presupposes that the teacher is engaged in practice. This involves authenticity as a fundamental element in teaching. In Chapter 1 we discussed the role of the facilitator/ teacher when developing the students' Academic Bildung and referred to Kreber (2014), who argues that there is a need for more authenticity in university teaching to address the students' personal engagement and their development to become academics. In her book *Authenticity in and through teaching in higher education*, she argues that "teaching is an ongoing transformative learning process that is intimately bound up with becoming authentic" (p. 5). Kreber understands that "authenticity in teaching" enables a much greater potential to develop the students' own authenticity. "Authenticity through teaching" refers to academic teachers moving towards greater authenticity with the ultimate goal of promoting students' learning, authenticity and development of Academic Bildung.

To safeguard the authenticity aspects of Academic Bildung, it seems important to make use of life, work and educational experiences as part of the students' learning activities within their learning environment. Case analysis, challenging problem-solving tasks, and interactive activities can stimulate the development of the students' own personal voices within higher education. To further develop the students' autonomy, it seems important to believe in them, to be curious about their thinking and who they are, to encourage and be there for them, with a trusting, supportive and authentic attitude. In my 2014 study, one of the interviewed teachers who strongly asserted the importance of the present and authentic teacher said it like this:

> Especially in the beginning of a net-based course, it's so important to be present and to set a standard on how we relate to each other, both socially and academically. All students should be treated politely and with respect. You need to set a tone, and to follow the students'

development. Personally, I follow for instance discussions to know where my students are, what they are struggling with and understand how they face challenges. The students also like me being present, even if I do not participate in the discussions. Sometimes a "smiley" is enough just to give them feedback, but other times it is necessary to ask new questions when I see that the students are not on track. Following the students' activities and progress more closely gives me a lot of feedback when teaching, supervising or making formative and summative assessments. Using IT can also facilitate a closer connection with the students, as it makes it possible to reach each and every one of them quite easily. Even though the use of "clickers" for instance can be seen as a technological tool, many students feel they are more activated and seen by me as a teacher.

(personal interview, my translation, in Fossland 2014)

This quotation is just one of several statements from my study of innovative teachers. This group of teachers can be said to be in the frontline of how technology is used in net-based education, and is therefore not representative of average university teachers. Nonetheless, when rethinking the role of an authentic teacher who encourages Academic Bildung, what stands out as an important foundation is genuine teaching in combination with structure and clear guidance. It does not matter how well suited the learning goals, teaching and learning activities, and technology are, if guidance is unclear or insufficient, and the students are not engaged and involved in an authentic learning process. Students need to develop their Academic Bildung, but cannot be left alone "in the open" to develop their own voice. Studies of adult learners (Fossland and Laugerud 2008) also demonstrate that even though this group of students is described as particularly mature, motivated, and self-regulated (in accordance to Meriam and Cafarella 1999), they too prefer structure and deadlines to help their progress and cooperation with others.

To sum up, we argue that there is a need to rethink the role of the teacher and the facilitator. When facilitating Academic Bildung, teachers need to engage students as persons. The approach is to encompass the whole person in his or her complexity. This is one of several reasons why the university cannot be constrained by an understanding of learning that emphasises only the acquisition of skills and specific knowledge. Rather, in the face of "an unknown future", and in line with thinkers such as Barnett and Pelikan, we argue that it is the university teachers' responsibility to foster the students' Academic Bildung. To answer my question: rethinking the teachers' role within net-based higher education seems necessary. To achieve this, engagement and authenticity seem like the most important key words.

Conclusion

The overall question in this book is "How can universities educate students through net-based education and at the same time facilitate Academic Bildung?" Inspired by this question, the findings in this book, and interviews with innovative teachers, the present chapter has outlined the broader picture and the pedagogical implications of our findings in order to answer affirmatively that there is a need to rethink net-based higher education in line with a four voiced pedagogy.

Even if there are no great changes in the understanding of how students learn and teachers teach, our findings and the use of technology invite us to rethink conditions for the facilitation of net-based learning. In this chapter I have argued that there is a need to rethink quality issues and pedagogy, learning outcomes, learning environments and activities, the role of assessment and the teacher's role – if our aim is to develop the students' Academic Bildung, and "move the students beyond learning" in net-based education. All four voices within higher education – "the voice of knowing", "the voice of doing", "the voice of being" and "the voice of the phenomenon" – must be interwoven in the facilitation, and the need for a more authentic approach to teaching and learning seems crucial in order to develop the students' Academic Bildung. In other words, technology invites us both to do what we always have done, but also to rethink the *conditions* for net-based education – if our ambitions are to facilitate Academic Bildung.

To address these findings at the strategic and educational developmental levels of higher educational institutions, it seems important that these institutions see the need for a rethinking of net-based education. We argue that there is a need to address the question of Academic Bildung. To develop net-based education questions related to Academic Bildung must be addressed in teacher training courses within higher education, to implement these important dimensions of rethinking to develop their approaches to net-based higher education.

Notes

1 See Barnett (2007), Hansen (2013) or Chapter 3 for a more detailed discussion on these concepts.
2 ENQA is an umbrella organisation which represents quality assurance organisations from the European Higher Education Area (EHEA) member states. ENQA promotes European co-operation in the field of quality assurance in higher education. For more information: http://www.enqa.eu/
3 http://unique.efquel.org/
4 https://www.qualitymatters.org/rubric
5 www.spsu.edu/instructionaldesign
6 http://www.spsu.edu/instructionaldesign/course_design/resources/best practices.pdf

References

Andersen, H. L. (2010). "'Constructive alignment' og risikoen for en forsimplende universitetspædagogik", *Dansk Universitetspædagogisk Tidsskrift*, vol. 5, no. 9, pp. 30–35.

Barnett, R. (1997). *Higher education: A critical business.* Open University Press: Buckingham, UK.

Barnett, R. (2007). *A will to learn: Being a student in an age of uncertainty.* Open University Press/McGraw Hill: Berkshire, UK.

Barnett, R. and Coate, K. (2004). *Engaging the curriculum in higher education.* McGraw Hill/Open University Press: Maidenhead, UK.

Beetham, H. and Sharpe, R. (2013). *Rethinking pedagogy for a digital age: Designing and delivering e-learning.* Routledge: New York.

Boud, D. and Falchnikov, N. (2007). "Developing assessment for informing judgement". In: Boud, D. and Falchnikov, N., eds., *Rethinking assessment in higher education: Learning for the longer term,* (pp. 180–97). Routledge: London.

Bryson, C. (2014). *Understanding and developing student engagement.* Routledge: New York.

European Communities. (2008). *The European qualifications framework (EQF) for lifelong learning.* Belgium: Luxembourg: Office for Official Publications of the European Communities. Available online at: http://ec.europa.eu/education/pub/pdf/general/eqf/broch_en.pdf (accessed 11 April 2014).

Fossland, T. (2013a). "Digitalisering er ikke nok- Digital vurdering, nye kvalitetskrav og institusjonelt ansvar". In: Nordkvelle, Y. T., Fossland, T., and Netteland, G., eds., *Kvalitet i IKT-støttet utdanning*, pp. 175–94. Akademika Forlag: Oslo.

Fossland, T. (2013b). "Sentrale prinsipper for kvalitet i diskusjoner på nett innen høyere utdanning". In: Fossland, T., Gjerdrum, E., and Ramberg, K.R., eds., *Ulike forståelser av kvalitet i norsk, fleksibel høyere utdanning – Teknologi og læring på og utenfor campus.* Norgesuniversitetet: Tromsø, NO.

Fossland, T. (2014). *Digitale læringsformer i høyere utdanning.* Universitetsforlaget: Oslo.

Friesen, N. (2013). "Bildung and educational language: Talking of 'the self' in North American education". In: Biesta, G., Edwards, R. and Allen, J., eds., *Making a difference in theory: The theory question in education and the education question in theory.* Routledge: London.

Gipps, C. (2002). "Sociocultural perspectives on assessment". In: Wells, G. and Claxton G., eds., *Learning for life in the 21st century: Sociocultural perspectives on the future of education,* pp. 73–83. Blackwell: Oxford, UK.

Hansen, F. T. (2013). "Dannelse forstået som taktfuldhed over for 'det sande og gådefulde' i tilværelsen". In: Pahuus, M., ed., *Dannelse i en læringstid.* Aalborg Universitetsforlag: Aalborg, DK.

Hattie, J. (2008). *Visible learning: A synthesis of over 800 meta-analyses relating to achievement.* Routledge: New York.

Havnes, A. (2002). "Hva gjør eksamen med studiene?" In: Raaheim, A. and Raaheim, K., eds., *Eksamen – En akademisk hodepine. En håndbok for studenter og lærere,* pp. 149–83. Sigma Forlag: Bergen, NO.

Kreber, C. (2014). *Authenticity in and through teaching: The transformative potential of the scholarship of teaching.* Routledge: London.

Meriam, S. B. and Cafarella, R. S. (1999). *Learning in adulthood: A comprehensive guide*, 2th edn. Jossey-Bass: San Francisco.

Nordkvelle, Y., Fossland, T. and Netteland, G. (2013). *Kvalitet i fleksibel høyere utdaning*. Akademika Forlag: Oslo.

Solberg, M. and Fossland, T. (2013). *Akademisk danning – Et mulig prosjekt for voksne studenter i fleksible studier?* pp. 46–62. Gyldendal Akademisk: Oslo.

Swedish National Agency for Higher Education. (2008). E-learning quality: Aspects and criteria for evaluation of e-learning in higher education [report]. Swedish National Agency for Higher Education: Stockholm. Available online at: http://www.viper.upc.umu.se/viper/resources/Workshop-Materials/DOCUMENTS%20&%20MATERIALS/SNAHE.Report200811R.pdf (accessed 5 April 2014).

Uvalić-Trumbić, S. and Daniel, J. (2013). *A guide to quality in online learning*. Academic Partnerships: Dallas, TX. Available online at http://norgesuniversitetet.no/files/newbooklet10_single.pdf (accessed 4 Sept. 2014).

Whitelock, D. (2010). "Activating assessment for learning: Are we on the way with web 2.0?" In: Lee, M. J. W. and McLoughlin, C., eds., *Web 2.0-based e-learning: Applying social informatics for tertiary teaching*. IGI Global: Hershey, PA.

Concluding remarks

Helle Mathiasen and Mariann Solberg

At the beginning of this book we asked: "How can universities educate students through net-based education and at the same time facilitate Academic Bildung?" We have discussed the question from a societal perspective, an institutional perspective, and pedagogical and didactical perspectives, and we also here suggest some new questions.

In Part I, the societal reasons for why the facilitation of Academic Bildung is more important than ever are discussed. It is argued that higher education needs to be rethought. In order to develop the academic orientation of the students, we need to address both challenges and opportunities within net-based higher education. We have to remind ourselves of the functions and contributions higher education has to provide for tomorrow's society and ask what knowledge, skills, and competences net-based courses need to offer to achieve this. In our approach, the students, teachers, universities, and society are all addressed. It is important to take into account that all are dynamic entities.

Furthermore, at the institutional level the changes and processes do not seem to have affected the potential space for Academic Bildung in a substantial way. Yet the trends in higher education are moving in a direction where this might be threatened by the massification of education and more managed and production-oriented institutions. In that sense, there might be some dark clouds in the foreseeable future.

From a pedagogical and didactical perspective it is vital for net-based education that net-based courses are run by faculty who have a close connection to research and are motivated and qualified to meet the specific opportunities and challenges of net-based teaching and learning environments. Educational technology carries values, and the complexities of net-based communication gives varied conditions for learning and Academic Bildung.

In Part II, the empirical studies showed the variety of approaches to the overall question, and we learned about the opportunities, constraints, barriers, and pitfalls for facilitation of Academic Bildung. The case studies come from pharmacy, IT educational design, business administration and healthcare, thus disciplines from different faculties are represented.

The discussions in Part III are based on the findings and perspectives presented in Part II. We found thirteen different, and to some extent overlapping, interpretations of Academic Bildung in the case studies. We take this as an expression of the empirical existence of Academic Bildung in these Scandinavian net-based courses. The case studies have found Academic Bildung to consist of: (i) professional proficiency, (ii) professional identity, (iii) autonomy in terms of being able to free oneself from didactical design, (iv) ability for perspective expansion, (v) exploration so as to achieve deep learning, (vi) ability to take an active part in a democratic society, (vii) being a whole person, (viii) acquisition of academic skills, (ix) acquisition of academic values, (x) acquisition of academic identity and behaviour, (xi) ability to think critically, (xii) ability to foster personal growth and maintenance, and (xiii) concern with the aims of a better society. These different traits cover both the autonomy and the authenticity sides of Academic Bildung, and are all important features in the development of the students in the respective courses and programmes.

We have thus found that different content will influence and shape the kind of Academic Bildung that potentially can and should be developed. This means that there is no privileged content to be found, all academic disciplines have a Bildung potential. In this way, the different disciplines and individual teachers will have to reflect on their specific ways to facilitate the development of Academic Bildung in their specific course or programme. The teaching and learning environment offered is pivotal for facilitation of Academic Bildung.

In conclusion, what can we say about facilitation of Academic Bildung in net-based higher education? What is the Scandinavian approach? Since our focus has been quite general in terms of not making divisions between different forms of teaching and learning environments, our emphasis has been on the pedagogical and didactic aspects, and not on the different technological solutions and mediations. In general, our empirical findings show us that facilitation of Academic Bildung is far from straight forward. The conditions for development of Academic Bildung vary depending on the concrete contexts. However, we have found that in terms of institutional conditions, net-based education is so far, to a large extent, a "bottom-up" movement, where the initiative still is in the hands of the academic staff. We have also found that teachers of Scandinavian universities have similar philosophical orientations of teaching and technology, where "the progressive orientation" dominates, "accompanied by comments revolving around their students' personal growth, and the connection to social systems". Moreover, they relate to technology due to "the uses and technological determinism orientation". We further suggest that the Scandinavian approach is to discuss theoretical, empirical, and normative premises for education, without giving definite answers, having the courage to remain in the open. When we used the empirical material (the case studies) to discuss Academic Bildung, we had a double aim: showing both *how* we discuss and *what* we discuss.

Thus the discussion in the case studies and in Part III could be seen as an opportunity to gain insight into Scandinavian ways of discursively constructing pedagogical and didactical perspectives.

We would like to invite you to take part in further investigation and discussion concerning both conceptual issues and empirical investigations. For instance, is the concept of Academic Bildung something immanent in persons, institutions and society or is it something that has to be constructed? If the approach to Academic Bildung has an ontological character, in the sense that Bildung is always already present, what conditions have to be present to allow it to grow? And if we take a constructivist approach to Academic Bildung, how can we facilitate development of Academic Bildung in specific teaching and learning environments? When we focus on the conditions for maintaining communication and offer fruitful teaching and learning environments, how can net-based and campus-based environments enrich each other?

We hope we have inspired you to reflect on the student's possibilities in your own disciplines and courses, and motivated new research projects that can expound the field.

Index

Note: The following abbreviations were used: *f* = figure; *n* = note; *t* = table